ALSO BY DENIS DONOGHUE

The Third Voice
An Honoured Guest: New Essays on W. B. Yeats (editor)
The Ordinary Universe
Swift Revisited (editor)
Emily Dickinson
Jonathan Swift
Yeats
Jonathan Swift: A Critical Anthology (editor)
Thieves of Fire
Memoirs, by W. B. Yeats (editor)
The Sovereign Ghost
Ferocious Alphabets
Connoisseurs of Chaos
The Arts Without Mystery
Selected Essays of R. P. Blackmur (editor)
England, Their England
We Irish
Reading America
Warrenpoint
The Pure Good of Theory

# THE OLD MODERNS

# THE OLD MODERNS

ESSAYS ON LITERATURE
AND THEORY

# DENIS
DONOGHUE

*Alfred A. Knopf   New York   1994*

THIS IS A BORZOI BOOK
PUBLISHED BY ALFRED A. KNOPF, INC.

Copyright © 1994 by Denis Donoghue
All rights reserved under International and Pan-American Copyright
Conventions. Published in the United States by Alfred A. Knopf, Inc.,
New York, and simultaneously in Canada by Random House of Canada
Limited, Toronto. Distributed by Random House, Inc., New York.

Owing to limitations of space, all acknowledgments for permission to reprint previously published material may be found on pages 301–3.

Library of Congress Cataloging-in-Publication Data
Donoghue, Denis.
The old moderns : new essays on literature and theory / by Denis
Donoghue.
p.    cm.
ISBN 0-394-58934-3
1. American literature—20th century—History and criticism—Theory,
etc.   2. English literature—20th century—History and criticism—
Theory, etc.   3. Modernism (Literature)   I. Title
PS228.M63D67 1993
820.9′1—dc20                                                    93-1391
CIP

Manufactured in the United States of America
FIRST EDITION

FOR FRANCES AND THE CHILDREN

# CONTENTS

[VII]

# Introduction

〰〰〰〰

**P**ope Pius X knew what Modernism was: it was an attempt by certain misled Catholics to bend the doctrines of the church to the authority of modern science. He issued an encyclical to put a stop to that folly. Since then, no one else has been clear about Modernism—what the word means or how it might be used on secular occasions. The concept of Modernism is an awkward device for describing modern English, Irish, and American literature; it is better established in Spanish and Italian than in English, and far more useful in relation to modern architecture and music than to literature. But we continue to use it as a swear-word or a cheer-word. It has been called upon to denote any of the following: the new desire for, or capitulation to, an art responsive to crises (any crisis, apparently); an attempt to reinvigorate an art deemed to have sunk into exhaustion and decadence; an art that exploits with verve the capacities of modern technology.

I once thought of writing a book called *Gasping on the Strand*, about the relation between modern literature and crisis. Instances of crisis were to be sought in politics, history, philosophy, economics, theology, and language. It seemed reasonable to suppose that certain forms of literature were developed in response to mass society, the Great War, the October Revolution, unemployment, inflation, the internal combustion engine, and other exacerbations. But the book didn't progress beyond its title; it was stopped by the consideration that many gifted writers managed to ignore crisis and to continue writing as if one day were much like another.

The title of the unwritten book comes from Yeats's "Three Movements":

> *Shakespearean fish swam the sea, far away from land;*
> *Romantic fish swam in nets coming to the hand;*
> *What are all those fish that lie gasping on the strand?*

Yeats's question is clarified by a note in his diary for January 20, 1932, six days before he wrote the poem: "The Passion in Shakespeare was a great fish in the sea, but from Goethe to the end of the Romantic movement the fish was in the net. It will soon be dead upon the shore." Yeats didn't name the gasping fish: they could hardly include Mann, Proust, James, Lawrence, Frost, Valéry, or Rilke.

*Gasping on the Strand* didn't survive much reflection. Talk of crisis seemed to issue from flirtation with the glamour of catastrophe. A few writers, notably Pound, Eliot, and in some moods Yeats, evidently thought the conditions of writing were unpropitious: their rage for order issued in further rage. But most writers decided that the conditions were tolerable and that the existence of one work of art made another at least conceivable. "We are conceived in our conceits." The much-announced "death of literature" and the "death of the author" were evidently compatible with the publication of many new books. I concede that there is no contradiction between those deaths and that sign of life. But the relation between crisis at large and novelty of forms in literature was hard to establish. I continued to write about "the modern," modernity, and Modernism, but with misgiving.

The essays I have gathered in this book reflect both the misgiving and the inclination to subdue it: the notion that Modernism is a mirage, and another notion, that it isn't; that the obstacles to serious writing are as troubling as Eliot thought they were. It is possible to resolve the question opportunistically. In *Required Writing* Philip Larkin asserts that the Modernism of Picasso, Pound, and Charlie Parker was a regrettable diversion and that Hardy, who practiced traditional forms and dictions, was incomparably the greatest twentieth-century poet who wrote in English. I don't agree with either of these assertions, but they can't be set aside merely by calling Larkin a Little Englander.

The only assertion I make in this book is that if there is a Modernist literature, it marks a relation between modern cities and those writers who felt beset by them. But feeling beset doesn't always mean feeling subdued. Some writers are exhilarated to discover in the conditions that apparently afflict them new emotions, more daring possibilities of expression. It is more important to them that the conditions permit work than that they permit happiness. Often the external circumstances prompt writers to imagine an adversary world and to compose their fictions in its service. They intuit a better life than the one they otherwise know. If they annotate the life they know, it is because the words they use insist upon doing so and have to be coaxed to go beyond this habit.

Later in the book I quote a lordly sentence from Yeats's introduction to *The Oxford Book of Modern Verse* (1936): "I too have tried to be modern." It is not clear why he thought being modern was something he ought to strive for, or what the signs of his success would be. I too have tried to settle upon one meaning of Modernism and to put up with the embarrassment of knowing that a different account of it would be just as feasible. If we start with the modern city and the friction of living in such a place, we quickly come to the question of subjectivity. What are the possibilities of a sentient life along crowded streets or in apartments? People who live in a city soon begin to feel that their apprehensions are private and can't easily be verified by being compared with someone else's. The status of those apprehensions makes a problem in epistemology. Not in ontology. The existence of city streets need not be doubted, but what my mind, eyes, ears, and feet tell me of those streets emphasizes my privacy rather than my sociality or my citizenship. It is harder to conduct a dialogue of the mind with other minds than a dialogue of the mind with itself. My true life seems to be the one I live inside my head. At least it feels irrefutable. But how can it be true? Solipsism is a risk, but it can be evaded. The question is: what makes my sense of the streets more persuasive (or less) than anyone else's? Of *The Waste Land* is it true, as Eliot said, that what Tiresias *sees* is the substance of the poem? Why is Tiresias's view more authoritative than the typist's? With these notions in mind, I think Eliot's "Preludes," Joyce's *A Portrait of the Artist as a Young Man*,

Yeats's "Vacillation," Woolf's *Mrs. Dalloway*, Valéry's "Le Cimetière marin," and Rilke's *Sonnets to Orpheus* are modern; they exemplify Modernism at least in the aspect I have indicated. The mind in those works is brooding upon the status of its feelings. Apparently external events become someone's experience: is this process entirely arbitrary? Should it be taken seriously, if only because no other consideration seems to have a stronger claim? Modernism is concerned with the validity of one's feelings and the practice of converting apparently external images and events into inwardness, personal energy. Whether or not these words are set in modern cities or allude to them, they presuppose the culture of cities as the inevitable form of modernity.

The corresponding process in literature is one by which writers mull over their own procedures and the mulling becomes a poem or a story. Poems issue from other poems, stories from other stories, because of the consanguinity writers feel between one style of mulling and another. The process is continuous with that of the Romantic imagination as Coleridge described its working: the imagination is the finite correlative of divine power, God in one vocabulary, Prometheus in another, Orpheus in a third. Modernism issues from Romanticism as cities displace villages.

My theme is Modernism, not postmodernism. If the word "postmodernism" makes a claim that Modernism has been discredited, dislodged, or otherwise consigned to a gone time, the claim is absurd. Nothing has been invalidated, the space of writing has not been taken over by new forms, there has not been a coup. There are some writers, a few, to whom the terms of Lyotard's *The Postmodern Condition* may be applied. They exhibit that "incredulity toward all metanarratives" which Lyotard proposes as the mark of postmodernism. In English and American literature I think of Nabokov (in his *Pale Fire* mode), John Barth, Coover (maybe), Donald Barthelme, Christine Brooke-Rose. Their relation to metanarratives is ironic, they keep their distance from such enchantments. The metanarrative about which they are especially ironic is the one I ascribe to Modernism, that of the redemption of time. Suppose we start with the subjective impulse or predicament; a mind lives and acts by converting apparently external events into itself. The experiences it produces or performs are whatever they are, but some few of them with luck seem irresistible. Joyce calls these epiphanies. Eliot's "Burnt Norton" woos them into being and broods on their spiritual value. Pound's "luminous moments" are similarly charged acts of perception. Beckett's *Endgame* has them, too, though Beckett deplores his susceptibility and, as in *Krapp's Last Tape*, belatedly erases them. Pater is the theorist of such epiphanies. Granted that they arise, a further range of experiences becomes possible. The mind, impelled by its visions, tries to "redeem the time"; that is, to find equally compelling evidence of value in other lives, the past, cave-drawings, Myron's *Discobolus*, wherever the creative energy of mind has left its mark. The literature I am writing about is attentive to these experiences and wishes to prolong them: it has this metanarrative and by reciting it aspires to a "culture of redemption." I take the phrase from Leo Bersani's book of that title, which denounces the Modernist project as pretentious. I don't agree with him.

In the first three chapters I have revised the Richard Ellmann Lectures I gave at Emory University in April 1990; they were published in a limited edition as *Being Modern Together* (Scholars Press, 1991), and I have retained the title. "The Use and Abuse of Theory" was the Presidential Address of the Modern Humanities Research Association, read at University College, London, on January 10, 1992 and published in *Modern Language Review*, October 1992. "The Political Turn in Criticism" was published in *Salmagundi* 81, Winter 1989. "The Sublime Blackmur" was the introduction to *Selected Essays of R. P. Blackmur* (New York: Ecco Press, 1986). "Translation in Theory and in a Certain Practice" appeared in *The Art of Translation: Voices from the Field*, edited by Rosanna Warren (Boston: Northeastern University Press, 1989). "On *The Golden Bowl*" was the introduction to that novel in the Everyman Library, 1992. "*William Wetmore Story and His Friends*: The Enclosing Fact of Rome" appeared in *The Sweetest Impression of Life: The James Family and Italy*, edited by James W. Tuttleton and Agostino Lombardo (New York University Press and Istituto della Enciclopedia Italiana, 1990). "The Modern Yeats" was published in *The World and I*, June 1988. "On a Late Poem by Yeats" is published here for the first time. "T. S. Eliot: The Communication of the Dead" appeared in *Antaeus* 63, Autumn 1989. "On 'Burnt Norton' " is published here for the first time. "On *The Idea of a Christian Society*" appeared in *The Yale Review* 78, no. 2 (1989). "Is There a Case Against *Ulysses*?" was published in *Joyce in Context*, edited by Vincent J. Cheng and Timothy Martin (Cambridge University Press, 1992); "Notes on a Poem by Stevens" in *Omnium Gatherum: Essays for Richard Ellmann*, edited by Susan Dick, Declan Kiberd, Dougald

McMillan, and Joseph Ronsley (Gerrards Cross: Colin Smythe, 1989). "Is There a Perennial Literature?" was a lecture at the Hebrew University of Jerusalem on March 4, 1992, in a series called "Periodization: Old Paradigms and New Perspectives" under the auspices of the Center for Literary Studies of the Hebrew University of Jerusalem. It is published here for the first time.

D.D.

# BEING MODERN
# TOGETHER

# THE MAN OF THE CROWD

֎ᴄ᷆ᴏᴄᴄ

I

It is a commonplace worth repeating that many of the ambitious writers of the early twentieth century regarded themselves as tormented by the conditions they had to meet. The time was never right, never as good as some earlier time when, as Henry Adams claimed in *Mont-Saint-Michel and Chartres*, the conditions supposedly made for unity and coherence. Ezra Pound looked to the Italian Renaissance of the sixteenth century, when intelligence was intimate with power. He did not dwell upon the fact that it was often on easy terms with murder. T. S. Eliot persuaded himself that something went wrong in the early to middle years of the seventeenth century—in England, it probably had something to do with the Civil War—and that not only literature but the culture at large had been disfigured, perhaps permanently. Wyndham Lewis, another admirer of Italian princes, thought that the conditions remained tolerable so long as the bounding line in art and the styles of satire in literature and painting retained their force—up to the age of Pope and Rowlandson. But some writers lived without a sense of crisis. Robert Frost asserted that "the time was neither wrong nor right"; if you were worth your salt, you would put up with the circumstances and survive them. Joyce confined his resentment to local exigencies: not enough money, too much family, church, and state. Virginia Woolf, who said that human nature

[3]

changed in or around December 1910, insisted that it was time to get rid of the methods of Arnold Bennett in particular and of naturalism in general, but she didn't think the age so bad that it couldn't be improved by a new belief, a decent chance for women, and more generally a change of heart. Henry James thought that the public terms an intelligent novel, short story, or play had to meet were a nuisance, but he didn't waste his energy describing some earlier state of happiness.

Adams, Pound, Eliot, and Yeats devised, each in his own style, a philosophy of history, or a form of historical prophecy, to impugn the modern forces and to account for them. Sometimes they invoked an earlier prophet to explain all: Vico, Joachim da Fiore, or some other. Yeats's two versions of *A Vision* (1925, 1937) made the most systematic attempt to account for historical and political change by reference to certain rhythms or sequences as fundamental as life itself. But he was also willing to be more specific. In his introduction to *The Oxford Book of Modern Verse* (1936), he listed the aspects of "Victorianism" that his friends denounced: political emphasis in Swinburne, humanitarian preoccupation in Arnold, scientific emphasis in *In Memoriam*, psychological curiosity in Browning, and "rhetoric" in everybody. But the mischief started, Yeats said, at the end of the seventeenth century, "when man became passive before a mechanized nature." This notion was based on a misreading of Locke, a partial reading of Hobbes, and an enthusiastic acceptance of Berkeley's repudiation of Locke and Newton. In an essay on Berkeley, Yeats wrote:

> The romantic movement with its turbulent heroism, its self-assertion, is over, superseded by a new naturalism that leaves man helpless before the contents of his own mind. One thinks of Joyce's *Anna Livia Plurabelle*, Pound's *Cantos*, works of an heroic sincerity, the man, his active faculties in suspense, one finger beating time to a bell sounding and echoing in the depths of his own mind; of Proust who, still fascinated by Stendhal's fixed framework, seems about to close his eyes and gaze upon the pattern under his lids.[1]

It didn't matter to Yeats whether man's passivity was caused by a mechanized nature or by the circumstantial contents of his mind. Either way, the active faculties were suspended. Yeats didn't need to be instructed by Blake or Nietzsche that the mind is most completely itself when it is in an antithetical relation to the conditions that thwart it. His imagination was theatrical in the sense that it flourished upon antinomies. He could rely upon his energy only when it was engaged in a conflict of principles, each of which might on another day gain the prize.

Sometimes the poet did not need to invent his conflict: it presented itself in social and public forms he could not help confronting. Yeats's dealing with the Abbey Theatre, Dublin audiences, businessmen, newspaper editors, and politicians gave him cause enough. But I suggest that for Yeats, Eliot, Pound, and many other writers, intimations of mechanized nature, the merely casual contents of one's own mind, modern forces of politics and economics, came together in a single but amorphous force, that of the crowd, specifically the modern urban masses. I must go back a little.

In the seventh book of *The Prelude*, Wordsworth writes of his residence in London, starting with the romance of the great city and moving on to the circumstances in which the romance was disfigured by misery and confusion. He writes with evident reluctance, and eventually invokes the city in its most repellent image:

> *Rise up, thou monstrous ant-hill on the plain*
> *Of a too busy world! Before me flow,*
> *Thou endless stream of men and moving things!*
> *Thy every day appearance, as it strikes—*
> *With wonder heightened, or sublimed by awe—*
> *On strangers, of all ages; the quick dance*
> *Of colours, lights, and forms; the deafening din;*
> *The comers and the goers face to face,*
> *Face after face; the string of dazzling wares,*
> *Shop after shop, with symbols, blazoned names,*
> *And all the tradesman's honours overhead. . . .*

It is as if, starting with the worst—the ant-hill—Wordsworth tried to take the harm out of his sense of the city by appealing to a vocabulary of natural life—streaming, flowing—that anticipates, but doesn't intimidate, the flowing crowd in the London of *The Waste Land*. But the most telling gesture in the passage is the face-about that goes from "face to face" to "Face after face," the first a dialogue, the second a sequence of isolates resolved in "Shop after shop."

> Meanwhile the roar continues, till at length,
> Escaped as from an enemy, we turn
> Abruptly into some sequestered nook. . . .

The ant-hill becomes an enemy, the audience in the theatre the "many-headed mass/Of the spectators"—Hydra, the nine-headed serpent slain by Hercules. Later in the same book, Wordsworth refers to "That huge fermenting mass of human kind," but in this passage he makes a desperate attempt to talk himself into comprehending the crowd:

> As the black storm upon the mountain top
> Sets off the sunbeam in the valley, so
> That huge fermenting mass of human kind
> Serves as a solemn background, or relief,
> To single forms and objects, whence they draw,
> For feeling and contemplative regard,
> More than inherent liveliness and power.
> How oft, amid those overflowing streets,
> Have I gone forward with the crowd, and said
> Unto myself, "The face of every one
> That passes by me is a mystery!"
> Thus have I looked, nor ceased to look, oppressed
> By thoughts of what and whither, when and how,
> Until the shapes before my eyes became
> A second-sight procession, such as glides
> Over still mountains, or appears in dreams. . . .

Second sight is work of the mind's eye or the soul's eye as distinct from the body's—a deeper vision, presumably, but also more abstract; the things seen are already receding or being distanced in favor of the mind that sees them. The mind is looking through the crowd in the determination not to be oppressed by it. In the next lines the process is impeded. Wordsworth sees—has to see—a blind beggar, and the scene loses its pageantry:

> lost
> Amid the moving pageant, I was smitten
> Abruptly, with the view (a sight not rare)

*Of a blind Beggar, who, with upright face,*
*Stood, propped against a wall, upon his chest*
*Wearing a written paper, to explain*
*His story, whence he came, and who he was.*
*Caught by the spectacle my mind turned round*
*As with the might of waters; an apt type*
*This label seemed of the utmost we can know,*
*Both of ourselves and of the universe;*
*And, on the shape of that unmoving man,*
*His steadfast face and sightless eyes, I gazed,*
*As if admonished from another world.*

It is only right that Wordsworth should feel himself admonished by the beggar, who came from another social world to the dismay of this one. The existence of the blind man poses questions that can't be answered by Wordsworth's values or anyone else's. Wordsworth is still invoking figures of nature—the might of waters, turning his mind upon disagreeables—to sustain him in facing what can't be faced. The remainder of this book of *The Prelude* is taken up with devices to remove Wordsworth's mind from the contemplation of such a figure as the blind beggar. He shifts the emphasis, as if he hoped to shift the moral burden, from the object seen to the mind seeing it:

*things that are, are not,*
*As the mind answers to them, or the heart*
*Is prompt, or slow, to feel.*

Wordsworth recurs again and again in this book to his sense of the indiscriminateness of the crowd:

*Oh, blank confusion! true epitome*
*Of what the mighty City is herself*
*To thousands upon thousands of her sons,*
*Living amid the same perpetual whirl*
*Of trivial objects, melted and reduced*
*To one identity, by differences*
*That have no law, no meaning, and no end—*
*Oppression, under which even highest minds*
*Must labour, whence the strongest are not free.*

Wordsworth's only way of dealing with this perception is to draw upon nature yet again to suffuse even such a fact as the blind beggar. In the last lines of the book he tries to see "the parts/As parts, but with a feeling of the whole." He asserts, against much evidence, the validity of "order and relation" in the world, vouched for by the apparent order of seas and mountains. In the end, the beggar is made to play his part in the divine plan, as if domesticated to the view from Westminster Bridge, September 3, 1802. Culture is made to appear compatible with nature:

> This did I feel, in London's vast domain.
> The Spirit of Nature was upon me there;
> The soul of Beauty and enduring Life
> Vouchsafed her inspiration, and diffused,
> Through meagre lines and colours, and the press
> Of self-destroying, transitory things,
> Composure, and ennobling Harmony.[2]

It is not convincing: it is one of the last occasions on which a poet relies upon a comprehensive sense of nature to encompass the miseries of the city. Modern literature begins, not from the seventh book of *The Prelude*, but from the experience of finding its harmonious resolution and its appeal to nature not at all persuasive.

But we need an even more dismayed occasion. In December 1840, Edgar Allan Poe published in *Burton's Gentleman's Magazine* a short story called "The Man of the Crowd." It is not one of the stories on which Poe's indelible if irregular reputation depends: "The Fall of the House of Usher," "The Pit and the Pendulum," "The Purloined Letter," "The Narrative of Arthur Gordon Pym," "The Gold Bug." It is still read, I imagine, by those who wonder why Baudelaire made so much of it in his essay on Constantin Guys, "The Painter of Modern Life." Baudelaire misread Poe's story, or read it as if he and not Poe had written it. So I propose to start with the story and let it lead me to Baudelaire and other writers.

The narrator is a man who has been ill and is now convalescing, taking things fairly easily and relishing the enhanced sensory power that is one of the happy attributes of convalescence. He is sitting at the large bow-window of a coffee-house in a hotel in London, smoking a cigar, reading a newspaper. It is an autumn evening. He looks at the people in the coffee-room, then at the crowds passing back and forth in the street, "the tumultuous sea of human heads," as he thinks of them. He starts deducing from their dress and demeanor that they belong to this or that profession: attorneys, clerks, gamblers, thieves, prostitutes, beggars. Suddenly he notices a man, old, decrepit, wild in appearance. On an impulse, the narrator takes his overcoat, hat, and cane and runs out to the street to follow him. He keeps a certain distance behind, but he doesn't let him out of his sight. As the evening becomes dark and wet and the gaslights are turned on, the man walks around the city, not dawdling or strolling but walking boldly as if he had somewhere to go. He crosses streets, comes back again, goes into a bazaar—it's now eleven o'clock—then down to the Embankment, past a theatre, out to one of the slums, into a pub, back to the street in central London where he started, still walking, varying his pace from time to time but never stopping or reaching a destination. He has passed the entire night in this way, and the following morning, midday, and it is coming on to evening again. But there is still no sign of a purpose or a motive. The story ends with this passage from the exasperated narrator:

> And, as the shades of the second evening came on, I grew wearied unto death, and, stopping fully in front of the wanderer, gazed at him steadfastly in the face. He noticed me not, but resumed his solemn walk, while I, ceasing to follow, remained absorbed in contemplation. "This old man," I said at length, "is the type and the genius of deep crime. He refuses to be alone. *He is the man of the crowd.* It will be in vain to follow; for I shall learn no more of him, nor of his deeds. The worst heart of the world is a grosser book than the 'Hortulus Animae,' and perhaps it is but one of the great mercies of God that 'er lasst sich nicht lesen.' "³

The evidence for associating the old man with deep crime is weak and would have been weak even in the middle of the nineteenth century, when people thought that by phrenology they could deduce evidence of character from bone structure and facial typologies. The narrator doesn't doubt that he has correctly deduced a concatenation of qualities in the old man:

Any thing even remotely resembling that expression I had never
seen before. I well remember that my first thought, upon beholding it, was that Retzsch, had he viewed it, would have greatly
preferred it to his own pictural incarnations of the fiend.

The reference is to Moritz Retzsch (1779–1857), the German artist
whose prints illustrated Goethe's *Faust*:

As I endeavored, during the brief minute of my original survey,
to form some analysis of the meaning conveyed, there arose con-
fusedly and paradoxically within my mind, the ideas of vast mental power, of caution, of penuriousness, of avarice, of coolness, of
malice, of blood-thirstiness, of triumph, of merriment, of excessive terror, of intense—of supreme despair. I felt singularly
aroused, startled, fascinated. "How wild a history," I said to myself, "is written within that bosom!"

So the narrator pursues the old man in the hope of detecting that wild
history and the motives at work in it.

The reference to the old man—"he refuses to be alone"—is clarified by the epigraph to the story, La Bruyère's elucidation of "Ce
grand malheur, de ne pouvoir être seul." But it is one thing not to be
able to be alone, and another to refuse to be alone. In *Caractères*
(1688), La Bruyère is concerned with social man, men and women so
far as they come into a social mode of understanding and description.
He is interested in finer discriminations than those of the major social
classes; in social groupings, coteries, socially recognizable entities. He
starts with the court and works his way down to the limits, quickly
reached, of social recognition. Roland Barthes has pointed out that the
feature common to the little worlds of La Bruyère's attention is enclo-
sure; he is concerned with social entities insofar as they are enclosed.
Each of them must have an inside and an outside. The inability to be
alone could mark the feeling of being suffocated by social rules and
nuances, the enclosures of particular desires and passions which define
one's social type. Pascal said (*Pensées* 1.8) that the sole cause of man's
unhappiness is that he does not know how to stay quietly in his room.
La Bruyère would not have said that, if only because he busied himself, more than Pascal did, with the fret of social life. But the man in

Poe's story insists on being in the crowd, even though he does not say a word to anyone or give the least sign of enjoying the throng.

Poe's story is usually interpreted as bearing chiefly upon the old man, the man of the crowd, rather than upon the narrator. W. H. Auden took it to be a story about "the state of chimerical passion, that is, the passionate unrest of a self that lacks all passion."[4] But that interpretation says nothing about the deep crime, the infernal quality, which the narrator ascribes to the old man. Presumably Auden means that a man lacks passion if he has many exacerbations but no motive in particular to define his life and give it unity of purpose, terrible or benign. But the story is more about the narrator than about the man he pursues. It is about the impulse to detect, to find out the meaning of the appearances that engage us; it is about the process of forming, as the narrator says, "some analysis of the meaning conveyed" by appearances and contingencies. It is a parable about the ambition of the human imagination to comprehend what it sees, and the opacity which, as in this case, thwarts it. The crowd is crucial to Poe's story and to Baudelaire's poems because it represents the conditions with which a particular modern imagination has to cope. City streets are the places in which social formations are for the time being dismantled: attorneys are no longer protected by their class but instead exposed to the proximity of clerks, thieves, and other orders. The story is a parable of imagination and reality, of what Wallace Stevens called the violence within in its dealings with the violence without.

Poe's story begins with a paragraph about expression and secrecy, opacity and interpretation, the first sentence being the problematic one:

> It was well said of a certain German book that "*er lasst sich nicht lesen*"—it does not permit itself to be read.

True, the narrator goes on to link this secrecy with crime, for no reason given. To speak of crime, deep or shallow, is to impose normative considerations upon a social or civil context, but by the end of the story we have been given no cause to believe that a crime has been committed or a criminal life secretly lived. The old man's refusal to be alone is what calls for explanation and it cannot be explained even by an intelligence bent upon detection. The crime seems to stand for a quality of human being, innate or otherwise ultimate, a metaphysical consideration.

Like many of Poe's stories, "The Man of the Crowd" is organized in a certain rhythm. We have a narrator, well qualified for the work of detection. He is evidently a man of cultivation, he alludes nimbly to episodes in the culture of Latin and Greek, French and German, to literature and art, classical and modern. He makes easy reference to Tertullian and Leibniz, to Parian marble and the Eupatrids, who corresponded in Greek society to the patricians in Rome. So he is thoroughly equipped as a modern intelligence. He has a triple rhythm of interests. When he has finished reading the newspaper, including the advertisements, he surveys the company in the coffee-room, and then turns his gaze upon the street and the crowd. There, too, the same rhythm obtains. "At first," he says, "my observations took an abstract and generalizing turn." "I looked," he says, "at the passengers in masses, and thought of them in their aggregate relations":

> Soon, however, I descended to details, and regarded with minute interest the innumerable varieties of figure, dress, air, gait, visage, and expression of countenance.

But this second regard allows him to make deductions only about the social classes passing before him, not about individuals. The logic of his rhythm entails his going further, descending to the single individual, the old man. The narrator's passage from the second to the third phase of his attention is prompted not only by the darkening of evening into night but by the lighting of the gaslamps, an episode in which the risks incurred by his narrower attention to individuals are prefigured:

> As the night deepened, so deepened to me the interest of the scene; for not only did the general character of the crowd materially alter (its gentler features retiring in the gradual withdrawal of the more orderly portion of the people, and its harsher ones coming out into bolder relief, as the late hour brought forth every species of infamy from its den), but the rays of the gas-lamps, feeble at first in their struggle with the dying day, had now at length gained ascendancy, and threw over every thing a fitful and

garish lustre. All was dark yet splendid—as that ebony to which
has been likened the style of Tertullian.

    The wild effects of the light enchained me to an examina-
tion of individual faces; and although the rapidity with which the
world of light flitted before the window prevented me from casting more than a glance upon each visage, still it seemed that, in
my then peculiar mental state, I could frequently read, even in
that brief interval of a glance, the history of long years.

The rays of the gaslamps have "enchained" the narrator to an especially close form of attention, but the capacity of the mind is neverthe-
less what we, like Poe, call the imagination; it is activated, according to
the strongest theories of Romanticism, by passion, and it proceeds
mainly by divination, not by attaching one concept to another. In some
theories, including those of Coleridge and Poe, it is the secular and finite correlative of the creative power of God. "The Man of the Crowd"
is about the power to imagine a life other than one's own, and the
limits of that power. The nature of the particular imagination is Shakespearean or Keatsian, according to a familiar distinction between these
writers and Wordsworth. In Shakespeare, Keats, and Hazlitt, the imagination is the will, withholding its life in favor of the other lives it at-
tends to or conceives. The Wordsworthian or egotistical imagination is
rarely willing to keep itself in abeyance. In Poe's story the narrator
tries to detect the old man. He begins by imagining a mode of life
other than his own, and in the end finds his imagination baffled.

    Guy Davenport has maintained, in *The Geography of the Imagina-
tion*, that Poe divided his imagery into three kinds and made his art by
moving between them. The three were the classical (his allusions to
Greece and Rome), the Gothic or grotesque (drawn mostly from
northern Europe, "my Germany of the soul," as Poe called it), and the
arabesque, which is Islamic or, however vaguely, Oriental. In "The
Man of the Crowd" the narrator associates himself with the classical
values, but when he sees the old man he thinks of Retzsch's illustrations of *Faust*, a northern swerve toward the Gothic or grotesque.
There is a turn toward the arabesque when the narrator describes the
old man:

He was short in stature, very thin, and apparently very feeble. His
clothes, generally, were filthy and ragged; but as he came, now

and then, within the strong glare of a lamp, I perceived that his linen, although dirty, was of beautiful texture; and my vision deceived me, or, through a rent in a closely-buttoned and evidently second-handed *roquelaire* which enveloped him, I caught a glimpse both of a diamond and of a dagger.

But even with an imaginative range as wide as the one Davenport ascribes to Poe, the narrator is shown defeated in the end by the old man's opacity. Whatever he is up to, it cannot be known.

The narrator is defeated by the crowd because the old man is its epitome. His refusal to be alone, his insistence on keeping going among strangers, means that his opacity is an emphatic version of the nature of the crowd. In "The Fall of the House of Usher" Poe refers to "that half-pleasurable, because poetic, sentiment, with which the mind usually receives the sternest natural images of the desolate or terrible." But the pleasure arises from a sense of poetic or imaginative comprehension of whatever is desolate or terrible; it can't continue once the imagination finds the reality it confronts impenetrable. That is the situation in Poe's story, and in many respects it anticipates the dread induced in many writers—not in all of them—by crowds. Many nineteenth-century and some twentieth-century writers have felt that the crowd, the masses, huddled or crushed or driven along together to the degree of anonymity, mark the forces in modern life that can't be comprehended—or can be understood only in abstract terms, as Poe's "aggregate." The London imagined by Poe has much in common with the city described by Wordsworth, Blake, Dickens, Mayhew, Conrad, and Engels. It anticipates the scene in *Sister Carrie* in which Carrie and Drouet watch the crowd from the parlor of the hotel; the scene in *The Great Gatsby* in which Nick follows the crowd; and the scene in *The Crying of Lot 49* in which Oedipa Maas follows the postman through the streets of San Francisco.

II

A distinctive modern literature arose not from the development of cities but from the experience of crowds on city streets; from the friction between the individual mind and appearances—city streets, crowds, anonymity—over which it had little or no control. Much of English

literature is predicated upon the values of rural and domestic life, vil-
lage communities, the working of the land—as farmers, tenant-
farmers, agricultural laborers—over many generations. The modern
city, as it developed in its late-eighteenth- and early-nineteenth-
century form, disturbed the rhythm of that literature and questioned
the continuities it took for granted. If we ask how the crowd, in Poe's
London, differs from the mob in *Julius Caesar* or the Roman people
for whom the tribunes spoke, the answer is that the modern crowd is
a particular social formation, the consequence of social and historical
forces which those in power were persuaded or compelled to recognize; once recognized, they had to be adopted and indeed promoted.
I mean the Industrial Revolution, the movement of reform from 1832,
the development of education, roads and railways, newspapers, the
penny postage, gaslamps. The first recorded use of the phrase "the
masses" dates from 1837; the contrast with "the classes" was first made
by Gladstone in 1886. The phrase meant the populace or "lower orders," people who supposedly acted upon impulse because they did
not identify themselves with any of the recognized social classes or accept a normative system of values. Marx and Engels determined to
give "the masses" a sense of companionship as a first step toward gaining power. They set out to give the masses their own narrative. But
the literature of the period shows that it was mainly the heterogeneity
of the urban crowd that had to be reckoned with, the lack of the system of differentiation that generally helped people to know who they
were and what they were about. The invention of the internal combustion engine made a difference; the motor-car enabled those who
could afford one to go about their business and take their ease with a
measure of privacy, the inside of the car resembling as far as possible
their home. But the crowd in Poe's story is a mixum-gatherum. The
best that can be said for it is that it provoked sensitive spirits—
Baudelaire, Monet, Toulouse-Lautrec—to new emotions.

### III

Whitman may appear to be an exception to the rule by which the
urban crowd is a source of dread. Doesn't he welcome every manifestation of life? It is true that he committed himself to hospitality, took
pleasure in every mode of communication, had a special interest in

bridges, roads, rivers, railways. But even in "Crossing Brooklyn Ferry," it is a condition of Whitman's recognition of persons and objects that they yield their individuality to his; they must allow themselves to become a constituent of the poet's prophetic voice at whatever cost to their own. In the eighth section of *Song of Myself*, Whitman acknowledges the heterogeneity of city streets but only by standing back from them and producing them by an act of survey. One event has much the same status as another. Actions become nouns, and the nouns fill the space about equally. If nothing stands out from anything else, it is because the poet's eye and the eye of the mind have determined that the picture will be thus and not other:

*The blab of the pave, tires of carts, sluff of boot-soles, talk of the promenaders,*
*The heavy omnibus, the driver with his interrogating thumb, the clank of the*
     *shod horses on the granite floor,*
*The snow-sleighs, clinking, shouted jokes, pelts of snow-balls,*
*The hurrahs for popular favorites, the fury of rous'd mobs,*
*The flap of the curtain'd litter, a sick man inside borne to the hospital,*
*The meeting of enemies, the sudden oath, the blows and fall,*
*The excited crowd, the policeman with his star quickly working his passage to*
     *the centre of the crowd,*
*The impassive stones that receive and return so many*
     *echoes . . .*[5]

What is on view in that passage is the process by which typical scenes of Whitman's New York yield their heterogeneity to the power of his mind. These events are observed, but it is a condition of their being reported that they are assimilated to the poet's voice. It would be wrong to say that the poet is like the impassive stones, receiving and returning so many echoes, but misleading to say that the poet "leans and hearkens" to each event and withholds himself in its favor.

IV

Baudelaire's sense of the swarming city—"Fourmillante cité, cité pleine de rêves"—required different strategies. I begin with "The Painter of Modern Life," published in 1863 but written sometime between November 1859 and February 1860.

The essay mainly expresses Baudelaire's appreciation of the sketches and drawings of modern life by Constantin Guys. Baudelaire did not claim that Guys was a great artist, but he was delighted by the artist's demeanor, his unperturbed, unmorbid way of being present to the city. A sketch, dashed off as if merely a scribble, showed that one could be charmed or thrilled by appearances, not necessarily intimidated by their profusion. Guys was at home in the crowd. The crowd was his element, Baudelaire says, as the air is that of birds and water of fish:

> It is his passion and his profession to merge with the crowd. For the perfect idler [*flâneur*], for the passionate observer, it becomes an immense source of enjoyment to establish his dwelling in the throng, in the ebb and flow, the bustle, the fleeting, and the infinite. To be away from home and yet to feel at home anywhere; to see the world, to be at the very centre of the world, and yet to be unseen of the world. . . . The observer is a prince enjoying his incognito wherever he goes. . . . It is an ego athirst for the non-ego, and reflecting it at every moment in energies more vivid than life itself, always inconstant and fleeting.[6]

By "modernity" Baudelaire means "the transient, the fleeting, the contingent; it is one half of art, the other half being the eternal and the immovable."

Baudelaire was a moody writer and it is possible to quote him to several contradictory purposes, but he saw the crowd as possibility rather than as threat. More often than not, he thought of the crowd on the streets of Paris as something interesting to be seen rather than as something hostile to be jostled by. The sense of sight works by holding objects at a certain distance, and it makes available the experience of sensing life as a spectacle, in congenial moments a circus or a *mardi gras*. This was especially the case for Baudelaire, many of whose poems have recourse to the sense of smell, rather than that of sight, for their richest and most evocative occasions.

It is significant, too, that in describing the poetical character, or in offering an account of it for general understanding, he presented it in close association with the curiosity of childhood and of convalescence. In "The Painter of Modern Life" he says that convalescence is like a return to childhood in its openness to every experience. Genius he defines as the ability to recover one's childhood at will. A complete poetry would involve the recovery of such experiences and the application to them of sustained analytic and linguistic attention. Always, indeed, on the understanding that the world is permeable to one's imagination. In one of the *Petits poèmes en prose* he writes:

> The poet enjoys the incomparable privilege of being able, at will, to be himself and an other. Like those wandering souls seeking a body, he enters, whenever he chooses, into everyone's character. For him alone, everything is vacant. And if certain places seem to exclude him, it is because he considers them not worth the bother of visiting.

It follows that Baudelaire, at least in this mood, regards the crowd as a gathering of individuals, each of whom is in principle hospitable to the poet's imagination. They have not—or not yet—congealed into a mass.

It is difficult to say when poets and novelists started feeling the large city, the urban mass, as an oppressive and suffocating thing. In Balzac's novels, as Calvino (echoing Shakespeare's Sonnet 94) has remarked of *Ferragus* (1833), the city is still feasible, "all the characters appear to be the owners of their faces." The era of the anonymous crowd has not yet begun, the city is still the place for curiosity, not for tragedy or even comedy. But Calvino accepts the common view that in Baudelaire we have moved into the fright of anonymity. I wonder. Baudelaire seems to me not yet oppressed by the city. This may account for the sense, well described by Walter Benjamin, that in *Les Fleurs du mal* and in *Le Spleen de Paris* neither the population nor the city is described—he is thinking of Victor Hugo as a master of such description—but the crowd is always secretly present, we can sense its presence, it doesn't need to be described. In the two "Crépuscule" poems we feel the swarm of people who have not yet thronged the boulevards; in the cold air of morning it is the absent people who shiver, rather than the dawn which is described as shivering— "L'aurore grelottante en robe rose et verte"—and the women who are not described are those who wear that rose-and-green dress. Baudelaire can be equable about crowds, letting them press with secret force upon his poems, provided he can believe that the imagination can see multiplicity and solitude as "equal and interchangeable." As he says in *Le Spleen de Paris*:

> Multitude, solitude: equal and interchangeable terms for the active and fertile poet. He who does not know how to populate his solitude does not know either how to be alone in a busy crowd.

It would be excessive to argue that the notion of the free-standing individual was invented in the middle of the nineteenth century. Such a person was invented or at least resuscitated in the last decades of the eighteenth century upon the experience of looking at a landscape that didn't seem to include him, or seemed to include him only under benign conditions of atmosphere, weather, and work. Given such happy auspices, it was easy to feel that a landscape was susceptible to the feelings it aroused. Felicities of the mind, in a congenial setting, might be too easily achieved to be significant. But the experience of a body confronting other bodies, crowded in a city street, made the question of subject and object a real test. In theory, the relation between one person and a crowd should not be too difficult: they all share a common species and perhaps a common social formation. Why not regard the issue as one of a subject confronting other subjects, different only in their multiplicity? But the issue was not simple: it became difficult to feel that crowds jostling along a city street were comprehensible in the same way as an individual might be comprehended. How this feeling arose, and why it came to be oppressive, could be understood by referring to an elaborate quasi-documentary literature from Malthus, John Stuart Mill, Poe, Le Bon, and Mayhew to Ortega y Gasset's *The Revolt of the Masses* (1930) and Canetti's *Crowds and Power* (1960). Baudelaire does not come into that history, if only because of the provenance in his work of the experience of being fascinated.

Fascination comes from the Latin *fascinum*, meaning a spell and having to do with witchcraft. To fascinate is to attract someone's attention and retain it by an irresistible influence. Wordsworth was interested in the leech-gatherer, for good reason, but he was not fascinated by him. The narrator of Poe's story was fascinated by the old man; he pursued him in the hope of being released from that bond. Many of Baudelaire's poems start from the experience of being fascinated by someone, often a woman in a crowd, and the poem is the process by which fascination is written out of itself and into something else, a different experience. That he wasn't afraid of the crowd is sufficiently explained by the fact that he felt sure he could write himself out of its witchcraft into some other mode of cultural life.

The poem "A une passante" is a case in point:

> La rue assourdissante autour de moi hurlait.
> Longue, mince, en grand deuil, douleur majestueuse,
> Une femme passa, d'une main fastueuse
> Soulevant, balançant le feston et l'ourlet;
>
> Agile et noble, avec sa jambe de statue.
> Moi, je buvais, crispé comme un extravagant,
> Dans son oeil, ciel livide où germe l'ouragan,
> La douceur qui fascine et le plaisir qui tue.
>
> Un éclair . . . puis la nuit!—Fugitive beauté
> Dont le regard m'a fait soudainement renaître,
> Ne te verrai-je plus que dans l'éternité?
>
> Ailleurs, bien loin d'ici! trop tard! jamais peut-être!
> Car j'ignore où tu fuis, tu ne sais où je vais,
> O toi que j'eusse aimée, ô toi qui le savais![7]

Baudelaire alludes to the crowd and disposes of it in a line: "The deafening street was screaming all around me." He relies upon the reader to fill the sentence with the recollection of any such noise: there is no need to be specific. From this setting, vague as it is, a particular woman emerges, but only after an adjectival line has prepared the way for her: "Tall, slender, in deep mourning—majestic grief." The woman passes along, but Baudelaire sees her in a gesture, as if she were someone in a sketch by Guys, her fastidious hand raising festoon and hem. Then he stands back a little to see her "agile and noble, with her statuesque body." The sequence of observations does not coincide with the divisions of the sonnet. The setting occupies the first line, the description of the woman the next four. The change from the description of the woman to the description of himself couldn't be more abrupt or self-assertive: "Moi, je buvais. . . ." Merely to look at the woman is not enough, he must drink the qualities he ascribes to her, "the gentleness that fascinates, the pleasure that kills." But before we know what qualities he drank, we have him seeing himself "contorted like a madman." Benjamin remarks that what makes the speaker's body contract in a tremor "is not the rapture of a man whose every fibre is suffused with *eros*; it is, rather, like the kind of sexual shock that can beset a lonely man." The shock is met in the woman's eyes—"that livid sky where the hurricane germinates." To see her eyes as the sky, livid, black and blue, the colors of distress and despair, source of the hurricane, is to give the woman—or rather the speaker's sense of her—a destiny entirely of his devising. It is emphasized in the rhyming of *statue* and *tue*, death inscribed on her body, the pleasure of which kills. Benjamin said this poem tells of the look "of the object of a love which only a city dweller experiences . . . and of which one might not infrequently say that it was spared, rather than denied, fulfillment."[8]

The sestet of the sonnet has a flash of lightning, then darkness, sign of the sudden passage of the woman's glance into eternity, having caused in the poet a rebirth that leads to nothing. "Shall I see you again," he asks, "only in eternity?"—a question that leads to regressions in space and time: "Far, far from here, too late, maybe *never!*"

*Because I do not know where you are fleeing, you do not know where I am*
*    going,*
*You whom I would have loved; you who knew that, too!*

In this poem, then, Baudelaire writes himself out of the fixity of fascination by imagining for himself and the woman a passionate history. The imagining moves the experience into a sequence not much the worse for being hypothetical or otherwise idle. Where Poe's narrator found the reality of the old man categorically opaque, such that the glance of apprehension turns into the glare of an anonymous object, Baudelaire's sense of the woman in the crowd is open to at least notional assent. In this poem he does not quarrel with appearances or imply that there is a better truth beneath them or apart from them.

## V

I have been distinguishing between Poe and Baudelaire in relation to their sense of the crowd. Poe set his story in London because no

American city he knew, neither Philadelphia nor New York, had the conditions of friction, of there not being enough room to stroll along the streets; he had to imagine such conditions and set them in a city that in 1840 had a population of two and a half million. Paris, too, was crowded, but not to the extent of jostling *flâneurs* off the pavements; Baudelaire could still think of himself as the center toward which appearances moved. Joyce's Dublin, too, was still small and slow enough to sustain idlers and gossips. But the dark side of the *flâneur's* experience is Baudelaire's *ennui*; it comes upon him when he feels not that the passing scene is dull but that its being interesting is not enough. So long as the question of a relation between appearance and reality is not raised, it is enough that a scene is interesting, but *ennui* marks the occasion on which a metaphysical question enforces itself. If there is no answer, then appearances lose the quality of being different, they become a repetition of the same. Spleen is the exasperation of having this happen.

A moral question has similar consequence. Auden's poem "The Capital" acknowledges the modern city with "your charm and your apparatus": it has abolished "the strictness of winter and the spring's compulsion." Auden spent much of his life in cities, from Berlin to New York, but his imagination soon turned them into Latin tropes. Neither traffic nor crowded streets engaged him, but the city of God and the music that turned Auden's mind into "a *civitas* of sound." Civilization was the work of cities, no doubt, but the metaphors with which Auden judged them were mostly rural, bucolic, natural, as in feasible landscapes. Heroes in the twentieth century, he believed, were not great demons but ordinary people who retained their faces and did good work. Auden used the words "civic" and "civil" as if Horace had invented them. But he feared one quality of the modern city, that it was ready to conspire with one's monsters. In "The Capital":

> So with orchestras and glances, soon you betray us
> To belief in our infinite powers; and the innocent
> Unobservant offender falls in a moment
> Victim to his heart's invisible furies.[9]

The city beckons like a wicked uncle to the farmer's children, offering them forbidden pleasures. The glow is visible far into the countryside. The children grow up to come to the city and take to its ways, but often find themselves living in rooms "where the lonely are battered/ Slowly like pebbles into fortuitous shapes."

VI

Heterogeneity is the sinister aspect of what in a more agreeable light is regarded as diversity. Part of the problem with crowds in the nineteenth-century city was that it was hard to discover who the people were, what they were doing, and why. John Lucas has argued in *England and Englishness* that in the Victorian age England was becoming unknowable, and he cites as evidence Hopkins's poem about the unemployed, "Tom's Garland." Lucas doesn't like the poem, and he takes particular offense at the verb "infest" in the last line. Hopkins starts with a description of laborers, men who have work and go home at night tired but not heartsore. Then he thinks of men who haven't a job; they can't feel that they have any place, even a lowly one, in the commonweal:

> *Undenizened, beyond bound*
> *Of earth's glory, earth's ease, all; no one, nowhere,*
> *In wide the world's weal; rare gold, bold steel, bare*
> *In both; care, but share care—*
> *This, by Despair, bred Hangdog dull; by Rage,*
> *Manwolf, worse; and their packs infest the age.*[10]

Hopkins explained those lines to Robert Bridges in a letter of February 10, 1888:

> But presently I remember that this is all very well for those who are in, however low in, the Commonwealth and share in any way the common weal; but that the curse of our times is that many do not share it, that they are outcasts from it and have neither security nor splendour: that they share care with the high and obscurity with the low, but wealth or comfort with neither. And this state of things, I say, is the origin of Loafers, Tramps, Cornerboys, Roughs, Socialists and other pests of society.

Figures of swarming life, infestation, and so forth, came easily to nineteenth-century poets, and not only to Baudelaire and Hopkins. It wasn't a simple matter of class distinctions, of knowing one's place, and of the mess caused by one's not knowing it. Class was one system of demarcation, typology another; what chiefly made writers anxious was amorphousness. Stevens has a trace of this nineteenth-century anxiety in "Farewell to Florida," where he refers to "a slime of men in crowds."

Lucas makes the point that when Victorian England became un-knowable, writers started getting fretful and looking for a "vision" of it. As long as the social facts were intelligible, a vision beyond or above them wasn't necessary. John Bayley has remarked that this anxiety troubles *Howards End*, where the most sensitive people are worried im-mediately about houses, places, gardens, trees, music, and repellent dis-tinctions of class, but ultimately about a vision of England beyond all that.[11] I'm not sure that this takes the harm out of Hopkins's line about the unemployed infesting the age. But it's silly to exempt oneself from this kind of feeling. In the poem, Hopkins gets himself into a se-quence that is bound to end with a dire superlative. The conjunction of idleness and despair begets "Hangdog dull"; that of idleness and rage breeds "Manwolf, worse." That leaves only the worst, the social generality that includes them and their kind, "and their packs infest the age." It is not surprising that a poet who set such store by individ-uality is nasty about crowds, though it is unchristian of him to blame the unemployed for the trouble they cause.

Certainly the poem gives every form of merit to the laborer or the navvy who has a job, works at it, and doesn't whine. He is allowed to trample upon thousands of thorns, which are thoughts, without a care, and to toss behind him the conditions of his life. Hopkins isn't convincing on these social matters, his language doesn't sustain his generalizations. It's true that Victorian poets didn't find a language to deal with social issues and discriminations; novelists were far more suc-cessful in that way. Hopkins's poem tries to deal, at least in its first lines, with the kind of feelings that Lawrence expressed in *Sons and Lovers*, but Lawrence's sense of English social reality—the world of la-bor, the mines, drink, family, fellowship, and rage—was more subtle than Hopkins's, not because it was closer to Lawrence's experience than to Hopkins's, but because the novel of Dickens, George Eliot, and Hardy was a readier form, much as Lawrence determined to change it, than any of the languages of Victorian poetry.

## VII

What poetry needed was a technique Ezra Pound derived from modern painting: juxtaposition of details to make a field of force, not an argument:

> IN A STATION OF THE METRO
> *The apparition of these faces in the crowd;*
> *Petals on a wet, black bough.*

The faces are isolated for imaginative attention but not for description. Apparitions can't easily be described, but "these" draws attention to the only point of concentration, the words in this order. The field of force is established by contrasts: underground, above ground; urban, rural; mechanical, organic. Accentual emphasis in each line directs equal attention upon four words, syllabically diverse.

## VIII

In *The Waste Land*, crowds come in two forms. The first:

> *Unreal City,*
> *Under the brown fog of a winter dawn,*
> *A crowd flowed over London Bridge, so many,*
> *I had not thought death had undone so many.*
> *Sighs, short and infrequent, were exhaled,*
> *And each man fixed his eyes before his feet.*

Eliot's note directs the reader to Baudelaire's "Les Sept Vieillards"— "Fourmillante cité"—and to the passage in the *Inferno* where Dante, led by Virgil into the woeful city—"la città dolente"—sees the wailing crowd, souls who, having lacked conviction, lived "without infamy and without praise." They make, Dante says, such a long train of people "that I should never have believed death had undone so many"—

> *. . . sì lunga tratta*
> *di gente, ch'i' non averei creduto*
> *che morte tanta n'avesse disfatta.*

To speak of a crowd as flowing over London Bridge is to enforce an irony, since the movement is so mechanically different from that of a river, even of the Thames, which runs softly in Spenser's "Prothalamion" but not quite as innocently in "The Fire Sermon" of *The Waste Land*. It was daring of Eliot to make an end-rhyme by repeating "so many" in successive lines. Dante's Italian doesn't do this. Calling a crowd "many" rather than great or large seems to have been prompted by the phonetic possibilities of a language rich in gestures of dismantling and set upon such a course by the "Un" of "Unreal" and the consequent internal rhyming of "Under," "London," and—one of Eliot's most brilliant rhymes—"undone." The dissociation of lives is further enacted in the passive voice of "Sighs, short and infrequent, were exhaled," and the stare of "And each man fixed his eyes before his feet." In "Les Sept Vieillards" the ghost that accosts the passerby in broad daylight turns into an appalling, broken old man, and then into another, the same, and into yet another, until at the seventh apparition the narrator rushes from the infernal procession. Again, Eliot's narrative *persona* is like Poe's rather than like Baudelaire's: it is the opacity of the crowd that dismays him, the repetition of purposes neither living nor dead.

William Empson said that *The Waste Land* is a poem about London, a city and a culture that had just barely survived one Great War and couldn't be expected to survive another. Certainly the poem is dark with the sense of defeated cities—

> *Falling towers*
> *Jerusalem Athens Alexandria*
> *Vienna London*
> *Unreal*

In this respect, like Ezra Pound, D. H. Lawrence, Wyndham Lewis, and many other writers, Eliot feared the modern crowd, the masses, and despaired of a civilization that gave in to them in the name of democracy. Augustine's *The City of God* testified to a more arduous vision, a spiritual empire or commonwealth, the pattern for which was formed in Heaven. Renaissance Italian cities, which elicited such fervor from Pound and Yeats, were merely comparisons from a relatively minor historical genre, not at all adequate to Eliot's vision, but they

were better than nothing. He was not content, like Auden, to quote
Horace.

The second form of the crowd, in *The Waste Land*, has a different
provenance. In 1919, Hermann Hesse gave a lecture called "*The Broth-
ers Karamazov* or The Decline of Europe"; it became a chapter in *Blick
ins Chaos*, published the following year. Hesse was distracted by his
sense of eastern Europe in the months after the October Revolution;
he was appalled to think that Europe, old and tired of itself, would
lapse from its intellectual and moral standards into a condition he described as Karamazovian. "The ideal of the Karamazovs," he claimed,
"a primeval, occult, Asiatic ideal, begins to become European, begins
to devour the spirit of Europe":

> In Dostoevsky's soul what we usually call hysteria, a certain illness
> and openness to suffering, has served mankind as an organ, an in-
> dicator, a barometer. Mankind is on the point of taking notice.
> Already half of Europe, at all events half of eastern Europe, is on
> the road to chaos. Intoxicated with a divine madness, it makes its
> way along the edge of the abyss and sings, sings drunken hymns
> as Dimitri Karamazov sang. The insulted citizen laughs that song
> to scorn; the holy man and the seer listen to it with tears.[12]

Eliot quoted those last sentences in Hesse's German as a note to *The
Waste Land*, glossing the passage that begins—

> *What is that sound high in the air*
> *Murmur of maternal lamentation*
> *Who are those hooded hordes swarming*
> *Over endless plains. . . .*

The word "horde" came into English sometime in the sixteenth century; its origins are in the languages of Turkey, Russia, and Poland,
and it means (according to the *OED*) a tribe of Tartar or kindred Asiatic nomads. Their being hooded suggests photographs of helmeted
soldiers, one of the most dreadful images of anonymity to Eliot's generation.

## IX

I have been suggesting that a distinctive modern literature arose in response to a certain situation, that of individuals finding their individuality threatened by mass society. People in a crowd were still people,
but human or subject-based analogies did not apply; the crowd seemed
to be an object, not a subject or a gathering of subjects. Crowds were
not permeable. According to the romantic rhetoric of landscape, we
live in a world hospitable to our sense of it. A landscape-poem by
Wordsworth or a painting by Turner stimulates that conviction to the
point of making it appear one's second nature. But with the development of the modern city, it became difficult to retain that confidence.
It took time and practice before people could persuade themselves that
artifacts of culture might be just as sustaining as the configurations and
colors of nature. As cities replaced communities, the natural world
came to be the place of one's vacation, not of one's ordinary life. You
could still have the sentiment of the picturesque, the beautiful, and the
sublime, but chiefly by going on a walking tour across the Alps, looking at Mont Blanc, or otherwise interrupting the rhythm of daily life.
The city provoked certain emotions, or gave them special emphasis:
shock, fascination, the piquancy of being among appearances and surfaces without inquiring beyond them.

    The city also disclosed formal possibilities. An artist could con-
sider not what naturally goes with what, but what could be placed
alongside what to cause a new sensation. Modern hospital-wards and
the science of anesthesiology made it possible for Eliot's J. Alfred
Prufrock to compare the evening, spread out against the sky, to a patient etherized upon a table, a comparison unavailable to the author of
"Ode to Evening." Invention of the acetylene lamp, *circa* 1895, made
it possible for Hart Crane to describe noon-tide sunshine on Wall
Street as "a rip-tooth of the sky's acetylene."

    In *On Photography* Susan Sontag notes that photographs "help people
to take possession of space in which they are insecure."[13] Tourists, for instance, coping with foreign countries, strange manners, difficult languages.
A crowded street presents every condition of one's insecurity: more force
than one can cope with, people who admit one's attention without returning it, anonymity accepted as if it were chosen. A photograph of a
crowded street represents not the passersby but the condition under
which the photographer wishes to see them—stationary, for once—or the

limits within which the photographer is willing to see anything. The feeling that one is in charge of the crowd is a pleasurable and brief illusion: that these people are the constituents of one's picture is a notion to play with. In a studio portrait, or in a domestic portrait, the conditions may be different, the sitter may resist the camera's invasion of his privacy. Photographs of Baudelaire, taken by Nadar, Carjat, and Neyt, show him responding to the camera's terms by asserting his own: even when he faces the camera, he seems to warn the photographer that further goodwill on his part is not to be counted on.

The "problem of communication" in modern literature arose as soon as the crowd could be thought of as readers—in England, after the Education Act of 1870 provided for compulsory universal education and ensured that thousands could read English at the level of skill commensurate with the daily newspaper. Fear of the crowd was not eased by the consideration that these people might read your prose; the restrictions the crowd was likely to impose corresponded to the friction, noise, and general hubbub in the street. Some writers—Shaw, Wells, Bennett, Chesterton—accepted the restrictions and made a virtuoso's best of them, a further condition being that these writers were not to think of themselves as modern. A writer who regularly travelled by tube, as Eliot did in London, found it impossible to believe that he could write for the people with whom he had merely a jostling and frictional relation. Modernity had to be an affair of cities, but the choice of being modern was incompatible with the satisfaction of the interests that corresponded to universal education. Eliot's wish for an illiterate audience has its bearing here, as upon the "strained time-ridden faces" adverted to with exasperation and dismay in the third section of "Burnt Norton":

> *Distracted from distraction by distraction*
> *Filled with fancies and empty of meaning . . .*

The city-world epitomized in the Underground is neither one thing nor another, neither daylight nor darkness. As a poet, Eliot found relief in extreme situations, sordid or sublime, either of life or of death, which had at least the merit of clarity, of coinciding with themselves. At every turn, he found himself immersed in indeterminacy, and longed to be released from it.

X

The Gloucester Road tube-station wasn't anyone's image of a good life, but there were some advantages in accepting that modernity had taken this form. If you accepted that the scene of reality in the twentieth century was the city—its human image the crowd, its economy an apparently thriving capitalism—then you could place yourself in some relation, however nerve-racked, to these situations. The fact that Eliot chose to live in London counts for something; at worst, it gave him endless provocation to imagine and pray for a better life. The fact that reality had come to take this urban, crowded form allowed many writers to regard it as a perversion of some truly civilized state of being: you had only to work out what this true state was, not necessarily by thinking in historical or nostalgic terms, though Pound, Eliot, and Yeats were ready to do this. But if you started from the modern city, you could envisage a better form of life somewhere else. London provoked Lawrence to Etruscan and Mexican visions. Conrad's sense of a better elsewhere came not only from his experience of the sea but from his exasperated, nervous sense of London. Yeats accepted that reality was as it was declared to be—urban, positivist, empiricist—and this enabled him to summon into existence an antithetical state of being, which he was willing to call Ireland so long as he could imagine it as pre-modern, poetic, occult, unsullied by reason or science. Hardy's novels and most of his poems are elegies for a defeated life, defeated by the forces that had London as their greatest success. The Universal Exhibition in Paris in 1889 was a triumphal parade of modernity. Poets were left free to come to terms with the victory, or to inquire of their feelings what vital forces had been suppressed in it.

XI

I come back to "The Man of the Crowd," mainly to put beside it a passage from Simone Weil's essay on *The Iliad* as "the poem of force." Weil defines force as "that x which turns anybody who is subjected to it into a *thing*."[14] In Poe's story, why does the narrator give up trying to understand what the man of the crowd is doing? It is because at that moment he feels the crowd only as the mechanical consequence of force, it has already become a thing. No one's particular will has turned individual people into a crowd; it has merely come to be the case, as if by an anonymous system of force. The narrator thinks of the man he is pursuing as a criminal; there is no evidence in favor of this, so the explanation is that the narrator's terms of reference and interpretation are social. According to one's civic sense, opacity is an indication of crime, just as translucence indicates innocence, sociality.

Simone Weil wrote her essay on force and deduced it from the evidence of *The Iliad* mainly to show that the exertion of force to turn people into objects is not a modern invention. The most acute temptation is to see force as the form necessity takes, the principle that Emerson and Stevens called *Ananke*, the necessity inscribed in human life as such. It is a temptation just as serious to remove the exercise of force from individual will, as Foucault did when he represented modern systems of power as anonymous and therefore incorrigible. Weil argued that it was wrong to regard Hitler as a freak of nature and his exertion of force as a bizarre infringement of the human norm. She argued, on the contrary, that the exertion of force is and always has been so rife in human action that it is virtually endemic; and for that very reason it must be known for what it is.

Writers who were dismayed by the crowd had no cause to blame the crowd for that dismay. Snobbery is an easy explanation for their doing so, but not an adequate one. If you posit the human situation as a relation, of whatever kind, between subject and object, it becomes inevitable to think of subject as spirit and object as matter, and to ascribe to matter an appalling force of oppression. The question then arises: how can subject, or spirit, resist that oppression? Or must it yield to it at every point?

# BEYOND CULTURE

∽∾∾∽

I

The Great Exhibition of 1851 was nearly as significant as the Reform Act of 1867: in both cases, a society felt sufficiently sure of itself to put its signs on display. The extension of the franchise in 1867 was important not because it gave power to the lower class but because it demonstrated that the middle class in Britain exercised power by seeming to disperse it: in any event, power remained in the same hands, and the populace continued to be interested spectators rather than participants. The shifting of parties, the relative disposition of Liberals and Conservatives in Westminster, did not mean that a different kind of person gained power. For many years, the working class allowed itself to be represented by its employers. Between 1851 and 1867 there were indeed "two cultures" in Britain: the predominant one was represented by the Great Exhibition; the second one was too poor to share in the images the exhibition presented to the world. The poor were "beyond culture" in a literal sense. In the Great Exhibition middle-class society defined itself and put on display the emblems of its culture. These were mostly household goods, the furnishings of a class that had not merely come into its own but had made a strong claim to identify its interests with those of the nation.

The significance of Arnold's *Culture and Anarchy*, which he wrote in 1867 and 1868 and published as a book in 1869, is that it reduced

the moral differences between the three major social classes by identifying each of them with its ordinary self. By calling the aristocrats
barbarians, the middle class philistines, and the working class the populace, Arnold made each class appear, morally, much the same. The
average self of the aristocrats tends to be low-minded; that of the middle class to be dull, intellectually penurious; and that of the toiling
class to be vehement in opinion and ignorance. Arnold then invokes
the best self in each class, and the best in every individual, and calls the
system of values to which he now appeals culture. That each of us has
a best self, Arnold takes pretty much for granted. Presumably it exists
because it must, and if only because Arnold can't bear to consider the
possibility that it doesn't. For much the same reason, he takes unques-
tioningly to the idea of perfection if only because the signs of imper-
fection are irrefutable: the necessity of perfection is a logical one.

Arnold's idea of culture is prescriptive: the qualities necessary to
its representative are sweetness, light, the harmonious development of
one's faculties toward perfection. Culture, he insists, is an inward
working of the mind and spirit, an individual mark or possession:

> The idea of perfection as an *inward* condition of the mind and
> spirit is at variance with the mechanical and material civilisation
> in esteem with us, and nowhere, as I have said, so much in es-
> teem as with us. The idea of perfection as a *general* expansion of
> the human family is at variance with our strong individualism,
> our hatred of all limits to the unrestrained swing of the individ-
> ual's personality, our maxim of "every man for himself."[1]

"Swing" does most of the diagnostic work in the last sentence. An
ideal society would be one in which every man and woman sought
perfection in the terms recommended by consideration of sweetness,
light, and harmony. Arnold's interventions upon public discourse in
Britain and the United States were attempts to persuade his readers to
pay attention to the value of culture, or to put to shame those who
lived contented in ignorance. In this spirit he disputed with friends
and enemies alike, arguing about education, religion, science, literature, the function of criticism, the necessity of order and authority.
Most of his disputes, such as those with Huxley, John Stuart Mill,
Sidgwick, and Francis Newman, were efforts to recommend a certain
kind of person, much like Arnold himself, and to suffuse the image of

such a person with a corresponding aura of value and bearing. Arnold's methods of persuasion were diverse: often he picked out a phrase from his opponent's program and repeated it for mockery; or he delivered a phrase of his own so often that he made it seem immune to irony by anticipating the irony it would attract. Often he proceeded by establishing boundaries: between reason and madness, good and bad taste, authority and anarchy, vehemence and urbanity.

But none of Arnold's interventions was intended to cast doubt upon the idea of society as such. If culture meant a certain inward working of mind and spirit in every individual, society was the public and objective harmony of that working. An improvement in education or law meant that intelligence had a better chance of prevailing. If a clear idea could be put into circulation, so much the better. Arnold was often angered by what he saw in the streets—the Hyde Park riot on July 23, 1866, for instance—but he never withdrew his credence from the idea of society. Many of the conditions at large he wanted to see changed. But he did not recoil from the conditioned character of social life, or demand that the objects offered for his attention should be different objects. In this respect, if in no other, Arnold is akin to such diverse figures as Marx, Freud, Engels, Dickens, and George Eliot: he had nothing against a social emphasis in the understanding, or indeed in the organization, of human life. He did not demand to be released from social conditions or to be allowed to determine new conditions on which he would agree to live.

The notion of such a demand may appear bizarre. But the writers we think of as modern are those who contemplated the possibility of seceding from society and disavowing the social understanding of human life. Not because they wanted more congenial social arrangements but because they wanted to escape from all social arrangements. I refer to situations in which desire, real or imagined, cannot be satisfied by any public form available for its apprehension, and, as a result, withdraws its credence from such forms. The best account of this situation is given by Lionel Trilling in *The Liberal Imagination*. Thinking of Stendhal's *Le Rouge et le noir*, and of Julien Sorel's speech to the Besançon jury in which he threw away his life, Trilling says that Julien's happiness and heroism came "from his will having exhausted all that part of itself which naturally turns to the inferior objects offered by the social world and from its having learned to exist in the strength of its own knowledge of its thought and desire." Trilling then makes a general observation about nineteenth-century fiction in consonance with that episode:

> The novel has had a long dream of virtue in which the will, while never abating its strength and activity, learns to refuse to exercise itself upon the unworthy objects with which the social world tempts it, and either conceives its own right objects or becomes content with its own sense of its potential force—which is why so many novels give us, before their end, some representation, often crude enough, of the will unbroken but in stasis.[2]

## II

In the sense in which Julien Sorel is modern, Arnold was not modern: he was not intransigent, he was willing to see his imagination constrained by the official forms and appearances. Speaking of culture as an inward working of mind and spirit, he knew that he risked implying that such inwardness offered a feasible alternative to the life lived in public and social terms. Presumably he thought the risk worth taking, or that the strain of living an entirely inward life would prove, in a particular case, intolerable. He trusted that people would be sufficiently gregarious to make any complete reliance upon inwardness repugnant to them. But he often feared that the movement of feeling between private and social life might be broken off. In certain moods he thought such a breach a distinctively modern predicament. Explaining, in the preface to *Poems* (1853), why he had decided not to reprint "Empedocles on Etna," he said of that poem:

> I intended to delineate the feelings of one of the last of the Greek religious philosophers, one of the family of Orpheus and Musæus, having survived his fellows, living on into a time when the habits of Greek thought and feeling had begun fast to change, character to dwindle, the influence of the Sophists to prevail. Into the feelings of a man so situated there entered much that we are accustomed to consider as exclusively modern; how much, the fragments of Empedocles himself which remain to us are sufficient at least to indicate. What those who are familiar only with the great monuments of early Greek genius suppose to be its ex-

clusive characteristics, have disappeared: the calm, the cheerfulness, the disinterested objectivity have disappeared; the dialogue
of the mind with itself has commenced; modern problems have
presented themselves; we hear already the doubts, we witness the
discouragement, of Hamlet and of Faust.[3]

In such a situation, the suffering "finds no vent in action," there is
"everything to be endured but nothing to be done."

    What Arnold means by action, as distinct from pathos, is clear
enough: he means the relation between our permanent passions and
the world in which they are expressed. I don't think he ever envisaged,
as Trilling did, that the will might refuse to exercise itself upon the objects presented to it by the social world. But he thought it possible that
the relation between private and public life would break down, and
that the will would find itself unable to escape from the prison of its
desire. Pathos, rather than action, would be its fate.

    Arnold was dismayed even to consider such a predicament, and
on one occasion he tried to talk himself out of it by revising the idea
of modernity to which he had alluded in the preface of 1853. On November 14, 1857, he delivered his inaugural lecture as Professor of
Poetry at Oxford under the title "On the Modern Element in
Literature." His theme was the degree to which the ancient literatures
of Greece and Rome could still offer modern readers "intellectual deliverance." Deliverance from what? Arnold describes two forms of
trouble. The first is the proliferation of historical facts and images that
somehow have to be comprehended. It is a consideration we find also
in Nietzsche, though Nietzsche offers to lighten the burden of the past
by turning our attention to the future: we seek, Nietzsche says in his
essay on the use and abuse of history, "a past from which we may
spring rather than that past from which we seem to have derived." Arnold never thought that our relation to the past could be disposed as
briskly as that. He believed that the only way to deal with the "vast
multitude of facts" which we have inherited is by discovering the general ideas which are the law of that multitude. We are intellectually
delivered, he says, "when we have acquired that harmonious acquies-
cence of mind which we feel in contemplating a grand spectacle
that is intelligible to us." The analogy Arnold has in mind is landscape painting, or any experience of the beautiful or the picturesque;
not an experience of the sublime, because the sublime is not intelligi-

ble, it is what drives us beyond ourselves, at once attracting and repelling.

The second burden that Arnold associates with modernity is debility, the cost of thought. It is yet another version of the dialogue of the mind with itself. Arnold finds it in the conclusion to the third book of Lucretius, a masterly expression of lassitude, except that it cannot master the lassitude it expresses. "What a picture of *ennui!*" Arnold exclaims, "of the disease of the most modern societies, the most advanced civilisations!" Lucretius is modern, therefore, but he is not—to use Arnold's reiterated word—adequate. He merely withdraws from the world: "There is no peace, no cheerfulness for him either in the world from which he comes or in the solitude to which he goes." He is like Arnold in "Empedocles on Etna." To find an ancient literature adequate to the conditions it had to meet, Arnold reverts to Sophocles, whose drama is adequate because "it represents the highly developed human nature of that age—human nature developed in a number of directions, politically, socially, religiously, morally developed—in its completest and most harmonious development in all these directions; while there is shed over this poetry the charm of that noble serenity which always accompanies true insight." Arnold is already working out the relation between private and public life, between reality and imagination, that he advances more spiritedly in *Culture and Anarchy*.

### III

The considerations that prompt the will to refuse to exercise itself upon the unworthy objects with which the social world tempts it are clearly outlined in Georg Simmel's *The Philosophy of Money* (1900). Simmel argues that "the modern division of labour permits the number of dependencies to increase just as it causes personalities to disappear behind their functions, because only one side of them operates, at the expense of all those others whose composition would make up a personality":

> On the one hand, money makes possible the plurality of economic dependencies through its infinite flexibility and divisibility, while on the other it is conducive to the removal of the personal

element from human relationships through its indifferent and objective nature.[4]

The result of these conditions is a conviction that one's autonomy
must be sought within, a sense that one's real life is lived in relation to
oneself, not in a relation to the facts and objects which make up the
external world. Simmel goes on to distinguish between the
eighteenth-century and the nineteenth-century concepts of individual
man. According to the eighteenth-century view, value is deemed to lie
in human beings "merely because they are human beings"; the absolute value of all individuals is the same. In the eighteenth century, the
individual as such gained his or her specific significance in relation to
the state, church, society, or guild, so that the ideal condition was the
independence of the individual. But in the nineteenth century, and as
a consequence of the interests embodied in Romanticism, the meaning attached to individualism lies in "the differences between individuals and their qualitative peculiarities." These differences came to be
valued in recognition of the "preponderance of objective over subjective culture." "Every day and from all sides," Simmel notes, "the
wealth of objective culture increases, but the individual mind can enrich the forms and contents of its own development only by distancing
itself still further from that culture and developing its own at a much
slower pace." What Simmel has in view is "the enigmatic relationship
which prevails between the social life and its products on the one hand
and the fragmentary life-contents of individuals on the other." Individuals pursue their development as an inner drama, rather than as a willing engagement with the contents of the objective culture. They
regard their objective, professional lives as chores, instruments of their
inauthenticity; their authenticity is to be sought as an inward possession, leisure its enabling condition, soliloquy its form.
 Simmel doesn't mention another consequence of the division of
labor which bears upon the cultivation of inwardness and the refusal of
the will to engage with social objects: it is the habit that Max Weber
has elucidated, by which the right of judgment in large areas of life—
science, morality, and art—is handed over to experts. As a result, the
crucial consideration becomes one's relation to oneself. In *The Portrait
of a Lady*, when Isabel thinks of the other people in her vicinity, the
first question she brings to bear upon them is their relation to themselves. In chapter 19, for instance, Isabel is thinking of Madame Merle:

If for Isabel she had a fault, it was that she was not natural; by
which the girl meant, not that she was affected or pretentious; for
from these vulgar vices no woman could have been more exempt;
but that her nature had been too much overlaid by custom and
her angles too much smoothed. She had become too flexible, too
supple; she was too finished, too civilised. She was, in a word,
too perfectly the social animal that man and woman are supposed
to have been intended to be; and she had rid herself of every
remnant of that tonic wildness which we may assume to have be-
longed even to the most amiable persons in the age before
country-house life was the fashion. Isabel found it difficult to
think of Madame Merle as an isolated figure; she existed only
in her relations with her fellow-mortals. Isabel often wondered
what her relations might be with her own soul.⁵

That is the 1881 text. When James revised it for the New York edition
twenty-seven years later, he emphasized further the criterion of one's
relation to oneself. "Isabel found it difficult," we now read, "to think
of [Madame Merle] in any detachment or privacy, she existed only in
her relations, direct or indirect, with her fellow mortals. One might
wonder what commerce she could possibly hold with her own spirit."⁶
In the first version Isabel assumes that Madame Merle had some relations with her soul, and she merely wonders what they might be. In
the final version she is not sure that Madame Merle holds any commerce with her spirit. Her being "not natural" is retained in both versions. Isabel doesn't doubt that being natural entails having commerce
with one's soul or spirit. She takes it for granted that we should retain
something of our tonic wildness despite the willing experience that
makes us social and sociable. She doesn't see that what appears as "being natural" may indicate the exhaustion of the gregarious will and a
refusal of sociality. Being natural may be a state before sociality or
after it; its insignia may be just as credibly assigned to *ennui* as to wildness.

Simmel is our best guide to these matters. But there is one respect in which he lets us down. Near the end of the book, he argues
that the will "is unable to effect anything at all unless it gains some
kind of *content* that is completely external to it." He maintains that the
contents of the world "are completely neutral, but at one point or another they unpredictably become coloured by the will." At that point,

they become the means by which the will defines a purpose. But Simmel doesn't allow for the situation described by Trilling, in which the will refuses to exercise itself upon any contents provided for it by the world; the will does this, however, without abdicating its sense of responsibility to itself. Simmel might argue that in such a situation we are not dealing with the will at all, that there is no will until someone's energy engages with an object external to it and for a purpose defined by that engagement. But we don't need Freud to instruct us, as he did, that an act of will may take the form of refusal, of going into exile, rather than deal with contents not at all neutral but degraded or otherwise sordid.

Simmel maintains that the contents of the world are neutral till one's energy pays attention to them and declares them a means toward a corresponding end. But there is a long-established tradition which holds that we ought to feel responsible for things on the analogy of our responsibility toward other people. One of the marks of the literature we think of as modern, however, is rejection of such responsibility; the will turns away from the things in front of it as if they constituted chiefly an obstacle to the relation between the will and itself.

IV

It is for this reason that we think of Pater as the most suggestive theorist of modernity, even though we may qualify his report by referring to Poe, Emerson, Baudelaire, Whitman, Mallarmé, and Hopkins.

In "The School of Giorgione" (1877) Pater gives his reasons for saying that all art constantly aspires toward the condition of music:

> Art, then, is thus always striving to be independent of the mere intelligence, to become a matter of pure perception, to get rid of its responsibilities to its subject or material; the ideal examples of poetry and painting being those in which the constituent elements of the composition are so welded together, that the material or subject no longer strikes the intellect only; nor the form, the eye or the ear only; but form and matter, in their union or identity, present one single effect to the "imaginative reason," that complex faculty for which every thought and feeling is twin-born with its sensible analogue or symbol.

It is the art of music which most completely realises this artistic ideal, this perfect identification of matter and form.[7]

The impulse which strives to be independent of the mere intelligence—or, in Wallace Stevens's version of Pater, resists the intelligence, almost successfully—is still a faculty of the mind, but it serves a different god. In one vocabulary, it is the imagination as distinct from reason; it is the mind in the enjoyment of freedom from the rules of sequence and order. As Stevens says in *The Necessary Angel* (1951), we live in concepts of the imagination before the reason has established them. But if that is true, "concepts" is not the right word. To make the distinction a little clearer, we might speak of the difference between reverie and reason, making it clear that one of the motives of reverie is to get rid of the mind's responsibilities to its subject or material. Reverie is the act of the mind which displaces attention from the object to the mind itself, its own processes and reflections. Perhaps the best description of it is in Yeats's essay "The Symbolism of Poetry." If the spirit of Symbolism were to prevail, he says, "we would cast out of serious poetry those energetic rhythms, as of a man running, which are the invention of the will with its eyes always on something to be done or undone; and we would seek out those wavering, meditative, organic rhythms, which are the embodiment of the imagination, that neither desires nor hates, because it has done with time, and only wishes to gaze upon some reality, some beauty."[8]

We are describing a state of mind that is not mere daydreaming but in which the will turns toward the objects held out to its attention, only to recoil from them. It is the state of mind that Yeats described as the gaze, distinguishing it from the glance. The glance is an administrative form of attention, engrossed in objects that it wishes only to deploy. The gaze is the mind's attention to its own processes and to objects only in passing and by necessity. The reason such a form of attention exists is that under certain provocations the mind is repelled by external objects, and wishes to pay attention to itself alone.

In the conclusion to *Studies in the History of the Renaissance*, Pater indicates what this form of consciousness entails:

In a sense it might even be said that our failure is to form habits: for, after all, habit is relative to a stereotyped world, and meantime it is only the roughness of the eye that makes any two persons, things, situations, seem alike. While all melts under our feet, we may well grasp at any exquisite passion, or any contribution to knowledge that seems by a lifted horizon to set the spirit free for a moment, or any stirring of the senses, strange dyes, strange colours, and curious odours, or work of the artist's hands, or the face of one's friend. Not to discriminate every moment some passionate attitude in those about us, and in the very brilliancy of their gifts some tragic dividing of forces on their ways, is, on this short day of frost and sun, to sleep before evening.

When Pater speaks of setting the spirit free "for a moment," he recognizes that the strain of such freedom couldn't be borne for much longer. The effort of analysis, apprehension, and discrimination could not be sustained. So Pater is committed to the desperate system of values by which the objects of the world are deemed mostly contemptible, and are attended to only till the mind, withdrawing from them, makes itself the better object of attention. The impression of burdensomeness in Pater's *Marius the Epicurean* issues from the strain of paying such attention to one's feelings.

In the passage I quoted from Trilling, he speaks of the will conceiving its own right objects—right, in contrast to the always wrong objects with which the social world tempts it. Much of the literature we think of as modern is an effort of the will to conceive right objects for itself, rather than the unworthy objects otherwise on display. Stevens's whole career, in poetry and prose, was an effort to conjure into existence a pageant of right objects displacing wrong ones, to create a secondary world that could hardly, in practice, dislodge the primary one but which would exceed it in finesse. Similarly, Pater's *Studies in the History of the Renaissance* is not an attempt to make sense, or better sense, of certain paintings, on the understanding that these have a demonstrably objective existence, but an attempt to describe the relation between these paintings and Pater's mind, on the understanding that the chief partner in the relation is his mind. Henry Adams's *Mont-Saint-Michel and Chartres* is not a study of Christendom or of France in the twelfth century or of Gothic architecture or of the Virgin Mary as force and object of conviction; it is a study of all these as right objects for a will disgusted by the official objects offered to its attention—the objects on display, for instance, at the Chicago Exposition in 1893. Pound's *Cantos* does not recite the history of ancient China, Renaissance Italy, John Adams's administration, or the execution of Mussolini as if these matters were of intrinsic or extrinsic interest. Pound is calling attention to these things, and pointing to the action of intelligence in the public worlds they denoted. But the episodes are in the first instance right objects that Pound's will conceives for itself, in place of the wrong objects that the objective culture offers as tokens of meaning and value. The philosophy of history that Yeats outlines in *A Vision* is his attempt, not to say how it was, as if he were a historian, but to indicate how historical events may be seen under the sign of a certain system of metaphors and other figures. The philosophy at work is exhibited in the mutual reflection of images and figures, not in an argument that might be deduced from them. The particular images and metaphors are right objects for the will they appease. These several works do not annotate a world common to us all; they constitute, in each case, a possible world, an adversary world sustained by the will that projects it in opposition to mere being and the official rhetoric in its favor. That is why these works are more persuasive as autobiographies than as works referring to a world we think we hold in common.

The other possibility to which Trilling refers is that the will may become content with its own sense of its potential force. Stephen Dedalus in Joyce's *A Portrait of the Artist as a Young Man* is a case in point. Here is a passage from the fifth chapter, where Stephen is walking, slowly indeed, toward the university and his classes in Stephen's Green:

> The rainladen trees of the avenue evoked in him, as always, memories of the girls and women in the plays of Gerhart Hauptmann; and the memory of their pale sorrows and the fragrance falling from the wet branches mingled in a mood of quiet joy. His morning walk across the city had begun, and he foreknew that as he passed the sloblands of Fairview he would think of the cloistral silverveined prose of Newman, that as he walked along the North Strand Road, glancing idly at the windows of the provision shops, he would recall the dark humour of Guido Cavalcanti and smile, that as he went by Baird's stonecutting works in Talbot Place the spirit of Ibsen would blow through him like a keen

wind, a spirit of wayward boyish beauty, and that passing a grimy marinedealer's shop beyond the Liffey he would repeat the song by Ben Jonson which begins:

*I was not wearier where I lay.*

His mind, when wearied of its search for the essence of beauty amid the spectral words of Aristotle or Aquinas, turned often for its pleasure to the dainty songs of the Elizabethans. His mind, in the vesture of a doubting monk, stood often in shadow under the windows of that age, to hear the grave and mocking music of the lutenists or the frank laughter of waistcoateers until a laugh too low, a phrase, tarnished by time, of chambering and false honour, stung his monkish pride and drove him on from his lurkingplace.[9]

The first sign that Stephen's will is content with its potential force is that the relation between his thoughts and the places which ostensibly call them up is arbitrary. In Stephen's mind and in no other mind in the world is there a connection between Baird's stonecutting works and the spirit of Ibsen. The marinedealer's shop and a song from Jonson's *The Vision of Delight* make company only in Stephen's mind. Stephen isn't interested in discovering why these and not other connections that might have equal or greater authority inhabit his thought. It is enough for him that he enjoys the arbitrariness of these relations, since the only authority in the case is then his own.

This explains the main difference between the stories in *Dubliners* and Stephen's story in *Portrait*. In *Dubliners,* Joyce accepts the objects provided by the social world. Or at least he is content to imagine objects contiguous to those, and to make little dramas of them. But in *Portrait* the objects offered by the social world are not given much authority. Stephen is shown disengaging himself from them, letting his will take pleasure in itself and its own potential force. The paragraph in which he imagines himself a doubting monk in the Elizabethan age is a little production of right objects; so we see his will moving here between two of its possibilities. What we see in the last forty pages of the *Portrait* is, to use Trilling's terms, a representation of the will unbroken but in stasis. The reason readers can't agree about these pages—and why some read them as sympathetic to Stephen and others as conveying Joyce's dismissal of Stephen's pretension—is that we don't know what status to give to the will when it hovers upon its potentiality and does not go forward to action. We don't know whether to regard it as mostly vain, as if making an empty claim for itself, or as a force fully entitled to project a future of its own in which it will indeed act.

There is another possibility, one that Trilling doesn't mention in his account of the refusing imagination. The imagination knows its potentiality but knows it only as conscious whirling in a void, and it comes to feel for itself mostly contempt. The most thoroughgoing example of this, precisely because he goes nowhere, is Eliot's J. Alfred Prufrock, the wings of whose consciousness beat in a void:

> *And I have known the arms already, known them all—*
> *Arms that are braceleted and white and bare*
> *[But in the lamplight, downed with light brown hair!]*
> *Is it perfume from a dress*
> *That makes me so digress?*
> *Arms that lie along a table, or wrap about a shawl.*
> > *And should I then presume?*
> > *And how should I begin?*[10]

Prufrock is a recognizable voice, a sensibility belated to every occasion, a series of gestures memorable for the pointlessness of their being made at all. But these transactions take place not in a common world stabilized by the attachment of words to things but in a language extraordinarily ready to substitute acoustic events for specifications. What we remember from the passage I've quoted is not a woman's bare arm glamorously lying along a table, but a voice—J. Alfred Prufrock's—aimlessly echoing among syllables: the emphatic end-rhymes of "dress" and "digress," the internal rhymes of "all" and "already" and "shawl," the ailing repetitions of syntax, "And I have known . . . And should I then . . . And how should I . . . ?" Eliot's language in the early poems is always dismembering itself, just as Prufrock dismembers women into eyes and arms. At any moment, the language is breaking up its full semantic capacity and exploiting one of its resources—usually the one that Eliot called incantation, with Poe, Tennyson, Swinburne, and Lewis Carroll mainly in mind—and all the while striving, in Pater's terms, to get rid of its responsibilities to mere subject-matter. Incantation is an exorbitance among the capacities of language; it testifies not only to a refusal of responsibility to subject-matter and reference but to an effort to constitute an adversary world, a world entirely verbal.

In her book on Valéry, Elizabeth Sewell says that "words are the mind's one defence against possession by thought or dreams; even Jacob kept trying to find out the name of the angel he wrestled with."[11] Eliot's early poetry is written upon that emphasis; upon words as such, their internal values and resonances. Their meanings constitute only one attribute among many.

V

It may be said that the refusing will or imagination is a harmless indulgence and that any reasonably comprehensive society could afford to have a few such idlers. Does their presence amount to anything more than the desire to escape from the middle class while continuing to enjoy middle-class felicities? Perhaps a question of bad faith arises; but whose faith is not in some respect bad? I should note, however, that the refusing or dissociating will has been regarded as sinister from at least two standpoints. In an essay called "The Angelic Imagination," Allen Tate declined to regard the refusing imagination as harmless. He denounced it as hypertrophy of the will, "the thrust of the will beyond the human scale of action."[12] Presumably the human scale of action consists of the objects, worthy or unworthy, which the social world offers the imagination. Tate believed that the imagination should stand well disposed toward that offer, and be willing to work with its images. He thought so well of the will in that state that he called it "the symbolic imagination" and saw it exemplified in Dante. But he called the refusing will "the angelic imagination" because angelism makes a direct claim upon essence, having no need of existence as an enabling or mediating element. Tate finds in Poe this circumvention of the human image. He says of the angelic motive in him:

> Poe's readers, especially the young, like the quotation from Glanvill that appears as the epigraph of "Ligeia": "Man does not yield himself to the angels, nor unto Death utterly, save only through the weakness of his feeble will." It is the theme of the major stories. The hero professes an impossibly high love of the heroine that circumvents the body and moves in upon her spiritual essence. All this sounds high and noble, until we begin

to look at it more narrowly, when we perceive that the ordinary carnal relationship between man and woman, however sinful, would be preferable to the mutual destruction of soul to which Poe's characters are committed. The carnal act, in which none of them seems to be interested, would witness a commitment to the order of nature, without which the higher knowledge is not possible to man. The Poe hero tries in self-love to turn the soul of the heroine into something like a physical object which he can know in direct cognition and then possess.

The second attack upon the refusing will is well represented by Fredric Jameson. A Marxist or post-Marxist critic, he is bound to be scandalized by the will that refuses to accept the world even to the extent of going out and changing it. In an essay on Wyndham Lewis, Jameson distinguished between two motives in the major artists of Modernism. According to one, which he finds in Lewis and the collage procedures of Cubism and Expressionism, the morality of the work of art consists in representing the plenitude of inwardness and subjectivity as illusory, and devising sentences and rhythms that underline the degraded character of objects in the social world. According to the other, which Jameson finds in Joyce and Eliot and associates with Impressionism and Symbolism, the work of art produces "strategies of inwardness" that "set out to reappropriate an alienated universe by transforming it into personal styles and private languages." Jameson argues that the procedures of Joyce and Eliot "reconfirm the very privatization and fragmentation of social life against which they meant to protest."[13]

This is the most tendentious part of the argument: it concerns the status and the value of private life. Jameson, like Adorno, denounces the private life as a spurious possession; it is just as degraded as the social world from which it flees. The only appropriate stance toward "the degraded world of commodity production and of the mass media," Jameson argues, is that of externality and satire, a jarring mimesis of the world the mind has to face. What Jameson denounces, therefore, is what he regards as a conspiracy between commodity culture and the devices by which people can feel themselves emancipated from it while leaving it unchanged. The readiest of such devices is a claim upon privacy. Jameson attacks any literature or art that practices

Impressionism, subjectivity, Symbolism, metaphor, aesthetics, unity of tone, the autonomy of individual life and individual consciousness. They are in collusion with the enemy.

The argument seems to me wicked when it denies individuals access in good faith to their subjectivity. Jameson has not shown that "strategies of inwardness" are bogus. What would constitute evidence? Reference to Stephen Dedalus, Leopold Bloom, and J. Alfred Prufrock is enough to show that the range of experience, within what counts as subjectivity, doesn't preclude critical discrimination. Eliot's poem acknowledges the possibility of individual consciousness, but it doesn't exempt its forms from criticism. The fact that Leopold Bloom muses about the commonplace objects and events he encounters to the point of keeping his mind busy is no cause for treating the process with contempt. Degraded objects are often the occasion of undegraded feelings, and not only in Bloom.

Besides, neither Joyce nor Eliot allowed the matter of inwardness and subjectivity to remain in those terms. Each of them became a major writer by virtue of the rational imagination he exerted upon his subjectivity. The poet of *The Waste Land* does not need instruction on the nature of a commodity culture, or on its mechanizing impact. But in *The Waste Land* and in the later poems, Eliot maintains the responsibility of individual consciousness and at the same time forces it to acknowledge, at every point, a higher perspective than its own. This is what the allusions are doing in *The Waste Land*. If we want a formula for it, we have one in Eliot's major essay on Dante, where he recommends that we accustom ourselves "to find meaning in *final* causes rather than in origins." Eliot is giving the back of his hand not merely to Freud, but to the common fixation upon origins as the place of explanation in every respect. It is important to try to understand one's feelings, but it is not sufficient to track them down to a putative origin in one's childhood or one's unconscious or in inherited traces as formulated by Darwin. The most important thing, according to Eliot, is to examine one's feelings in the light of one's end, the validity of human life in relation to God. From "Ash-Wednesday" to "Little Gidding," this emphasis is explicit; but even before "Ash-Wednesday" Eliot neither dismissed individual consciousness nor left it unexamined.

It would be easy to take Eliot's word for it, in "Tradition and the Individual Talent," and say that the best curb upon one's consciousness, if a curb is needed, is "the historical sense," "which we may call nearly indispensable to anyone who would continue to be a poet beyond his twenty-fifth year." But nothing that Eliot says about the historical sense, in that essay or elsewhere, solves any of the problems of the philosophy of history which have persisted, despite the best efforts of Hegel, Dilthey, Gadamer, Habermas, and many other writers. History, in the sense intended by any of those writers, is deeply compromised by the unworthy objects with which it deals and the materials of the objective culture variously described by Marx, Simmel, Weber, Adorno, Benjamin, and others. It would be implausible to claim that Eliot gave much credence to a philosophy of history which had to work with such materials. He valued the historical sense, and for much the same reason that he valued the power of memory: because each of these capacities enables us not only to recover certain moments that have meant a great deal to us but to recover them in a new context, the present, which alone confers meaning upon them. The meaning of an experience does not coincide with its happening. Meaning is what an experience becomes when, removed from its immediacy, it can be recovered and, for the first time, understood.

The point is to escape from one's immediacy, to achieve a certain distance, a saving gap of time. Memory is one such device. The best escape is by considering ultimacy. In the passage from *The Republic* that Eliot thought of using as an epigraph to *The Waste Land*, Glaucon asks Socrates if the ideal city can be found in this world, and Socrates answers: "Well, perhaps there is a pattern of it laid up in heaven for him who wishes to contemplate it and, so beholding, to constitute himself its citizen."

## VI

The essay I have been quoting, Trilling's "Art and Fortune," was published in 1948. Like the other essays collected in *The Liberal Imagination*, it was written as part of Trilling's effort to speak up for the will, against those intellectuals, those "fellow-travellers" as he later described them, who "cherished the idea of revolution as the final, all-embracing act of will which would forever end the exertions of our individual wills."[14] These people, weary of moral vigilance, saw in Stalin's Communism "the promise of rest from the particular acts of will which are needed to meet the many, often clashing requirements of democratic society." Trilling was convinced, on the contrary, that life was always the better for putting a high valuation on the will. He also believed that the major works of nineteenth- and twentieth-century literature arose from the engagement of the writer's will with the conditions, social and personal, it had to meet. The will could choose to confront the conditions at large, as Jane Austen, Dickens, Balzac, and Henry James did, or make a principled refusal to deal with them. Either of these choices would mark the continued vitality of the will.

Temperamentally, Trilling was more comfortable with the first choice than the second. He believed that the novel became a major achievement to the degree to which it directed the force of will upon the conditions that surrounded it. He admired Howells's novels for that reason. But he also respected the literature that exhibited the will in the act of refusal. This respect is clear in *The Opposing Self* and *Beyond Culture*. Trilling thought it entirely appropriate that literature should take an adversary stance toward the society that provoked it.

But he came to feel considerable misgiving not so much about the writer's will in the act of refusal but about the apparent ease, the glibness of the act: it was in many instances an unearned felicity. It is not now thought that Trilling invented the phrase "Modernism in the streets," but it describes well enough his conviction that what started as a heroic effort of the literary imagination was now available in cheap imitations. His misgiving first appeared in an essay on Hawthorne published in 1964. At one point in the essay Trilling distinguished between Hawthorne and Kafka. "Never," he said, "in a secular culture, has the inner life seemed of such moment as it does in our culture."[15] The modern relation to Kafka seemed especially to bear upon this sentiment. Where Hawthorne, in the end, emphasizes "not the power of the artistic imagination but the intractability of the world," Kafka exhibits the boldly autonomous imagination that conceives of nothing that can throw it off its stride. Kafka's work "gives very little recognition, if any at all, to the world in its ordinary actuality, as it is the object of our desires and wills, as we know it socially, politically, erotically, domestically." He is an exemplar of the intransigent imagination that takes no notice of mere conditions.

In the same essay, Trilling argues that the modern understanding of Hawthorne is the reverse of James's:

The modern consciousness requires that an artist have an imagination which is more intransigent than James could allow, more spontaneous, peremptory and obligatory, which shall impose itself upon us with such unquestionable authority that "the actual" can have no power over us but shall seem the creation of some inferior imagination, that of mere convention and habit. Our modern piety is preoccupied by the ideal of the autonomous self, or at least of the self as it seeks autonomy in its tortured dream of metaphysical freedom.

For this reason, the modern hero is Kafka rather than James or Hawthorne.

I can't claim to be familiar with Trilling's sense of the years after 1964; the war in Vietnam, his response to the *événement* of the spring of 1968, the student disturbances at Columbia University, where he taught a course on modern literature. But a lecture he gave at Cambridge University in 1973, "Art, Will, and Necessity," expressed his sense that something had changed. There was now no reference to Kafka, to modern insistence on the autonomy of the self, or the aggressive disengagement from society that sent many people "beyond culture." Trilling was now concerned with the symptoms he took as evidence that the will, in many people, had resigned. Instead of the nineteenth-century tension between will and necessity, there seemed to be a reduction, a devaluation, in the general sense of both terms. Necessity figures in the contemporary imagination, according to Trilling, not as a condition endemic to life but as a contingency: it is widely regarded as an anomaly that persists "not because it cannot be mastered but only because we have not yet put ourselves with sufficient energy to getting rid of it." What corresponds to this axiom of the merely contingent character of necessity is the fact that the will has lost virtually all its former standing. Trilling appeared to say that in 1973, as in 1948, intellectuals were looking for conditions and forces in which they could submerge the individual will.

Trilling's argument in the Cambridge lecture seems to me persuasive. But the only evidences he offered for it were an essay by Robert Scholes on contemporary fiction and a collection of essays on modern art by Harold Rosenberg. Rosenberg argues that capitalism has appropriated modern art; as a result, the ostensibly free, subversive spirit of art merely lends the color of spirituality to the capitalist enterprise.

Scholes's essay celebrates a new kind of fiction that makes a greatly reduced demand upon the individual will. He refers to the emergence
of Structuralism and to a form of fiction—he meant chiefly John
Barth, Thomas Pynchon, John Fowles, and Robert Coover—
according to which human existence is presented as a structure, in
Trilling's words, "a discernible pattern of reiterated destinies in which
personal intention is but one of several formal elements."

There is more to be said about these matters than I propose to
say. It is doubtful if any cultural conclusions can be drawn from contemporary painting, a proliferation of objects palpably compromised
by the collaboration of corporate money, gallery owners, dealers,
agents, advertising, and the media. As for Structuralism: it has receded
from any common range of interests. No particular privilege is now
claimed for the novels—with the exception of *The Sot-Weed Factor* and
*Gravity's Rainbow*—that Scholes described. What most clearly emerges
from Trilling's Cambridge lecture is his nostalgia for a time and a literature in which the crucial issue was the conflict between a society
deemed to be inescapable and the heroic will of certain writers in
confronting it.

In the end, Trilling was dismayed not by the desire of an intransigent will to secede from culture but by the apparent ease with which
the secession could be effected. My own sense of the matter is that our
feeling of being "beyond culture" is a valuable sentiment, provided
we acknowledge that it would be better still to be within an enlarged
or enhanced culture. Modern literature gives some indication of what
a transformed culture would be. But literature suffers from the disability that reading is a private act: we cannot read in a crowd or even in
a group. At a concert, a play, or a football match, one is obviously
within culture, but the experience of reading a novel or a poem is private. Current debates leave one free to regard the truth of consciousness as the experience of introspection, a decision not at all
undermined by scientific descriptions of the act of the mind as neuro-
nal activity in the brain. Reading is a provocation to introspection, if
only because the necessity of continuously interpreting the words
makes the act of reading an inward experience. It is mischievous to de-
grade the character of reading by presenting it as merely yet another
bout of subjectivity, the consolation prize of bourgeois liberalism. The
best way of countering this attitude is by showing that introspection is
not the puny, self-regarding act it is commonly said to be but an act

of ethical and moral bearing. When Baudelaire spoke of populating one's solitude, he meant the act by which the mind, in privacy, imagines lives other than its own. Conscience is the capacity by which we reflect upon our actions in the light of our sense of justice. There is no reason why we should allow ourselves to be put out of countenance by attacks upon this sort of subjectivity.

We revert to the dialogue of the mind with itself. Arnold was afraid of it, or nervous about it. He associated it with doubts, discouragement, anxiety, Hamlet and Faust. But Plato, both in the *Sophist* and the *Theatetus*, represented thinking as the silent dialogue of the mind with itself; the mind, in thinking, is talking to itself. Not in a state of doubt or discouragement. Arnold placed a high valuation upon thought, but only as a preparation for action in the world. Thought was valid because it improved our prospect of acting justly. The reason why Pater, and not Arnold, is the begetter of modernity in English literature is that he showed how thinking could be valued as an intrinsic satisfaction. Thinking, feeling, reverie: the pleasures of these are self-evident, they don't have to be judged upon their results or upon their consequence as action in the world.

# ARIEL AND HIS POEMS

ༀ༐ཾ

I

In 1983, Foucault gave a lecture in Paris under the title "What Is Enlightenment?"; it started as a commentary on a short essay of the same title that Kant published in November 1784. I am not concerned with Kant's essay but with Foucault's argument that modernity is a consequence of the Enlightenment. He spoke of "the extent to which a type of philosophical interrogation—one that simultaneously renders problematic man's relation to the present, man's historical mode of being, and the constitution of the self as an autonomous subject—is rooted in the Enlightenment."[1] Foucault accepted, as Kant did, that the Enlightenment refers to a set of events, historical processes, and social institutions sustained by a project of knowledge as the result of unaided reason, quasi-scientific inquiry. But the feature of the lecture on which I want to concentrate is Foucault's assertion of continuity, if not identity, between the Enlightenment and modernity. He was not concerned, at least on that occasion, with questions of historical development or of sequence: it was not a matter of significance to him that he located the Enlightenment in the eighteenth century and modernity in the nineteenth. He was far more concerned with a certain attitude which he offered to describe. It is not surprising that he quoted, as texts of modernity, two essays by Baudelaire, "The Painter of Modern Life" and "On the Heroism of Modern Life." I've commented on one of these, but I propose a further remark in the light of Foucault's transaction with both essays.

Foucault commented on three aspects of modernity, as Baudelaire construed it. The first is that when Baudelaire associates modernity with "the transient, the fleeting, the contingent,"[2] he means that the distinctive modern sense of these appearances consists in recapturing something eternal that is not beyond the present moment but within it. In Guys's drawings, as Baudelaire says, "things seen are born again on the paper, natural and more than natural, beautiful and better than beautiful, strange and endowed with an enthusiastic life, like the soul of their creator." When Baudelaire speaks of the heroism of modern life, he means that it is heroic in the degree to which the mind finds interest and value not in the established past but in the unofficial present, a time vulnerable because fleeting, hardly a time at all except that it is neither past nor future. Modernity, Foucault said, "is not a phenomenon of sensitivity to the fleeting present; it is the will to 'heroize' the present." The heroic quality is the mind's willingness to stake everything upon the chance of appearances and upon the choice of paying attention to them. We have adverted to another form of heroism, according to which the will refuses to have anything to do with these appearances—it is Trilling's theme. But Baudelaire's hero doesn't merely stroll around the city. He looks at an object and gives it a different life, imagines it as other than it is.

Foucault noted the passage in "The Painter of Modern Life" in which Baudelaire celebrates the dandy, the one who determines to create "a personal form of originality, within the external limits of social conventions." The dandy belongs to periods of transition, as Baudelaire says, "when democracy has not yet become all-powerful, and when aristocracy is only partially weakened and discredited." Dandyism is a setting sun, the last flicker of heroism in decadent ages. Foucault goes a little further than Baudelaire in saying that modernity involves taking oneself as an object in the same spirit in which Guys transformed the objects he looked at. One produces or even invents oneself by an elaborate act of asceticism; it corresponds to Pater's idea of *ascesis*, an inward discipline in the cause of one's development. To these observations, Foucault added a crucial consideration. Baudelaire, he said, does not imagine that the heroic acts of modernity have any place in society, or in the body politic: "They can only be produced in another, a different place, which Baudelaire calls art."

Foucault's strategy in the lecture was to translate into twentieth-century terms Baudelaire's three motifs—emphasis on modern hero-ism, the transfiguring play of freedom with reality, and the ascetic elaboration of the self—and to represent them as work to be done, consistent with Kant's Enlightenment. Kant's question was that of dis-covering the limits that knowledge had to make sure not to transgress; the modern question is: "In what is given to us as universal, necessary, obligatory, what place is occupied by whatever is singular, contin-gent, and the product of arbitrary constraints?"

## II

There are strategic advantages in making modernity seem to consist of a certain attitude and the projects that it attracts to itself. There are ad-vantages, too, in making these seem the fulfillment of the Enlighten-ment. But there is a flaw in Foucault's argument, or rather, an anachronism in his definitions. The Enlightenment was a confident program of the application of reason to life. Reason was to be put to the task of detecting illusions and superstitions, the "empire of error," as Hegel called it. The aim was to achieve, by way of knowledge, mas-tery over the natural world. The type of such knowledge was empir-ical science. But it is clear from Hegel's *Phenomenology of Mind* that Enlightenment suffers a certain embarrassment, since it can't avoid re-garding the social world as a cave of error, and the *philosophe* as the only enlightened mind on view. How the *philosophe* came to rise above otherwise universal confusion is not clear. In the section of the *Phe-nomenology* about the "Struggle of the Enlightenment with Supersti-tion," Hegel says, in effect, that the believer is in just as strong a position as the *philosophe*:

> How are deception and delusion to take place, where conscious-ness in its very truth has directly and immediately the certitude of itself, where it possesses itself in its object, since it just as much finds as produces itself there?[3]

There may be no defect in consciousness, but the *philosophe* hasn't sole access to its certitude.

In any case, the attitudes that Baudelaire brings together in his account of modernity are incompatible with a strictly empirical or experimental science. His interest in the ephemeral, the fleeting, and the transitory is not under the jurisdiction of knowledge. These appearances present not a problem of being or even of knowledge but opportunities for the emotion we have already come upon as fascination. Fascination is a scandal to the *philosophe* because it displaces knowledge. The experience of fascination is the thrill of being seized by an appearance, indifferent to origin or end; it is destined only to pass out of sight, and is therefore exempt from the rule of being judged. Fascination is the thrill of not having to know. One experience of being fascinated differs from another in intensity because that is the only scale of interest which arises: there is no question of subjecting those experiences to the criteria of knowledge.

That is one of many reasons why the major Romantic poets, indebted as they were to the Enlightenment, were not content with its program or its methods. The concept of reason is highly mobile in Romantic writers, but their use of the vocabulary of vision and imagination expresses, on the whole, their dissatisfaction with the Enlightenment. No self-observing *philosophe* would have looked at an object and tried to imagine its being different; he was concerned only with its being the same. Lyotard has done well to point out that the essential factor in modernity is not reason but the insinuation of the will into reason.[4] Romantic writers do not insist on finding every experience intelligible, or on detecting illusion in dreams, fantasies, and visions. Indeed the Romantic writer is especially open to experiences of the sublime, which drive beyond reason, or of fascination, which eludes it. Besides, the will insinuating itself into reason may choose to see the crowd not as anonymous victim of the social and economic system it sustains, but as making a lively picture. Baudelaire's *flâneur*, in this respect like his dandy, is not concerned to detect experience or to expose it as illusion by rational criteria. His criteria are those of taste, not of intelligibility; and taste is a flair for making arbitrary choice among sensory occasions, not for separating truth from error. Lyotard notes, too, that Kant himself spoke of reason's urge to go beyond experience; at that point the concept of reason isn't sufficient, we need a different name. The new name, whether we call it imagination, vision, or something else, is meant to accommodate not merely the power of observation but of sympathy, the ability to imagine one's being someone else.

Among the English Romantic writers, Coleridge and Hazlitt are preeminent theorists of this sympathetic or dramatic imagination. In these and other writers, projects of reason become projects of the will, and the fundamental impulse of Romanticism is to make the mind feel not that it is in command of the natural world but that it is at home in a world at once natural and human; that there is a "wooing both ways" between the mind and the world. Suffused with this conviction, the mind thinks of itself as sensibility. The condition that imposes the most severe test upon the mind is, as I have suggested, that of the crowd, the mass society, and the mind that has to deal with it.

The insinuation of the will into reason makes a difference so emphatic to nineteenth-century literature that it calls for description in terms quite different from Foucault's. Knowledge as the work of unaided if not unprejudiced reason is the project of science. Hostility between literature and science, or rather between concepts of education that gave privilege to one more than to the other, was inevitable until an agreed division of labor made communications between them feasible. Wordsworth tried to make peace by saying, in the preface to the second edition of *Lyrical Ballads*, that if the time should ever come when "what is now called Science" shall be ready to put on "a form of flesh and blood," the poet "will lend his divine spirit to aid the transfiguration." He means that if a scientific discovery becomes a human property, part of ordinary lore, then the poet will take as much interest in it as in leech-gatherers and forsaken Indian women. But when Arnold, Huxley, and Sidgwick were arguing about education, scientists were claiming to know what the world was, and the claim was commonly if not universally accepted. What poets claimed to know was the working of affections and desires, the unofficial but irrefutable transactions between one person and another, and between the mind and itself.

Over the years, Wordsworth's offer was taken up. A few scientific discoveries became common lore if not common knowledge, and artists accepted them for the new metaphors they provided: this is Gillian Beer's theme in *Darwin's Plots*. Whitman shows that when knowledge becomes lore, it offers itself to the poet alert to such occasions; where it came from doesn't matter. Knowledge of psychoanalysis is a rare possession, but the lore of psychoanalysis is in everyone's ears and, unfortunately, in nearly everyone's mouth. As lore, it is available to writers and readers, much as Wordsworth predicted.

I am not implying that literature and science settled their differences and agreed that scientists would take over the Enlightenment and keep the franchise on reason and knowledge, letting writers do what they might with unofficial modes of being. It has always been possible to regard reason as a puny capacity: "Reason? That dreary shed, that hutch for grubby schoolboys!" as Theodore Roethke called it in "I Cry, Love! Love!"[5] Possible, too, to regard science as having a largely predatory interest in the objects it examines, by contrast with the poetic imagination, to which John Crowe Ransom ascribed the faculty of contemplating the world's body, "things as they are in their rich and contingent materiality."[6] Science and literature did not agree to divide the spoils between them. But during the years in which science achieved remarkable success and gained a high degree of mastery over the natural world, writers and artists took comfort in discovering that they could deduce a world from their own inwardness. That was not their sole comfort; it was possible to move about in the world, as artists, without incurring a charge of naiveté. But the writers we think of as modern—a short description of them would be the writers who affected to despise Bernard Shaw—made of the private life their true estate and theme. The practice of one's consciousness upon its own processes became, as Saul Bellow once said with some dismay, the most available form of virtue. Virtuous or not, poets blundered upon "a wonderful instead."

Of these blunderers the most resourceful was Stevens, who saw that you could make a world, or at least a globe, a semblance of a world, not by examining the external world, proclaiming the discovery of a circumference and divining a center for it, but by starting with the self as center and summoning to its presence enough appurtenances to make up another globe. Strictly considered, Stevens had little to say. Like the God of *Exodus*, he merely said, "I am that I am." But Stevens repeated the statement so often, in so many moods and tones, that we hardly think of counting the repetitions a disability. The poetry he wrote in this spirit disclosed not only a feasible way of passing the time and living one's life but a method of inventing an adversary world, boldly set off against the one apparently held by science, technology, and politics.

## III

Stevens's *Collected Poems* was published on October 1, 1954, the day before his seventy-fifth birthday. In the final section, *The Rock*, there is a poem, "The Planet on the Table," which he published in the Summer 1953 number of the magazine *Accent*: we are free to imagine that the planet on the table is the large typescript of the *Collected Poems*, or the galleys, or the page-proofs. We may think of Stevens looking at the bulk of his poetry and thinking of it as amounting to a world, a planet, a globe, his life not as heterogeneity but as form and now as composure.

In those late poems, Stevens's effort is to come upon the worst he can't avoid thinking of—old age, impending death—and then by a heroic gathering of energy to encompass even that fate within the grasp of his imagination. His motto for this effort is in "The Plain Sense of Things":

> Yet the absence of the imagination had
> Itself to be imagined.[7]

Sometimes, as in "Of Mere Being," it is a relief to give up thinking, and to let the natural world continue on its way without one's mind in attendance. But more regularly Stevens wants his imagination to be even more comprehensive than the poverty of substance it seems increasingly to have to meet.

"The Planet on the Table" begins:

> Ariel was glad he had written his poems.
> They were of a remembered time
> Or of something seen that he liked.

It is judicious that Stevens speaks of himself, or at least of the author of these poems, as Ariel rather than as Prospero. In *The Tempest*, Ariel is "an airy spirit," an angel in an irregular tradition of magical practices. He is also Prospero's servant, and he doesn't much like his servitude but is assured by his master that "after two days" it will end and he will be released to the air, his choice element. Prospero is a magus and a scientist, so the powers we see Ariel wielding come from his master. If Stevens is Ariel, it is because his imagination partakes of an even greater power, the poetic imagination as such, the supreme and supremely human capacity, or so he encourages us to believe. In *The Ethics of Romanticism*, Laurence Lockridge describes as "expressivist" a particular mode of the author as agent. In this mode, the production of a poem is "an act as real as other acts in the world" and equally open to "being judged in part by moral criteria." With the development of expressivist theories of poetry, as in Coleridge and Wordsworth, there comes "a larger sense of responsibility for the act of writing."[8] The poem discloses the moral reality of the poet, and the poet may be judged upon that evidence. Theories of the poetic *persona* have been invoked to give the otherwise merely biographical self of the author a certain latitude. Emerson's distinction between *psyche* and *pneuma* works to the same purpose: the *psyche* is one's personal or psychological character; one's *pneuma* is the divine spark of creativity which takes possession of one person rather than another and makes that person a genius. By calling himself Ariel, Stevens keeps his genius within the expressivist mode and places it at a certain distance; he is merely a messenger, after all, though he serves a divine master.

In other poems, according to the same tradition, as in "The Auroras of Autumn," Stevens speaks of the poet as scholar, "the scholar of one candle," the candle being the poetic capacity of vision, the scholar its adept. Stevens got the word "scholar" in that sense from Emerson's "The American Scholar" and from Pater's essay "Style"; like Pater, Stevens used the word to refer to a vocation, a discipline somewhat cloistral, as he understood poetry to be. In *The Rock*, the rock means everything that is the case, what can't be evaded, though its terrors may be mitigated to the point of their seeming to vanish:

> . . . *the poem makes meanings of the rock,*
> *Of such mixed motion and such imagery*
> *That its barrenness becomes a thousand things*
>
> *And so exists no more. This is the cure*
> *Of leaves and of the ground and of ourselves.*

There is, in a prosaic sense, no cure, no remedy for dying, but the act of writing poems, of making meanings of the rock till the last breath, is what these poems do.

When Stevens says that Ariel's poems were of a remembered time or of something seen that he liked, he doesn't mean that his poems were about these things. "Of" is the most difficult word in Stevens. It sometimes means "about," and separates the mind from the object in the case. More often, it is the partitive genitive, according to which something is part of something else and therefore inseparable from it. Sometimes the relation between the part and the whole is so intimate that even to distinguish them in this way is misleading. Ariel's poems are of a remembered time in the sense that they are part of that time. They don't claim to be as extensive as the time, but to be its epitome; they are not something seen that he liked, but the gist of the experience of seeing it.

I propose to skip to the end of the poem, to the point where Stevens indicates the system of values upon which a claim for poetry—and for that way of spending one's life, if one is a poet—may be sustained. He says of Ariel's poems:

> It was not important that they survive.
> What mattered was that they should bear
> Some lineament or character,
>
> Some affluence, if only half-perceived,
> In the poverty of their words,
> Of the planet of which they were part.

In Stevens's poetry generally, affluence is an attribute of diction, the pleasure he took in the gaudiness of the coat of many colors he wore, especially in his early poems. A poet's words are part of the larger affluence of being alive and living on this planet. The poems are part of the planet, in the sense that they do not exist aside from it. They are not mere annotations or footnotes to a planet complete without them. A poet's words, as Stevens claimed in *The Necessary Angel*, "are of things that do not exist without the words."[9] That is to say, the authority the words claim is not that of denoting things in the common world. It comes from the language of which the words are parts, and from the capacity that Ariel's imagination discloses by moving between them.

The writing of poems is therefore a project of the self; its aim is to discover and to bring forth the capacities of the self. Reasoning is necessary but not sufficient. Or rather: the will has insinuated itself so resourcefully into reason that it has made reason its servant; the substance of the mind is desire, to an even greater extent than it is cognition or ratiocination. If Stevens is in any sense a philosophic poet, it is because his poems are moments or motions in a phenomenology of desire. Not truth, but pleasure, especially the pleasure of self-production and self-disclosure, is their business.

But this does not give us any warrant for treating Stevens's poems as if they were music, or as if they met no resistance in their flight to fictiveness. He was enamored of fictions, provided they were his own, and he loved them so much that he protested he believed in them, or at least in a few of them and especially the one he deemed supreme. But he knew that the expressivist mode in literature makes the poet responsible for everything he produces. The chief characteristic of the mind, as Stevens repeated after Henri Focillon, is "to be constantly describing itself." The artist may transform us into epicures, as Charles Mauron said, but as epicures we still incur a moral judgment, and so does the artist who effected the transformation. Stevens accepted this responsibility in the late poems of *The Rock* more clearly and more gravely than in any earlier book; this is the main reason that these, and "The Course of a Particular," which he overlooked in assembling *The Rock*, are Stevens's greatest poems. He still cultivates the fictions, but he acknowledges, too, how obdurate the rock is, and that it cannot be cured merely by his wanting to cure it. He knows the force exerted by things as they are—in "Les Fenêtres" Mallarmé says, "Ici-bas est maître"—even though he determines to talk himself through this knowledge.

In Stevens's poems, the mind describes itself by setting up fictions; that is, statements or narratives arbitrarily conceived, such that the question of their correspondence to any situation in the world does not arise. In a realistic novel, the novelist tries to make us forget that the fiction is fictitious. But in Stevens's poems, no attempt is made to ground the fictions upon anything we already know of the world: their authority is a function of the poet's will, and of the internal accord he makes among the words. If the words seem to acknowledge anything in the world, or to denote something we recognize, then the poet starts the process he calls abstraction. According to a motive we have already seen in Pater, Stevens liberates the will from its responsibility to things. That is the process he calls, in "The Creations of Sound," making the visible a little hard to see.

IV

Stevens's master in this process is Mallarmé. In "Crise de vers" Mallarmé relegates the acts of describing, reporting, and recounting to the merely commercial function of language; it is honorable so long as we are involved in ordinary communications. We distribute our words much as we pass coins across the counter. But the poet's task is to engage in the process by which a natural object appears to be conjured out of its material existence; it become an idea, a fiction:

> Je dis: une fleur! et, hors de l'oubli où ma voix relègue aucun contour, en tant que quelque chose d'autre que les calices sus, musicalement se lève, idée même et suave, l'absente de tous bouquets.
>
> Au contraire d'une fonction de numéraire facile et représentatif, comme le traite d'abord la foule, le dire, avant tout, rêve et chant, retrouve chez le Poëte, par nécessité constitutive d'un art consacré aux fictions, sa virtualité.[10]

We load the dice a little if we put this passage beside another one, from Mallarmé's "Mystery in the Art of Letters," where he says that "the thing to which we grant a character of immediacy and nothing more is vulgar." Leo Bersani has shown, in *The Death of Stéphane Mallarmé*, that Mallarmé's dealings in the journalism of themes and subjects are more complex than they appear; he did not divide his culture as strictly as we have assumed into high and low, the poet and the crowd.

But the word we need from the passage I've quoted is "virtuality." Mallarmé doesn't define it, but it denotes the process by which the elements of an art are disengaged from their ordinary purposes and given the particular destiny appropriate to that art. The word "flower" is used in mundane transactions of communication—a flower may be named, bought, put in a vase, given to someone—but the poet's task in the spirit of Mallarmé and Stevens is to use the word in such a way that, along with other words similarly chosen, it expresses his own spirituality rather than an object in the world. Let us suppose (though it's a large supposition) that the predominant character of a word is its punctuality, the lucidity with which in ordinary communications it points to things, objects, and conditions. What color is that lime? It is green. The word "green" in that reply doesn't distinguish one shade of green from another, but presumably it is an adequate description for the immediate purpose. It would not be adequate for Stevens in *Notes Toward a Supreme Fiction,* in the passage about the planter and the island-orchard left after his death:

> *A few limes remained,*
>
> *Where his house had fallen, three scraggy trees weighted*
> *With garbled green. These were the planter's turquoise*
> *And his orange blotches, these were his zero green,*
>
> *A green baked greener in the greenest sun.*

The process by which "green" is eased out of its punctuality begins with "garbled." The first meaning of "garbled" is sifted or culled; it became a prejudicial word only late in its career. Garbled green is green blotched with other colors, a mess but still green. Zero green depends upon our sense of "zero degree" in Stevens's poems generally, an honorable state of poverty but not destitution. The movement, in the last line, from green to greener sends it on its inevitable way to "greenest." Greenest as an adjective in the superlative character is odd with "sun" as its noun. No sun looks green. But at this point even the sun is thought of as suffused with greenness; it is the color of the planter's element, and for that reason it is the color of the limes and of everything else. Stevens has removed from green its local responsibility: "greenest" has a different affiliation now. The force of mind at work is chiefly Stevens's will, testifying to desires other than those appeased by rational description.

I am emphasizing virtuality because it is the character of words—or indeed of any of the substances of art—when they are released from their responsibility in the daily life of the world. Release is most difficult to achieve in literature, because a trace of mundane observance adheres to words no matter how resourceful the poet is in removing it. "Greenest" tries to be an adjective qualifying "sun," and fails only because the pure formality of green, greener, greenest and the semantic clash of "greenest" and "sun" makes us look elsewhere for its provenance. It is because we expect suns to be red or gold that "greenest" makes us think further about its ideal relation, in this context, to sun.


V

The best account of virtuality I have come across is in Susanne K. Langer's *Feeling and Form*, a theory of art largely based on music. "All music," Langer says, "creates an order of virtual time, in which its sonorous forms move in relation to each other—always and only to each other, for "nothing else exists there."[11] Virtual time "is as separate from the sequence of actual happenings as virtual space from actual space." Virtual space, "the primary illusion of all plastic art," exists for vision alone; it has no continuity with "the space in which we live." The elements of a work of art are "created only for perception." That is the point. In daily life we have many purposes and obligations, so we need words as currency; we have to practice domestic and social economy. But literature does not help us in those transactions. It arises from excess, more energy than we locally need. It is a luxury of words, not a necessity. Perception is only one of our purposes, and it may not even be the most urgent one. In a work of literature, the words are chosen and arranged "only for perception." A poet does not make statements, even if statements appear to be made. "The poet's business," as Langer puts it, "is to create the appearance of 'experiences,' the semblance of events lived and felt, and to organize them so they constitute a purely and completely experienced reality, a piece of *virtual life*." The elements of a work of art will not organize themselves spontaneously in this way, if only because the first obligation of each of them is to facilitate the immediate transactions of our lives; literature comes later and at leisure.

I am not claiming that the notion of literature as virtual life rather than as actual life was an invention of modernity. Emphasis on virtuality is just one way of putting it: much the same understanding of literature could be reached by taking seriously the idea of form or the idea of rhythm. The only advantage of talking about virtuality is that it keeps us mindful of the risk of confusing elements of art with elements of life—the sense of time and space, the provenance of statements, assertions, meanings. All of these factors take place in a work of art, but under different auspices and obligations. The literature we regard as modern defined itself in a mainly adversary relation to reality as commonly construed—as construed, notably, by politics, science, and commerce. It was crucial to discover how a word, worldly in its first consideration, could be prevailed upon to become an element in a poem and serve there the sole purpose of perception. Mallarmé and Stevens are best appreciated in that enterprise.

But this is not the end of the story. Modernity is not a fact of historical life or of chronology: it is not something that happened at a particular time. Nor is it a cause, such that everything else in its domain became a consequence. The name refers to a stance, an attitude, a choice. By definition, the invitation could be declined. If modernity is defined in constraining terms, it becomes clear that a writer has always been free to ignore the considerations which it apparently entails. It is not necessary to be modern. If the early Eliot and the early Joyce are deemed to have embodied in their writings a predicament and a set of devices to deal with it, and if that relation of predicament and device is regarded as constituting at least a version of Modernism, then it is obvious that many writers took no notice of the predicament. In poetry, Frost, Robinson, Graves, Edward Thomas, Auden, and many other writers ignored what Frost ironically called the larger excruciations—alluding to Eliot, I assume—and went about their different business. It has always been possible to ignore what other people regard as the "spirit of the age." It may be a chimera.

At the same time it is clear that the devices we think of as modern in literature resemble the procedures in Western philosophy from Kant to Husserl. I put the matter inaccurately: many philosophers, and not only Nietzsche and William James, refused the official "direction" of philosophy. But, by and large, from Kant to Husserl and Heidegger, philosophy proceeded, at least in Europe, as a metaphysics of subjectivity: it concerned itself chiefly with the subject positing itself in knowledge and encountering objects apparently to be known. Among poets in English and American literature, Stevens is the one who most elaborately pursued that paradigm. His aim was to discover to what extent the individual mind can posit, invent, produce, perform itself by "insinuating the will into reason," and to disclose the little planet the mind thereby appears to create.

VI

A metaphysics of subjectivity is not self-evidently what philosophy should be engaged in. And even if philosophy from Kant to Husserl and Derrida has been a major achievement, there is no reason to think that it must continue in that spirit. Habermas has argued in *The Philosophical Discourse of Modernity* that the "paradigm of the philosophy of consciousness is exhausted."[12] He has reached this conviction after an analysis of Kant, Hegel, Schiller, Nietzsche, the Frankfurt school, Husserl, Heidegger, Derrida, Bataille, and Foucault. I do not see how his account of these philosophers, and of the discourse of modernity in which they have played major parts, can be much faulted. I am not sure about his own proposal—that philosophers, having abandoned the philosophy of consciousness, should take up a different project, that of "mutual understanding between subjects capable of speech and action." As Gandhi said when asked what he thought of Western civilization: "It would be nice." Habermas assumes that the language in which such communications would take place is translucent, equally available to all its speakers as if in a perfectly simultaneous system of translation. But Lyotard has a better argument, that language is a highly complex archipelago, involving regimes of discourse so different—descriptive, prescriptive, evaluative, and so forth—that they are opaque to the program Habermas has in view.

Even if the philosophy of consciousness were to be abandoned, as Habermas recommends, the validity of introspection would not be undermined. Habermas is not as forthcoming about this as I would like him to be. His descriptions of the communication he recommends have their main resonance in social and political action, but it would be a pyrrhic victory if he had in view the devaluation of inwardness. Levinas says in *Totality and Infinity* that the "inner life is the unique *way* for the real to exist as a plurality," and, again, that interiority constitutes an order in which "what is no longer possible historically remains always possible."[13] It would be wrong to remove that possibility, or try to make people ashamed of themselves for enjoying it.

It is in Levinas, rather than in Habermas, that one finds the necessary—the necessarily radical—change of bearing. In *Totality and Infinity* and *Otherwise Than Being* he proposes not only to put aside the Western fixation upon ontology and epistemology, upon being, the same, the one, totality, and the claims of power which they enforce, but to ground philosophy upon the radical imperative of ethics. His maxim is: ethics precedes ontology. A philosophy of ethics would differ from Habermas's philosophy of communicative action in several respects. Some of them are indicated in an early essay by Levinas on Proust and a slightly later one on Michel Leiris. "The Other in Proust" was published in 1947, at a time when it was widely felt that solitude and the breakdown in human communication were the fundamental obstacles to universal brotherhood. Collectivism searched for a term outside individuality to which each person could contribute so as to found a community.

Levinas didn't remark, as Trilling did, that the idea of a collectivity had for many people the particular charm that they could relax their will in its embrace. Levinas wasn't cynical about the desires approved by collectivity, but he knew that the easiest way of forming one was, as in Hitler's plan, to name a common enemy. His most emphatic objection to a collectivity was that it was sought as a fusion:

> One begins with the idea that duality must be transformed into unity, and that social relations must culminate in communion. This is the last vestige of a conception that identifies being with knowledge, that is, with the event through which the multiplicity of reality ends up referring to a single being and where, through the miracle of clarity, everything that encounters me exists as coming from me. It is the last vestige of idealism.[14]

Proust's most profound vision, on the other hand, "consists in situating reality in a relation with something which forever remains other, with the other as absence and mystery, in rediscovering this relation in the very intimacy of the 'I.' "

In the essay on Leiris, "The Transcendence of Words" (1949), Levinas says that modern philosophy and sociology have accustomed us to underestimating the social link between persons who speak; they have emphasized silence or the complex relations, such as customs or laws, prescribed by civilization:

> This scorn for words certainly has to do with the way language can degenerate into a prattle that reveals nothing but social unease. But this scorn cannot triumph over the situation Robinson Crusoe is privileged to experience when, in a magnificent trop-

ical landscape, where he has continued to maintain civilization through his tools and his morality and his calendar, he still finds in his encounter with Man Friday the greatest event of his insular life. It is the moment when finally a man who speaks replaces the inexpressible sadness of echoes.

Several years after Levinas's essay, and independently, Elizabeth Bishop wrote one of her most telling poems, "Crusoe in England," in which she imagines Crusoe returned now to England and thinking of the two islands of his experience and of the archipelago in his dreams. His theme is the inexpressible sadness of the loss of echoes, the silencing of the speech of objects:

> *The knife there on the shelf—*
> *it reeked of meaning, like a crucifix.*
> *It lived. How many years did I*
> *beg it, implore it, not to break?*
> *I knew each nick and scratch by heart,*
> *the bluish blade, the broken tip,*
> *the lines of wood-grain on the handle . . .*
> *Now it won't look at me at all.*
> *The living soul has dribbled away.*
> *My eyes rest on it and pass on.*[15]

Bishop's Crusoe doesn't interrogate the knife or try to appropriate it in the form of knowledge. The object is not required to return to the subject, or to demonstrate the subject's power in comprehending it. The complaint, if there is one, is an issue of justice, and the analogies invoked are moral ones. The knife once spoke to Crusoe, and now that it has gone silent, it won't even look at him. When Crusoe looks at it, it does not return his look. It may be true, as another poem by Bishop ("One Art") talks itself into saying, that the "art of losing isn't hard to master," but it is a terrible discovery to make, and the keenest sense of justice cries out against it.

Levinas's philosophy is a metaphysics of the will, but not the will-to-knowledge or (the same thing) the will-to-power. The most fundamental act is that of welcoming the other; the jurisdiction entailed is that of justice, the principles engaged are those of ethics. The principles of logic are never called upon to sustain acts of respect and welcome. In *Totality and Infinity*, Levinas insists that there is no point in formally distinguishing will from understanding, will from reason, when you decide at once to consider as goodwill "only the will that adheres to clear ideas" or that makes decisions only out of respect for the universal. If will is accompanied by anything in Levinas's account of it, it is by "the primordial face to face of language." Knowledge is not derided, but it is placed under the authority of justice.

## VII

Nothing I have quoted from Habermas or Levinas implies that the literature of Romanticism, Symbolism, and Modernism is superannuated. To appreciate that literature, it is necessary for a reader only to imagine being different and speaking that difference. As Coleridge said, let us not introduce an Act of Uniformity against poets. Besides, even if poetry from Wordsworth to Stevens seems to have conceived a purpose not much different from the purpose taken up by philosophy from Kant to Husserl, there is a difference: philosophy acted upon that purpose in a far more officious and single-minded spirit, as an epistemology in league with an ontology. The poets pursued this aim in the spirit of amateurs, as well they might, and they held themselves ready to respond to any prompting, turning aside from their task. They took their duty lightly, whereas the philosophers took it gravely. So it is not surprising that when formal philosophy came to a crisis, as it did with Husserl, no such crisis afflicted the poets. Stevens went on writing, getting stronger as he wrote. Many younger poets, notably John Ashbery and A. R. Ammons, have proved themselves entirely capable of writing in Stevens's spirit and of finding their own voices partly by listening to his.

Indeed, I feel no misgiving about the poetry that culminates in Stevens; it hasn't come to an end with him. I feel misgiving only when Stevens's accomplishment is described in prescriptive terms; when his critics represent what he did as the only thing worth doing in poetry, a program of self-invention or self-production that seems worthy until too much is claimed for it. At that point it begins to seem an essay in vanity. It is not that. But one can hardly avoid thinking that it might be, when faced with the claim that the true spirit of America is the Protestantism of Emerson, which reached its most emphatic form of self-invention in Stevens's *Notes Toward a Supreme Fiction*.

VIII

What, then, is a writer's responsibility? What should Ariel be doing? He should be writing poems, taking only sufficient precaution to en-sure that they are poems rather than editorials or slogans. My remarks on virtuality were designed to suggest not the form of that precaution in any particular case but the responsibility itself. It would have been just as valid to say with Adorno that form is that through which phe-nomenality is determined, whereas content is what determines itself. But content doesn't quite determine itself, it aspires to a destiny in form. All over the world we are witnessing the collapse of collectivities and recognition of smaller social units. There are forms. They are em-barrassing not only to Marxists but to those sages who insisted, against much evidence, that nationalism had died. On the contrary, people are forming themselves into groups, communities based on nationality, re-ligion, language, tradition. The most appalling problem in the world is starvation, a state of being so dreadful that every other, by comparison, seems trivial. No condition is trivial, except comparatively. If starva-tion could be prevented—if people could survive and then begin to live—most people, all over the world, would want a common culture, provided that it resembled what we call bourgeois liberalism. Russian Communism has collapsed not because of the force and reiteration of the ideas directed against it, but because of the dearth of food and clothes and consumer goods, and the realization—through television mainly—that such things are plentiful in other countries. The deter-mination of East Germany to join with West Germany was prompted by the breakdown of its own economy and by clear evidence of wealth in the West.

I mention these events not with any intention of doing justice to them but to make the point that social formations, never quite as static as we think, are more effectively altered by imagery than by argument. The content of such imagery does not determine itself; nor does it arise spontaneously. An image, like a poem, is made. The question is:

under what jurisdiction, if any, is the image made? Levinas argues, as we have seen, that the first consideration is ethical, and that the true jurisdiction is that of justice. I can't disagree with him. This does not mean that every writer must write about the Holocaust, but that the crucial system of values is that of ethics and justice.

# IN THEORY

# THE USE AND ABUSE OF THEORY

ﾟﾟﾟﾟﾟﾟﾟﾟﾟﾟﾟﾟﾟﾟﾟﾟ

I n March 1937, René Wellek published in *Scrutiny* a challenge to the author of *Revaluation*: would Dr. Leavis please expound and defend the principles upon which the book was based? Would he offer a theory of literature to explain how he had arrived at the judgments of the several poems analyzed? Wellek intimated that without such a theory the judgments could have only whatever authority a reader was willing to concede to Dr. Leavis's personality. Leavis's reply to Wellek mainly consists in his assertion that the author of *Revaluation* is a literary critic, not a philosopher: "Literary criticism and philosophy seem to me to be quite distinct and different kinds of discipline—at least I think they ought to be," he asserted. The business of the literary critic "is to attain a peculiar completeness of response and to observe a peculiarly strict relevance in developing his response into commentary: he must be on his guard against abstracting improperly from what is in front of him and against any premature or irrelevant generalizing—of it or from it." "I think I have gone as far in explicitness," Leavis said, "as I could profitably attempt to go, and . . . I do not see what would be gained by the kind of explicitness [Professor Wellek] demands (though I see what is lost by it)." What is lost by it, Leavis maintains, is the cogency of concrete analysis, the organization of "similarly 'placed' things, things that have found their bear-

[77]

ings with regard to one another, and not a theoretical system or a system determined by abstract considerations." Leavis speaks of the danger of "blunting of edge, blurring of focus and muddled misdirection of attention: consequences of queering one discipline with the habits of another."[1]

I have recalled that exchange between Wellek and Leavis, familiar as it is, mainly to remark that Leavis has usually been supposed to have had the better of it. I have never met anyone who argued that Leavis should have worked out a theory of literature in advance of the need of it or a poetics ready to be applied on every occasion of commentary. It has generally been agreed that the close work of analysis must come first, and that the development from practice to theory may well be postponed. I share this prejudice, for the reasons Leavis has given. But I wonder, if the exchange between Wellek and Leavis were to take place today, whether the privilege that Leavis claimed for the literary critic would still be granted; or indeed whether the relation between the theory and the practice of literary criticism would be thought to be a matter of any moment. Many students would find the argument between Wellek and Leavis quaint. They would say that theory is one thing and practical criticism a different thing. They would not observe any important relation between the two or understand why Wellek and Leavis troubled themselves with it.

If I were to claim that an argument between Wellek and Leavis more than fifty years ago retains an interest not merely historical, I should have to explain to my students that in 1937 there was a notably close relation between the literature represented by Eliot, Pound, Yeats, Joyce, and Lawrence, on the one hand, and, on the other, the particular forms of criticism developed to deal with it; that the New Criticism, as it was called in the United States, was designed as a response to a literature still thought to be new and difficult; readership, in the universities and, beyond them, in the reading public, was a matter of urgency. Eliot was the crucial figure, by virtue of *The Waste Land* and the poems surrounding it; by virtue, too, of the essays in *The Sacred Wood*. The scale of Eliot's achievement was acknowledged and clarified in Leavis's *New Bearings in English Poetry*. This is commonplace, but it marks a situation that doesn't now obtain. Literary criticism is no longer impelled by a new literature. No literature written in the past forty years has called for a new method of reading, a distinctive critical response such as was required to cope with the formal organization of *The Waste Land*, *Ulysses*, the *Cantos*, and *Finnegans Wake*. Critics don't feel impelled to devise new procedures to deal with current poems and novels. Nor do poets and novelists show much interest in the theory and practice of criticism. There are many books that call for sustained attention. *Gravity's Rainbow* is at least as difficult as, say, *The Waves*. But *Gravity's Rainbow* proceeds independently of criticism in respects that do not apply to *The Waves*.

Yet certain issues that were for centuries determined by a general reading public have now been removed to the universities: the current argument about the canon, for instance. So far as there is a canon of literature, it has been formed by the fact that certain writers have been important to other writers: Spenser to Milton; Milton to Wordsworth, Keats, and Blake; Shelley to Browning, Hardy, and Keats; Dante to Eliot. These relations were verified by readers who paid attention to them. During the years in which Eliot's central significance was accepted, it was not considered eccentric to propose a revision of the canon in his favor. Cleanth Brooks offered a revised history of English literature in this respect in *Modern Poetry and the Tradition*. Now that there is no such contemporary writer—no writer upon whose work the future of literature in his or her language appears to depend—the question of the canon is open to much more diverse considerations. It is no longer considered self-evident that there are distinctions to be made between High Literature and Popular Literature, or between the values expounded by literary criticism and those brought to bear upon the sociology of literature. It may be that such distinctions can still be established, but they cannot be taken for granted or imputed to common knowledge. I am not complaining.

Nor am I complaining that the context of these arguments is not what it was. The university has become an epitome of the world, so far as the world is discursive. So it is not surprising that the university is now a place in which diverse worldly interests are pursued. Some of our colleagues may be dismayed to find that libraries have to find space not only for the *Oxford Standard Authors* but for *The Norton Anthology of Literature by Women*, various collections of black writing, and *The Faber Book of Gay Short Stories*. But this merely reflects the fact that the university deals with its interests by recognizing their multiplicity, by regarding them as we regard lobbies in the political world, as groups speaking for special interests. Those in the university who cherish the notion of a canon, a syllabus held in common and reflective of a common culture, may take comfort in the thought that the great authors are still those who satisfy the diverse interests of many writers and of large groups of readers otherwise disparate. These classic authors are still found to be, in Frank Kermode's phrase, "patient of interpretation"; their works may be read in many different ways and subjected to disparate considerations.

My sense of the university, then, is that it is no longer an institution in which certain topics of research are pursued in different ways by many people but, rather, a place in which many groups of people—constituencies—pursue special interests among which there is little or no communication. It may be that over a longer period these groups will discover relations between one interest and another and combine to articulate them, but for the moment there is little communication.

The word in current use to describe these interests is "theory," though I am not sure that it is correctly used. A passage from J. Hillis Miller's *Hawthorne and History* shows how the word is commonly called upon. He is speaking of literary theory, but a little extension of his account would be enough to accommodate "critical theory":

> I mean by "literary theory" the shift from the hermeneutical process of identifying the meaning of a work of literature to a focus on the question of how that meaning is generated. When there is a general consensus about literary theory, if there ever was such a time (for example in that mythical time at the beginning of the present epoch of literary studies when the "new criticism" was more or less universally accepted in the United States), theory tends to be effaced, latent, presupposed. One just goes to work doing or teaching "close reading." When a multitude of conflicting critical theories call for attention, and when in addition there is confusion over the canons and the curricula of literature, as at the present time, then literary theory, rather than being something that can more or less be taken for granted becomes overt, exigent, even, some would say, strident. Theory tends to become a primary means of access to the works read. These works now tend to be redefined as "examples" demonstrating the productive effectiveness of this or that theory. In such a situation, literary theory even tends to become a primary object for study itself, as in that ever-increasing number of courses and

programs these days in critical theory as such, sometimes treated historically, sometimes as a matter of current concern.[2]

In that statement, urbane as it is, a number of distinctions have been elided. The New Criticism was never a matter of such consensus as Miller implies: think of the disagreements that enlivened the proceedings of the Kenyon school of criticism, and the published disputes between Ransom, Tate, Richards, Burke, Blackmur, and Empson. But Miller is, broadly speaking, correct; the New Critics thought of themselves as engaged in "the common pursuit of true judgment"—in Eliot's phrase—and their efforts were turned upon a provocative literature deemed to be held in common. I wish Miller would explain, though, how theory "tends to become a primary means of access to the works read." In his own work it does, but he is exceptional in this respect. Generally, it seems to me that theory, far from being a primary means of access to the works read, becomes a primary means of endlessly postponing access to them. Or if works of literature are read, they are read merely as illustrations of a theory already fixed: it is the fate of the theory merely to be fulfilled, and of the work of literature merely to gratify the theory. Miller is on firmer ground in saying that theory becomes "a primary object for study in itself."

Miller's slide from literary theory to critical theory gives occasion to ask what he means by theory. The shift from the hermeneutical process to a focus on the question of how the meaning of a work of literature is generated is not entirely clear. I take it that "the hermeneutical process" is one in which the aim is a valid—or at least a productive—interpretation of the work of literature. When we move from that consideration to the question of how the meaning of the work is generated, we are concerned with the process by which one meaning rather than another is arrived at and in some sense enforced, given whatever authority is ascribed to it. We would be concerned to discover, as a case in point, not what Leavis thought of "Ash-Wednesday" but the process by which his sense of that poem acquired a certain authority. I don't think the word "theory" registers that interest.

To make sense of the matter, we need to distinguish between two words that offer themselves in this context: "theory" and "principle." They are not synonymous, but the difference between them is hard to maintain. I. A. Richards's *Principles of Literary Criticism* could not reasonably have been called *Theories of Literary Criticism*. If it were, it would have had to include a survey of the many theories in the vicinity of criticism. Instead, it tried to establish one set of values in preference to another. The dictionaries do not help us very much here. They tell us that principles are those first or founding considerations from which later elaborations and applications are derived. The word is often used to refer to moral or ethical principles, such as principles of natural justice, on which specific judgments may be made in other fields of interest. When we say that Dr. Johnson was a moralist, we intend not only to say that his criticism is directed by the moral claims he acknowledged but to explain why he censured the mythological allusions in *Paradise Lost* as "not being always used with notice of their vanity."[3] It would be trivial to think of that judgment as having issued from a theory.

The difference between a principle and a theory depends upon a difference in the scale of the matter under consideration: where the matter is grand, we think of a principle; where it is relatively minor or local, we think of a theory in its behalf. Jean Starobinski's distinction between a theory and a method is valuable here. He takes a theory to issue from an act of intellectual contemplation, on the analogy of certain procedures in the natural sciences. Theory is a predictive hypothesis—concerning the nature and internal relations of the object under examination; or it means the general contemplation of an ensemble, or the comprehensive system governed by an intelligible order.[4] A method is, then, the scrupulous coding of certain technical procedures; it develops into a reflection on the aims to be proposed.

These definitions are useful, especially as they make us wonder whether those who proffer a literary theory or even a critical theory are not hoping to gain a certain advantage they do not deserve. Theory, as Starobinski encourages me to use the word, has an air of speculation about it: it is not to be treated casually, but it is notional, hypothetical, or, as we say, heuristic. We use a theory for what it is worth, and we drop it when it has served its day. We do not hold to it for dear life, as if it were a belief. But when I read Terry Eagleton's *Literary Theory*, I find it not at all speculative. He is bent upon an ideological program, and uses literature only as a means to a political end.

I should make it clear that I am objecting not to the politics or the ideology, but to their furtherance in the guise of theory. I should also try to explain why essays in theory so often include an attack on the literature of High Modernism. I have remarked the disjunction between theory and contemporary literature. Much of the energy of theory is provoked by disappointment, the apparent failure of High Modernism to achieve its aims—or rather one particular aim: its attack on bourgeois liberalism.

The antithetical, subversive character of modern literature is a commonplace. Trilling remarked that the social purpose of modern literature was to enable its readers not only to criticize the achievements of middle-class culture but, if they so wished, to live some part of their spiritual lives beyond that culture. The possibility of adopting an antithetical stance, or an attitude of dissociation, was disclosed in the art and literature of Modernism. From Pater and Mallarmé to Yeats and Eliot we find this possibility held out as a vision, its emblem the ostensibly self-animating poem, the passage of murmuring, self-beguiling prose. In poetry: difficult forms, language brooding upon itself. In prose: passages in which the mind is engrossed in a dialogue with itself. One might expect modern critics, then, to approve such efforts and to thank the modern writers for maintaining, in poems and fictions, the possibility of a "world elsewhere." Surely they would endorse the efforts of James, Conrad, and Proust rather than those of Wells and Shaw? Instead, we find critics complaining that Yeats, Eliot, Joyce, and Pound not only failed to make middle-class society feel ashamed of itself but, all the while, were in secret league with the society they claimed to oppose.[5]

What form would such a charge take? Here is one example of it. Some years ago the critic John Guillory published an essay called "The Ideology of Canon Formation: T. S. Eliot and Cleanth Brooks." The gist of it is that Eliot's cultivation of Donne, Herbert, and other poets culminating in Dryden (rather than in Milton) was in the service of religious and political "orthodoxy," a term Eliot came to use instead of the "tradition" of "Tradition and the Individual Talent." Cleanth Brooks's *The Well-Wrought Urn* then becomes a reinterpretation of several major poems from Donne to Yeats in the light of Eliot's canonization of Donne. By presenting poetry as paradox, as the reconciliation of opposites, Brooks raises it above science and associates its saints with the miracle of a neo-Christian resurrection. I shall quote a substantial paragraph of Guillory's essay to give a sense of its tone. He is commenting on the chapter in *The Well-Wrought Urn* in which Brooks brings together Donne's urn, Shakespeare's phoenix, and the prophetic figure of the resurrected Christ. Brooks's implication is, according to Guillory, that one day soon the suppressed truth of poetry will be recovered, removed from the control of scientists and positivists, and handed into the keeping of true priests, the ordained teachers of poetry in colleges and universities. Guillory writes:

> The elaboration of the ideology into such allusive structures yields up the New Criticism to the service of the liberal pluralism which is the regnant ideology of the academy and which the pedagogy in no way contradicts. The technique of formalist interpretation subtends a larger ideology, satisfying within a narrower domain of practice the longing for consensus, for a metaphysics of the same—a longing expressed by the posited "unity" of the literary work. . . . It would appear that we mean by consensus what Eliot meant by orthodoxy.
>
> The canon participates centrally in the establishment of consensus as the embodiment of a collective valuation. . . . The phoenix image emerges from the exemplary text as an emblem of the canonical principle. . . . The assimilation of "The Phoenix and Turtle" foreshadows a systematically ideological reading of the canon, a reading capable of absorbing what Eliot's more primitive rule had excluded: the major English poets.[6]

So far as I understand the phrase, "a metaphysics of the same" refers to the act of knowledge by which the mind, encountering an object, engages with it on the understanding that no threat to its own autonomy is entailed: the mind returns to itself at the end, justified and strengthened in its self-understanding. A consensus is the civic equivalent of this experience.

Guillory's attack not only on Eliot and Brooks but on the ideology of liberal pluralism that they allegedly endorse is bound to appear odd. It comes as a surprise to hear that Eliot gave support to liberal pluralism. But Guillory's terms are not wild. What appears eccentric is his assumption that the replacement of "the same" by "difference" as "our central critical category" will solve our problems. In our colleges and universities, the rhetoric of difference, and its corresponding pedagogy, merely take the form of establishing groups to express different viewpoints and, as we used to say, different lifestyles. The establishment of courses in women's studies, African-American studies, Minority Discourse, feminist studies, Marxist studies, and so forth, seems to recognize difference; and so it does till the members of each group sink their difference in yet another rhetoric of the same. Consensus is sought within the group on the sole ground of its difference from the group in the next seminar room. Within the group, membership implies the experience of fusion: the terms sought are those that have been found sinister in the world at large—unity, "the same."

There is no merit, no justice, in being tendentious. I am not sure, however, what form a conversation with Guillory would take. The critical problem has to do with the status of fictions: how to teach students to deal with fictions and not to change them into concepts. It is hard to persuade students that a poem is not an editorial or a campaign-manifesto. There was a time when it was convincing to quote Eliot's admonition that if you read literature it is as literature: you must read it and not as another thing. But many of our students don't understand what Eliot was talking about or what it means to read literature "as literature." They read literature as they read everything else, as matter for conversation on themes that happen to interest them apart from literature.

Unless we can establish the fictive and the aesthetic as calling for a distinctive form of attention, we cannot teach literature. We can present poems and novels as illustrations of human experiences that can then be discussed independently of their provenance in literature; but that is indeed another thing. So how may we proceed?

We may start, as so often, with Kant's third *Critique*, especially with the passage in which he describes an aesthetic idea as "that representation of the imagination which induces much thought, yet without the possibility of any definite thought whatever, i.e. *concept*, being adequate to it."[7] The imagination, to Kant, is the mind's power of invention, of producing what nature has not given, a distinctive *copia* free and freely enjoyed, independently of concepts. It follows that a work of art is exempt from determinant or cognitive judgment, the judgment by virtue of which thinking is turned upon being and deemed to be veridical by being so turned. Schiller extended Kant's sense of art by appealing to the experience of play as an act of the mind superior to both the impulse to sense and the impulse to form, removing the deficiencies of each. A person is only and completely a person while at play. The source of play is excess of energy, beyond need. We have the basis of a theory of aesthetics if to Kant's third *Cri-*

*tique* and Schiller's *Letters on the Aesthetic Education of Man* we add Goethe's letter to Louise Seidler (February 1818) in which he describes that excess as the emotions of hope, anticipation, and astonishment. The condition of art, Goethe said, is probability, "but within the realm of probability the highest ideal must be supplied which does not otherwise appear."[8]

What I have said of Kant, Schiller, and Goethe is not intended to be adequate to the theory of aesthetics they imply; it is designed merely to say that there is such a theory. It has not been ignored. Much recent theory has been an effort to disqualify it or, if that is not possible, to compromise it by associating it with the allegedly fascist politics of "aesthetic ideology." I cannot go far into these arguments, but I shall try to represent them in a few sentences. It is alleged that Kantian aesthetics is tainted by his idealism and by its ministering to bourgeois hegemony. It is also alleged that this aesthetics claims to transcend political difference and to embody "the universal formal identity of the human."[9] What corresponds to the autonomy claimed for the aesthetic object is the autonomy felt by the subject, the mind that contemplates the object. This mind escapes from history, politics, economics, and all such forces or at least has the sentiment of escape. So the human subject is recuperated on the ground of universality as freedom enjoyed at once individually and in common. The mind can exert this claim to freedom by observing it also in natural or organic processes, as well as in *l'imaginaire*, a place all the better for its not yet existing; it is the site of an "as if" that is not embarrassed by its fictiveness. Kantian aesthetics is then declared guilty, because it allows its adepts to feel that they embody the essential truth of human life, free of political and other constraints, that they are at once individual and universal, and that their felicity in the contemplation of aesthetic objects is authenticated by nature.

The argument is more elaborate than I have implied, but I may refer to one occasion in Derrida's *La Vérité en peinture*. There are two main emphases. In the first, Derrida takes the work of art as requiring a frame to hold it separate from everything else, and he shows the problems entailed by trying to hold the frame in place. He then removes the frame and declares "the political" or "the sublime" to be everything that is the case. The frame is contradictory because it cannot be held. It seems to me that it is theoretically no more difficult to have an aesthetics than to have a politics, unless you queer the issue by deeming one or the other to be axiomatic or self-evident. Derrida's argument against Kant's aesthetics depends upon his taking politics as self-evidently unbounded. There is no reason to think it is. In the second part of the argument, Derrida maintains that Kant's third *Critique* "depends in an essential way . . . on a pragmatic anthropology and on what could be called in more than one sense of the term a reflective humanism." This anthropology, Derrida argues, "weighs massively by its content on the supposedly pure deduction of aesthetic judgment."[10] But the reference to "pure" deduction is misleading. Kant claims not that such a judgment is pure but that it is not covered by a concept. Kant's claim is strengthened by the fact that Derrida does not produce a concept capable of dealing with aesthetic experience in any of its recognized Kantian forms: the beautiful, the picturesque, the sublime.

But a question persists. How can we teach our students to read, assuming that they have not even begun to read so long as they are merely extracting themes and discussing them in isolation from their formal destiny in novel or poem? There are two issues. The first is to decide whether to cede to the ideologues the definition of reality in political terms or to hold out against this concession as reductive. The definition of reality in political terms is, I maintain, false. Herbert Marcuse has argued, in *The Aesthetic Dimension*, that Marxist orthodoxy has committed a serious mistake in interpreting the quality and truth of a work of art in terms of the prevailing relations of production. He claims that art, by virtue of its aesthetic form, is largely autonomous in relation to the given social relations. Literature is revolutionary "only with reference to itself, as content having become form." Marxism has erred in placing a low value upon subjectivity, not only upon the rational subject but upon inwardness, the individual imagination, the private emotions. It was a mistake to dissolve the subjectivity of individuals into class consciousness, because the need for radical change "must be rooted in the subjectivity of individuals themselves, in their intelligence and passions, their drives and their goals." Marxists should have understood that the world imagined in art, far from being inauthentic, is the very reality that is suppressed in every official definition of reality. It follows that "the critical function of art . . . resides in the aesthetic form." The truth of art consists in its power to break the monopoly that those in power exercise by defining what is real. The supreme merit of art is that it contradicts the version of reality that obtains in social and economic life.

The purpose of Marcuse's book is to defend the integrity of art by assigning high value to the freedom—the forms of a free life—that it imagines. Like Ernst Bloch in *Geist der Utopie* and *Das Prinzip Hoffnung*, Marcuse turns that freedom toward a future, utopian if we want to call it that. So we have a "defence of poesy" in various vocabularies from Bacon and Sidney through Kant, Schiller, and Goethe, to Bloch and Marcuse. Common to these otherwise disparate figures is the acknowledgment of the freedom of fiction.

This brings me to the second and last consideration. If, as teachers, we are not obliged to accept a political or otherwise ideological definition of "the real," it follows that we make a claim for art as proposing new images, new thresholds, new antinomies. The next question is: how can we teach our students to understand these inventions and to stop suppressing them in the interests of the common discourse of politics? There are several possibilities. Cleanth Brooks's theory of literature concentrates upon the language of paradox, mainly to claim that the sense of experience which a poem embodies is more complex, more subtle, than the judgments we make in our economic or appetitive lives. Empson's *Seven Types of Ambiguity* works in the same spirit: the words of literature are "complex words." It is also possible to find the poetry in the precise form of a particular poem, though it remains a matter for tact, in each case, to decide what constitutes the form and how much to claim for it. Strictly accounted, form is every consideration that gets the poem from its first word to its last. The form of *The Waste Land* is not that of "The Red Wheelbarrow." Each requires to be shown in action.

As teachers, we should start with a simple proposition. I quote it from John Crowe Ransom's *The World's Body*:

> Poetry is a kind of language, and therefore a kind of experience. It distinguishes itself by an act of will from prose, which is also a language and an experience. Probably that is its whole intention. If there were no prose, there would not have to be poetry; and the more ubiquitous the tyranny of the prose, the more necessary it is to undertake the poetry, and the harder.[11]

It is a simple proposition, that poetry is a kind of language. But it is sufficient if we use it to invite our students to ask the next question: what kind of language is it, in the particular poem we have chosen to read? These questions are far better than those more commonly asked: was Eliot anti–Semitic, on the evidence of "Gerontion" and *After Strange Gods*? Was Yeats a fascist, on the evidence of *On the Boiler* and the last stanza of "The Statues"? Was Larkin politically acceptable?

I hope I have made it clear that I am not "against theory." Not to have a theory is to have someone else's. But I wish theorists would challenge themselves more severely than they mostly do. The kind of challenge I have in mind is suggested to me by two literary occasions, one an old one, the other very recent. In his essay "Poetry and Abstract Thought," Valéry defended his theoretical meditations by claiming that "there is no theory that is not a fragment, carefully prepared, of some autobiography."[12] Most of the theories I read could not be fragments of any autobiography: they are fragments of a political program. It would make a far healthier intellectual situation if we asked theorists to speak from their personal experience, rather than pretend to what Valéry called "a knowledge that is entirely impersonal, an observation with no observer."

For the second challenging occasion, I quote a passage from a recent *Times Literary Supplement*, in which Geoffrey Hill reviewed Isabel Rivers's *Reason, Grace, and Sentiment: A Study of the Language of Religion and Ethics in England 1660–1780, Volume 1: Whichcote to Wesley*. The passage reads, in part:

> Whichcote wrote that "by wickedness [a man] passes into a *Nature* contrary to his own." I am willing to claim as an empirical fact that when you write at any serious pitch of obligation you enter into the nature of grammar and etymology which is a nature contrary to your own. You cannot extricate yourself from this "contrary nature" by some kind of philosophical fiat or gesture of spiritual withdrawal. Hobbes categorized "Compleasance" as a "Law of Nature": "That every man strive to accommodate himself to the rest." In the palpable contrariness of *strive/ accommodate* one recognizes the working of intelligence at a more than conceptual level. . . . [Dr. Rivers] simply assumes the concurrence of language with one's expectations.[13]

This passage from Hill's review is not an essay in theory, but it implies a theory of language and a theory of literature. The phrases he quotes from Whichcote, the Wesleys, George Herbert, and other writers are not merely illustrations of a posture already taken up: they are acts of mind at one with acts of language, the English language in a certain phase of its contrariness. We might well discuss with our students such questions as these from Hill: what is the nature of grammar and etymology such that, entering it, you engage with a nature contrary to your own? What is entailed by assuming the concurrence of language with one's expectations? What precisely is going on in Hobbes's "strive to accommodate"?

# THE POLITICAL TURN IN CRITICISM

ႢᢏᢏᢦᢏᲪ

I

In the January–February 1953 issue of *Partisan Review*, John Crowe Ransom, reviewing R. P. Blackmur's *Language as Gesture*, took issue with him upon one consideration: that in appraising the social and political issues which inhabit Yeats's major poems, Blackmur remarked only their function within the work, not the ideas as such, even though they might be "ideas from which, at the very moment, out in the world of action, the issues of life and death are hung." Blackmur, according to Ransom, was repudiating "the ideas as ideas, and reckoning their usefulness for the poem."[1]

Ransom had especially in view "The Later Poetry of W. B. Yeats" (1936), in which Blackmur spoke of Yeats's "Byzantium" as "the poetry of an intense and condensed declaration of doctrine, not emotion put into doctrine from outside, but doctrine presented as emotion." Blackmur spoke, too, of the companion-poem, "Sailing to Byzantium," as exhibiting "the doctrine in action, the doctrine actualized in a personal emotion resembling that of specific prayer." He concluded the essay with a large consideration:

> When we call man a rational animal we mean that reason is his great myth. Reason is plastic and takes to any form provided. The rational imagination in poetry, as elsewhere, can absorb magic as

a provisional method of evocative and heuristic thinking, but it cannot be based upon it. In poetry, and largely elsewhere, imagination is based upon the reality of words and the emotion of their joining. Yeats's magic, then, like every other feature of his experience, is rational as it reaches words; otherwise it is his privation, and ours, because it was the rational defect of our society that drove him to it.[2]

This little episode between Ransom and Blackmur anticipates many of the issues I shall try to describe. We might clarify them by requiring each of the disputants to be somewhat more forthcoming. We might ask Ransom what status he assigned to ideas as such, and how they acquired such privilege, and whether or not he thought ideas remained intact in that character during and after their involvement in the poem. Are they already a virtual poetry, or merely, as Blackmur seemed to imply, raw material for a possible poem? We might ask Blackmur whether he was really content to regard the production of ideas as a matter of ad-libbing, of informal play before the commitment of the words is made. Was he content to give the poet every latitude till the play transpired in decisive words, and to judge the result by an unexplained correlation of emotion and rhythm? When Blackmur says that Yeats's magic is rational as it reaches words, he seems to mean that the poetical character is wayward till it finds a proper syntax for its emotions. Nothing that has preceded the finding matters, every caprice is forgivable as merely auxiliary to the order arrived at. But we might ask Blackmur how he could be sure that the syntax found is the order of the rational imagination and not of some sinister force that has assumed the mask of reason in order to appear plausible. Blackmur's answer would probably invoke the evidence of form; as, in writing of Allen Tate, he said that for Tate events do not become experience till the imagination creates them in objective form, and further that "the act of experience, in the arts, transpires only in form." What has not transpired in its particular form cannot be said to have been experienced. For Blackmur, ideas in a poem have merely instrumental value. For Ransom, the question was: must they not also have constitutive value, and be judged by strict criteria?

## II

It is a commonplace that recent critical theory has taken a political turn. After twenty years in which theory was in a dependent relation to epistemology, linguistics, anthropology, and psychoanalysis, it now proceeds in a parasitic relation to politics, either of the Right or the Left. For the time being, the ideological wind is blowing from Germany more strongly than from France: the main sources of authority are Marx and the neo-Marxist Frankfurt critics, especially Benjamin, Adorno, and Horkheimer, with selective acknowledgment to Lukács. Debates among Habermas, Gadamer, and Ricoeur are best understood in that setting. The Frankfurt way of being serious has displaced the Parisian way of being rueful.

## III

I shall cite two examples of the political turn, the first from close to home. In Ireland, readers of Yeats, Joyce, and Synge are interrogating these writers in a far harsher spirit than any I recall. It is regularly suggested that Yeats bears some responsibility for the violence and death-dealing in Northern Ireland since 1968. Seamus Deane has argued in his *Celtic Revivals* (1985) that Yeats turned a misreading of Irish history into a myth which is being acted out by young people who have perhaps never read a word of his poetry. Yeats, that is, construed the Protestant Ascendancy as an aristocracy, so that he could endow it with the power and grace he ascribed to Italian Renaissance princes, while in fact the Ascendancy was "a predominantly bourgeois social formation." To fulfill the logic of his enterprise, Yeats also conjured into existence the Irish peasant, so that the kinship of peasant and aristocrat, predicated on the working of land, would provide a paradigm of an Ireland heroic in its difference—most tellingly, in its difference from an England given over to science, positivism, empiricism, and industrialization. It follows, according to Deane, that Yeats derived a politics from an aesthetics; he sought "to obliterate or reduce the problems of class, economic development, bureaucratic organization and the like, concentrating instead upon the essences of self, community, nationhood, racial theory, Zeitgeist."[3] To some extent, therefore, Yeats is responsible for the situation in the North, where political actions are propelled by myths, images, and symbols.

In this spirit, Deane refers to Yeats's "Ancestral Houses." The poem, he says,

> owes its force to the vitality with which it offers a version of Ascendancy history as true in itself. The truth of this historical reconstruction of the Ascendancy is not cancelled by our simply saying No, it was not like that. For its ultimate validity is not historical, but mythical. In this case, the mythical element is given prominence by the meditation on the fate of an originary energy when it becomes so effective that it transforms nature into civilization and is then transformed itself by civilization into decadence. This poem then appears to have a story to tell and, along with that, an interpretation of the story's meaning. It operates on the narrative and on the conceptual planes and at the intersection of these it emerges, for many readers, as a poem about the tragic nature of human existence itself.[4]

Deane repudiates what he calls this humanist reading of the poem on the grounds that it claims that a work of literature "can arrive at a moment in which it takes leave of history or myth . . . and becomes meaningful only as an aspect of the 'human condition.' " It endorses, he maintains, the humanist conviction that literature, in its highest forms, is free of ideology.

I shall comment a little on Deane's position before citing my other example of the political turn. It strikes me that his distinction between history and myth is itself ideological because he has not established it, he has merely assumed it. Whether we approve or not, myth is as real as history; language offers hospitality to both, with little show of favor to one more than the other. Neither of them is given by nature or arises spontaneously. Nor has Deane established that a consideration of Ireland in terms of class, economic development, and the like is ideologically innocent by comparison with discriminations in terms of caste and race which are ideologically guilty.

Besides, there are indeed human experiences of which the appropriate account is not historical but mythological. I am persuaded by Northrop Frye to distinguish between mythology and ideology in this respect. An ideology, he says, "expresses secondary and derivative human concerns"; ideologies are derived from mythology, "which expresses the primary desires of existence, along with anxieties attached to their frustration."[5] The ground of the distinction is biological: it is based upon one's bodily form and its relation to the earth; upon a metabiology rather than a metaphysic, to invoke a distinction by Kenneth Burke. Mythology, in Frye's sense, doesn't float free of history; it may be verified upon historically acceptable evidence at any moment. But it calls, too, for a description that recognizes the primordial character of the experiences it expresses. "Ancestral Houses" posits a certain mode of experience, which Yeats regards as analogous to an organic sequence—birth, growth, maturity, decay, death—and which, he is hardly obliged to prove, may be verified by recourse to historical evidence. I can't see that Yeats's rhetorical position is more vulnerable than Deane's or mine.

## IV

My second witness is Fredric Jameson, a critic for whom a political passion provides every incentive—literature, film, and architecture giving him occasions of acting upon it. In his essay on *Ulysses*, his study of Wyndham Lewis, and *The Political Unconscious*, Jameson has developed a theory of Modernism according to which many of the received works of modern literature constitute only a scandal.[6] Briefly, he argues that Anglo-American Modernism has been dominated by an impressionistic aesthetic that issues from Symbolism, which Jameson regards as featuring "the illicit transformation of existing things into so many visible or tangible meanings."[7] Illicit because the transformation surreptitiously brings into a single act of perception the experienced and the intelligible. Any work of literature, therefore, that is founded upon Symbolism is to be rejected, since it offers to turn a predicament into a privilege; it provides an otherwise alienated reader with an unquestionable recourse to his own subjectivity, and encourages him to feel that his truth is to be found and enjoyed there. In *Ulysses*, whatever Bloom encounters is mediated through his subjectivity, and the whole is "unified by the stylistic tone in which all contradictions are ironically resolved as well as by the overall unity of Bloom's personality." So "the Joycean phantasmagoria, even in the Nighttown chapter, serves to reconfirm the unity of the psyche, and to reinvent that depth-psychological perspective from which these private fantasies spring."⁸ Joyce has played into the hands of the enemy; he has given his reader the prize of a restored subjectivity.

Jameson's reading of *Ulysses*, to go no further than that book, is disabled by his insistence that literature will serve a political cause—what the cause is, it makes no theoretical difference to specify. Jameson's immediate authority for his rejection of Symbolism, I think, is the passage in *The Origin of German Tragic Drama* where Benjamin juxtaposes the allegorical and the symbolic ways of seeing, much to the moral advantage of allegory:

> Whereas in the symbol destruction is idealized and the transfigured face of nature is fleetingly revealed in the light of redemption, in allegory the observer is confronted with the *facies hippocratica* of history as a petrified, primordial landscape. Everything about history that, from the very beginning, has been untimely, sorrowful, unsuccessful, is expressed in a face—or rather in a death's head. And although such a thing lacks all "symbolic" freedom of expression, all classical proportion, all humanity—nevertheless, this is the form in which man's subjection to nature is most obvious and it significantly gives rise not only to the enigmatic question of the nature of human existence as such, but also of the biographical historicity of the individual.⁹

(I might note that *"hippocratica"* denotes the livid, shrunken image of the body immediately before death; it is so named because Hippocrates was the first to describe it.) It follows that the moral superiority of the allegorical vision consists in its refusal of comfort, redemption, and unity; according to Benjamin, the occasional felicities of man in nature are specious, anthropomorphic delusions, to be set aside by a relentless sense of history as death. Allegory testifies to a refusal to be appeased; it resents every token of unity, the seeming conjunction of existence and meaning. So Jameson contrasts *Ulysses* with *The Childermass*, much to the advantage of the latter because Lewis refuses to be comforted, seeks the dispersal rather than the unification of subjectivity, takes precaution against homogeneity of tone, "composes by phrase, by larger word-units drawn from various sources which are never completely subdued and mastered by the overall form of the sentence itself."¹⁰

Jameson's comparison of Joyce and Lewis serves a political purpose. It doesn't matter that Lewis's political attitudes were flagrantly right-wing. What matters is that he devised a style which refuses to conspire with personality, subjectivity, homogeneity. The resentment that is the most evident feature of his common style can be dealt with later; for the moment, Jameson can produce him as the *facies hippocratica* of a modern literature otherwise rotten with inwardness.

V

My objection to Deane and Jameson would be just as severe if they served another political cause: they compromise the literature they read by subjecting it to a test of good behavior. They defeat the literature in advance. But the question arises: what form would a serious engagement with literature take, if not a political form that turned it into propaganda? In approaching an answer, I disclaim any originality for it by alluding to its constituents, these being the work of other hands. I merely bring the pieces together to suggest a program all the better for its slightness.

I begin with a passage from "Yeats and the Language of Symbolism," where Frye distinguishes between the natural man and poetic man:

> Once a poet finds his mask, and it becomes the outward form of his creative life, it loses all real connection with his natural life. . . . The poet, by presenting us with a vision of nobility and heroism, detaches that vision from our ordinary lives. He thus works in a direction exactly opposite to that of the political leader who insists on trying to attach it, and so perverts its nature, as fascism perverted the Nietzschean gospel of heroic virtue into the most monstrous negation of it that the world has ever seen. . . . The artist, of course, is always, like Narcissus, apt to become enamored with the reflecting illusion of his own mask. Yeats himself did not possess every kind of high intelligence, and some affectations resulting from a pedantic streak in his make-up led him into a certain amount of social and political dithering. But for all that we should not be too quick to plaster a fascist label on Yeats's myth merely because a conspiracy of thugs happened to debase

that myth instead of some other one. . . . Poetic symbolism is language and not truth, a means of expression and not a body of doctrine, not something to look at but something to look and speak through, a dramatic mask. "The poet," said Sir Philip Sidney, "never affirmeth": when he does affirm, he not only ceases to be a poet, but is as likely to be wrong as anyone else.[11]

I assume that when a poet affirms, in Frye's sense or Sidney's, he voids the distinction which Hegel makes, in the *Encyclopedia of Philosophical Sciences*, between imagination and reason: "Imagination . . . is reason, but only a nominal reason, because the matter or theme it embodies is to imagination *qua* imagination a matter of indifference; while reason *qua* reason also insists upon the truth of its content."

This implies—and it leads me to the second constituent, a passage from Frank Kermode's *The Sense of an Ending*—that a poet does well to remain among his fictions, and to regard them as "heuristic and dispensable."[12] A myth, in Kermode's sense but not in Frye's, is a fiction that has congealed because the poet has forgotten that it is a fiction and proposes to put it into practice as if it were true. *King Lear* is a fiction, anti-Semitism a myth. Kermode aptly quotes Sartre's observation that "the final aim of art is to reclaim the world by revealing it as it is, but as if it had its source in human liberty." The "as if" is the grace note that prevents a poet's fictions from becoming myths.

The third constituent is compatible with Frye and Kermode; it is a composite factor, a motive common to Ernst Bloch's *The Spirit of Utopia* and Herbert Marcuse's *The Aesthetic Dimension*. Bloch defends modern art and literature: they represent the future of mankind by expressing mankind's desires, especially the desire for freedom. Bloch's work is a philosophy of hope, of futurity, or utopia, a stirring of possibility. Marcuse is more specific: when the subjectivity of individuals is dissolved into class consciousness, a major prerequisite of revolution is minimized, namely, the fact that the need for radical change must be rooted in the subjectivity of individuals themselves. Marxist theory was mistaken, according to Marcuse, in interpreting subjectivity as a bourgeois notion:

But even in bourgeois society, insistence on the truth and right of inwardness is not really a bourgeois value. With the affirmation of the inwardness of subjectivity, the individual steps out of the network of exchange relationships and exchange values, withdraws from the reality of bourgeois society, and enters another dimension of existence. Liberating subjectivity constitutes itself in the inner history of the individuals—their own history, which is not identical with their social existence.

Marcuse goes on to defend art for art's sake "inasmuch as the aesthetic form reveals tabooed and repressed dimensions of reality: aspects of liberation." The domain of art is the freedom of inwardness and subjectivity. This freedom is not, Marcuse says, illusory; it is just as real as the public reality it contradicts. "Art breaks open a dimension inaccessible to other experience, a dimension in which human beings, nature, and things no longer stand under the law of the established reality principle." But this does not mean that the world according to art is a fantasy or an illusion. It is that of another "reality principle," of estrangement "and only as estrangement does art fulfil a cognitive function: it communicates truths not communicable in any other language; it contradicts."[13]

The only remaining constituent I see as necessary is a certain capacity in the reader: imagination. It is a sufficient justification of art that it enables us to imagine experiences which we have not had and to participate in those experiences within the limits of form.

Is there a clear objection to this program, apart from the obvious one issuing from theorists who lay violent hands upon the work of art on behalf of a political aim? The only one I have found is in Paul de Man's introduction to Hans Robert Jauss's *Toward an Aesthetics of Reception*. As in his "Hegel on the Sublime," de Man repudiates "any valorization of aesthetic categories at the expense of intellectual rigor or political action, or any claim for the autonomy of aesthetic experience as a self-enclosed, self-reflexive totality."[14] I am content with that; especially in a work of literature, where the saving commonness of language, the heterogeneity of every work, makes the dream of totality and self-enclosure absurd. In the introduction to Jauss, de Man argues against any "concatenation of the aesthetic with meaning-producing powers of language." The aesthetic, he says, is by definition a seductive notion "that appeals to the pleasure principle, a eudaemonic judgment that can displace and conceal values of truth and falsehood likely to be more resilient to desire than values of pleasure and pain." It is strange to find de Man saying this, since according to his normal view, all such values are merely different functions of language, they have no independent character. But in any case de Man brushes the aesthetic category aside; aesthetic reactions are interesting only as symptoms. "Whenever the aesthetic is invoked as an appeal to clarity and control, whenever, in other words, a symptom is made into a remedy for the disorder that it signals, a great deal of caution is in order."

But de Man's idea of the aesthetic is specious. "It is impossible to conceive of an aesthetic judgment that would not be dependent on imitation as a constitutive category," he claims. Why? Because the easiest notion of form is that of a visible object, and the easiest notion of cognition is the apprehension of such an object? De Man refers to "Hegel's massively misunderstood treatment of the aesthetic as a provisional (*vorläufig*, a word that also occurs in Benjamin) form of cognition" and says that it is "entirely in the spirit of his continuators Kierkegaard and Nietzsche."[15] But it is not misunderstood if we relate it to the other activities I have invoked as constituents of an aesthetic stance: provisional cognition, nominal reason, the production of "consciously false" fictions, imagery of a future consonant with desire, and the antithetical function that Marcuse called estrangement or contradiction.

## VI

I'll make a few remarks about "Ancestral Houses," since Deane has given it a distinctly ideological reading. Not that I think it a great poem; by Yeats's standards, much of it is flaccid, and in that character best taken as the dispirited beginning of a series of meditations, in the last and best of which Yeats shakes himself out of a weary mood by thinking of "eyes that rage has brightened." Deane and I differ in our readings of the poem. Whereas he is scandalized by Yeats's movement from bad history to no-history-at-all, I read the poem as expressing one of Yeats's recurrent moods, his worry that the next phase of history may not be the antithetical one he prophesied and longed for; it may continue to be the primary culture he partly despises, partly fears, the Christian culture of meekness, the common many, democracy. Great men, out of phase, may be brought low by the common herd.

We have a poem in five stanzas, eight iambic pentameter lines each, end-rhyming strictly in the sequence *abababcc*. Each stanza coin-cides with a long, complex sentence, although a repeated phrase at the beginning of the second—"Mere dreams, mere dreams!"—postpones its sentence for a moment. It is possible to follow Harold Bloom in taking the poem as sardonic on the whole, as if Yeats were scorning the aristocrats for not holding on to their possessions. But that inter-pretation ignores the degree to which Yeats recognizes the satisfactions—the sweetness, the gentleness—which also mark the de-feat of once-great men.

The first stanza invokes the familiar Romantic contrast between organic and mechanic form. The distinction is most readily found in Coleridge, but its imagery comes from Shelley, to whom water was the great symbol of existence, according to Yeats's "The Philosophy of Shelley's Poetry"; and from Blake, who says in *The Marriage of Heaven and Hell* that "the cistern contains: the fountain overflows." In "The Philosophy of Shelley's Poetry," Yeats refers to Blake, "who was always praising energy, and all exalted overflowing of oneself." It is decent of Yeats to ascribe to the rich man the powers to be admired; at least he doesn't suggest that anyone might have them merely by taking thought. The stanza is a reply to Yeats's "Adam's Curse"; it makes no bones about the exhilarating conjunction of power, inherited property, and genius, as if it might stave off the inevitable decay of beauty and other proud forms of achievement.

The second stanza begins with the most rueful concession—"Mere dreams . . . "—but it sets it aside at once by invoking Homer, Yeats's type of another conjunction, that of genius and the natural or unchristened heart, the poet of life itself with nothing but his own conviction in its favor. This stanza contains the first crisis; the fountain of life becomes "the abounding . . . jet," but it is then given up, as if Homer were now defeated. The proper symbol, Yeats admits, is the "marvellous empty sea-shell." In "The Island of Statues" Colin ad-dresses the shepherd boy:

> *Who art thou?—speak,*
> *As the sea's furrows on a sea-tost shell,*
> *Sad histories are lettered on thy cheek.*

The sea-shell has been flung "out of the obscure dark of the rich streams," so it can speak with authority of everything it has been

through, but now it can only recite its sad history, shadowing "the inherited glory of the rich." This stanza goes back not only to the worn
shell of "Adam's Curse" but to every instance of greatness brought
down.

In the third stanza, Yeats celebrates the Renaissance princes and
the artists and architects they employed, and here a major disjunction
is recognized, between the artists, "bitter and violent men," and the
sweetness and gentleness of their creations. In "Ego Dominus Tuus"
and *Per Amica Silentia Lunae* Yeats is fascinated by artists whose works
are entirely different from themselves, by William Morris and by
Landor, the latter a man of notable violence who "topped us all in
calm nobility when the pen was in his hand." Or in the version of
Landor that Yeats gives in *A Vision*: "The most violent of men, he uses
his intellect to disengage a visionary image of perfect sanity . . . seen
always in the most serene and classic art imaginable."[16]

This third stanza contains another crisis: a violent artist may
produce works of surpassing gentleness, and satisfy that in us which
longs to be appeased, but his master's power, in a generation or two,
may lapse, his descendants decline into mice; it is a theme of several
poems, including the next meditation of the sequence, and *Purgatory*.

The fourth and fifth stanzas brood upon the same fear, that these
works of grace and beauty may domesticate our greatness as thoroughly as our violence and bitterness. The beauty Yeats celebrates is
that of women, the gardens where they walk, their patron, Juno:

> *O what if gardens where the peacock strays*
> *With delicate feet upon old terraces,*
> *Or else all Juno from an urn displays*
> *Before the indifferent garden deities.*

(I assume a "that" after "all"; meaning all the beauty and high-
spiritedness that the figure of Juno displays, attended by the peacocks
sacred to her.) The sentence has to wait through three rather slack
clauses before finding its verb, "take," in the last line; it is an extrav-
agance of suspended revery, repeated with less risk to the grammar in
the final stanza, which anticipates a similar revery in "To Dorothy
Wellesley." These beautiful women were always a danger to Yeats's
syntax.

It is a mark of his rhetorical power that it turns into terms of praise many words normally held for rebuke: "violent," "bitter," "haughty," and in many societies "rich." This effect is achieved in "Ancestral Houses" by setting up a concatenation of values that go together only when compelled to do so: the attachment of "life" to Blake's imagery of flowing fountains, and the greatness commonly ascribed, in Pound as in Yeats, to Renaissance patrons of the arts. Yeats's word "greatness" asks us to acknowledge this concatenation as a single force, even though we would ordinarily want to distinguish its constituents according to an un-Yeatsian system of values. Marvell's "Horatian Ode upon Cromwell's Return from Ireland" makes it similarly difficult to dissent from the values he celebrates: active virtue— another equivocation—is ascribed to Cromwell, only aesthetic decorum to the defeated Charles.

Deane maintains that "Ancestral Houses" takes leave of history and becomes meaningful only as an aspect of the "human condition." In fact, it doesn't take leave of history; it refers vaguely but clearly enough to eighteenth-century accomplishment—"a haughtier age" points in that direction. There is no need to assume that Yeats meant Ascendancy Ireland, even though in "Blood and the Moon" the haughty man praised is Burke. The theme is the alleged decline of culture between the Augustan age and our own; the anomaly that gives the poem whatever life it has is the fact that the images which please our passivity are those, now long domesticated, which we have inherited from great and violent men.

More thoroughly than most other poets, Yeats knew that a vocabulary, a diction, incorporates a totalizing ambition. When we bring together a few cognate words, we think their kinship so compelling that we let them take over the world. So much so, that by apt choice and repetition of such words it is easy to convey a conviction that this way of construing the world is ordained by natural law. Yeats recited his high words so imperiously that his poems nearly prescribe a way of being in the world: like a cavalry officer, assured of rank, dignity, and power. The experience of reading any of these central poems is one of imagining a world other than one's own, assenting to it at least provisionally, and holding back from it, swaying while the reading lasts between assent and refusal.

As for the "human condition": it is a reasonable merit to ask of a poem that it spill over from its local circumstances and speak of the universal fate of being human. We value Donne's poems and Shakespeare's and Hardy's because, whatever the local circumstances that provoked them, they transcend that origin and speak beyond their occasion. Besides, to read "Ancestral Houses" it is only necessary to imagine what it would be like to be different, to feel differently, to live by another system of values, according to which Yeats's word "greatness" would exert for the time being a particular claim. Once we read the poem as offering an imagined experience, we are free to discard every piece of merely local evidence in its favor: it is not necessary to remain infatuated with the greatness of a Renaissance prince. Deane's reading of the poem, like Jameson's reading of *Ulysses*, would ensure that these works are censored in advance.

## VII

I revert to the disagreement between Ransom and Blackmur. Ransom argued that "there are substantive as well as formal values" in a poem, just as there are in a novel where their existence is generally admitted. He did not mention that, in writing about Eliot's criticism, Blackmur had been more specific in defining the several relations between thought, experience, belief, feeling, and emotion; so that in Eliot's context, rather than in Yeats's, Blackmur's notion of "doctrine presented as emotion" becomes clear. It is hardly surprising that Blackmur ascribed to Eliot a program much the same as his own. Eliot, according to Blackmur, "excluded thought *as such* from poetry and said that poetry dealt with the experience or feeling of thought which might or might not—probably *not*—have been the poet's thought; and similarly he said that poetry dealt with belief as the experience or feeling of belief which probably had to be, from the nature of belief, the poet's own belief."[17] A page or two later Blackmur gave working definitions of feeling and emotion. Feeling "is the fundamental term: concrete, sensory, nuclear, somehow in experience, whether actual or imagined, always particular." Emotion is "feelings organized by a force whether within or without the psyche"; "feelings organized, generalized, abstracted, built into a form, theoretic or not." Doctrine presented as emotion may be translated now to read: an apparently systematic body of ideas, presented so far as they are feelings, which in superior poems is far enough. The feelings are sufficiently organized, the writing of the poem is the mode of organizing them within the constraints of language. Otherwise put, in Blackmur's terms: emotion is the theoretic form of feelings which, lacking that form, are disordered and personal beyond redemption. Blackmur says of the theoretic form, the emotion, that it is good only in that instance; which I take to mean that the defect of an idea is that it claims to be good in every instance. This is Deane's error, and Jameson's: that, having arrived at an idea—a political stance, a position which can only be reasserted since its history as an idea is already complete—they insist that it is good in every instance.

So the question to ask about "Ancestral Houses" is not: do I find its political attitude congenial? But rather: am I willing to read it, and to let it at least provisionally read me? If I am willing to read it in that spirit, I suspend for the time being not my disbelief but my economy, the nearly automatic disposition of attitudes I for the most part practice.

# THE SUBLIME BLACKMUR

In 1941, John Crowe Ransom published *The New Criticism*, a study of T. S. Eliot, I. A. Richards, William Empson, Yvor Winters, and R. P. Blackmur. He claimed not that these critics formed a school or a movement but that they exhibited loose kinship while each went about his business. Ransom had an interest in showing that a critic would find his sustenance, and most of his vocabulary, by positing a privileged relation between literature and something else, some other body of preoccupations and lores. Such a body would likely be found among the stricter concerns of philosophy, such as those of logic. Each of these critical procedures would be a partial affair and would hold out a possibility that it didn't itself fulfill and which Ransom called for in the final chapter. Wanted: an ontological critic. Or, in the terms common to *The New Criticism* and an earlier essay, "Criticism, Inc.," Ransom wanted a critic who would assume that the writing of a poem is a desperate ontological or metaphysical maneuver.

In daily life, a poet has practical interests much the same as anyone else's: he has to live, he has to use the material at hand. Only in poetry is he free to celebrate the natural or human object "which is real, individual, and qualitatively infinite." An ontological critic would respect the poet for this tenderness and value the poem for being a special form of discourse and embodying a special kind of attention.

Ransom proposed that such a critic would think of a poem as having a logical object or universal, which might be produced as an imagined scene or story, and, in addition, "a tissue of irrelevance" from which the object would not really emerge. The tissue of irrelevance would testify to the plenitude of sentiment with which the object is suffused.

None of the five critics was sufficiently ontological, by Ransom's exacting standard. But Blackmur could have protested that his interest in literature did not issue from a prior interest in something else. He was not, like Richards, a psychologist who resorted to literature for evidence; or a logician, like Winters, who judged literature upon its capacity to make impeccable statements. Blackmur's approach to literature was technical; it featured a concern for language and form, the adequacy of the arranged words to do everything they had to do. Completeness was not for him the supreme value it was for Ransom. He never spoke, as Ransom often did, of the companionship of structure and texture. But I am running ahead of myself. It is enough to say for the moment that *The New Criticism* placed Blackmur's work in company he was happy enough to keep, though later he repudiated the orthodoxy ascribed to him as a New Critic.

Blackmur's first steps in criticism were taken in 1927 when he became one of the editors of *Hound and Horn* and a frequent presence in its pages. He reviewed Eliot, Santayana, and Wyndham Lewis. In 1928, on the occasion of the presidential election, he wrote an essay—in the form and spirit of *The Education of Henry Adams*—denouncing Herbert Hoover and recommending Al Smith. With Hoover's victory, Blackmur withdrew from comment on political matters and confined himself to literature, an institution he could hope to understand. Many years later he enlarged his survey again, pronouncing upon the social and cultural situation and the many forms of trouble-making he saw at large. But in Hoover's America, Blackmur concentrated on reading literature and thought the best work he could do would be close to the page. For the time being, his method was the one Eliot recommended, that of being very intelligent. High intelligence and exegetical zest amounted to the only credo he acted on.

Over a few years, Blackmur published close work on many writers, mostly modern poets but also a few prosers—Samuel Butler, Henry Adams—who caught his mind for one reason or another. Eliot was never out of his interest for long. Blackmur gradually took up the notion of writing a big book on Adams. After many years, still incomplete, it became a thorn, a burden, a broken promise. He made forays into it, published several essays on Adams, and left it unfinished upon his death; it has now been published in a form adequate to the gist of what he had to say. Henry James was a companionable figure to Adams—*Hound and Horn*, like *The Little Review* and other journals, brought out a special issue on him, and he remained exemplary to Blackmur for the rest of his life in criticism.

These and other figures inhabited Blackmur's mind, and were always available for reference and provocation. He liked to set them in relation, one to another, as he set James in relation to Adams on the consideration that James's mind was willing to let the pattern of experience emerge as the amassed record of the experience itself, while Adams insisted on having the pattern in advance. "James imagined human reality always through dramatizing the bristling sensual record of the instance—almost any instance that had a story in it—and let the pattern, the type, the *vis a tergo*, take care of itself, which under the stress of the imaginative process it commonly did." The only problem was to know what would make a story, or how the story would stretch all the way from its constituents to the pattern they would, taken together, manage to imply. "Adams, on the other hand, tended in a given case to depend on his feeling for human type and pattern—for history and lines of force—as the source of drama, and hence saw the individual as generalized *first*." To put it another way—and Blackmur liked putting his perceptions in several ways—"Adams's set of intellectual instruments more or less *predicted* what he would discover, James resorted to instruments only to ascertain what his sensibility had *already* discovered."

Blackmur worked such relations for all they seemed to be worth. He wanted to know what would happen in his own mind if he set Eliot in relation to Dante and really worked the relation. Stevens and Pound, Stevens and Eliot. These comparisons were rarely elaborated; Blackmur was content to catch from them a glint, a sharpened insight good for the moment. In *Anni Mirabiles 1921–1925*—lectures he gave at the Library of Congress in January 1956—he nearly turned comparison into a method, and guarded himself against the danger by making most of the instances eccentric. So he compared Faulkner and Proust, Hart Crane and Stevens, Pound and Whitman (a common comparison, this), Cummings and Dryden, Auden and Tennyson, Byron and William Carlos Williams. Sometimes he surrounded a poet with two comparative figures, setting the glints running up and down and all around the town. Hart Crane was accompanied by Baudelaire and Whitman, Marianne Moore by Keats and D. H. Lawrence, Henry James by Joyce and Proust. These happenings relied on the authority of tact.

But no procedure amounted to a method or depended upon a theory. It is odd and exhilarating that we are reading Blackmur more ardently than ever in conditions which he would have reproved. He flourished in an Age of Criticism, but he would not have borne in patience an Age of Theory in which literature and criticism are nearly dissolved in favor of the theory of each. In "A Critic's Job of Work," Blackmur compared criticism with walking, observing that both need a constant intricate shifting and catching of balance, and that neither is done very well. The fact that Blackmur in his later years walked little—and that little with difficulty—makes the comparison the more telling. Most men in our day, he said, prefer "paved walks or some form of rapid transit—some easy theory or outmastering dogma." Not that he would have approved a hard theory; he didn't want a theory near him or pressing upon him any more than he wanted a dogma, though he accepted that some minds think themselves in need of both. Again, in "A Critic's Job of Work":

> For most minds, once doctrine is sighted and is held to be the completion of insight, the doctrinal mode of thinking seems the only one possible. When doctrine totters it seems it can fall only into the gulf of bewilderment, few minds risk the fall; most seize the remnants and swear the edifice remains, when doctrine becomes intolerable dogma.

If you hand your mind over to a theory, he seems to say, you have only yourself to rebuke when your theory hardens first into doctrine and then into dogma. Even if it doesn't, you can't do anything with your theory but apply it, forcing it upon your poems as if they could have no other desire than to receive such overbearing attention. No wonder Blackmur thought the best kind of mind the most provisional, and Montaigne the finest exemplar of it, revelling in mobility of perception. Poetry does not flow from thin air, Blackmur said, "but requires always either a literal faith, an imaginative faith, or, as in Shakespeare, a mind full of many provisional faiths"—the last being the best kind of mind, he didn't consider it necessary to say. When he wrote his early essays on Adams, Blackmur made him seem far more mobile than he was, assimilating him to an idiom he had resorted to, with more cause, in describing Montaigne. He described Adams's skeptical intelligence as "restless but attentive, saltatory but serial, provisional in every position yet fixed upon a theme: the theme of thought or imagination conceived as the form of human energy."

It follows that Blackmur's values can be made to coincide with an attitude, a preference subjected to the mobility of mood and standing well back from a doctrine. He despised "romantic egoism" and took it as asserting that "whatever I experience is real and final, and whatever I say represents what I experience." He was irritated by poems that proclaimed their spontaneity, and thought it no praise of Whitman and Pound to say that "each remained spontaneous all his life," because that condition, too, was just as congealed as dogma. He was not impressed by minds that offered "an easy vault from casual interpretation to an omnivorous world-view." Like Eliot, and perhaps instructed by him, Blackmur thought that ideas as such had no place in a poem, and were a nuisance, killing the feelings they pretended to stand for.

It follows, too, that Blackmur valued literature as far as it presents experiences in forms which enable us to know them. "All his life long," he said of James, "and in all but his slightest work, he struggled to use the conventions of society, and to abuse them when necessary, to bring himself directly upon the emotion that lay under the conventions, coiling and recoiling, ready to break through." The tragic character of thought, Blackmur said, is "that it takes a rigid mold too soon" and insists upon a destiny long before it has become necessary to choose one. Hence the value of irony, which postpones destiny and keeps our minds on the stretch, so that even when we succumb to an idea we are not so besotted as to stick to it. Hence, too, the supreme value of imagination, in any of the attributes Blackmur described as rational, dramatic, or symbolic. In a poem, what precedes the words— obsession, self-delusion, or plain nonsense—doesn't matter, so long as its presence in the poet's mind is provisional and not dogmatic. Dante's imagination "enabled him to dramatize with equal ardor and effect what his doctrine blessed, what it assailed, and what, at heart, it was indifferent to."

But I am merely indicating in Blackmur a broad preference or a prejudice that helped him to get his work done and kept it fresh. Between the prejudice and the sentences of his criticisms as they come together in particular essays, we find his idiom. Some readers think it a nuisance and wish he had written the kind of prose that cats and dogs can read. He was often as lucid as anyone else. He could even be aphoristic: after several sentences on Adams's faith, he said that "he had no faith, but only the need of it." He noted of Henry James that "he began at once to cultivate what his father had planted in him, the habit of response across any barrier—the more barrier the more response." In depreciation of *The Bostonians* and *The Princess Casamassima* he said that these novels "have a strangely transformed air of protecting themselves from what they are really about." Remarking that there is no sex in Marianne Moore's poetry—"No poet has been so chaste; but it is not the chastity that rises from an awareness—healthy or morbid—of the flesh, it is a special chastity aside from the flesh—a purity by birth and from the void"—Blackmur listened, a page or so later, to the word "aside" and said that Moore's sensibility "constitutes the perfection of standing aside."

But there is still an obstacle; not, as a general thing, the quirky verbal play that Ransom and other readers of Blackmur have shaken their heads over, but the words and phrases that, because Blackmur uses them with an emphasis designed to be cumulative, amount in the end to his diction. Like any poet's diction, it begins to be recognizable only when its recurrence constitutes a problem; till then we take the words as they come. But they come not in single file but in relations, sometimes specified, often assumed; hence the problem. Perhaps I can dispose them in categories, bringing together the words that are synonymous or nearly so.

There is, to begin with, the set of terms that refer to the "firstness" of experience, the earliest stirrings of sentient life before it knows what it is or why it is stirring. Sometimes Blackmur calls this "emotion," as in the sentence I quoted about James's use and abuse of conventions; sometimes "sensation," "momentum," "intuition," and very often "feelings" or "behavior," the last of which is virtually a technical term in Blackmur. "Behavior is the medium in which our lives take place"; elsewhere it is "the actual momentum in which the form of life is found." It is our impulse, and it is anarchy unless we want to mitigate the sentence and say, as Blackmur says in "Between the Numen and the Moha," that behavior "may merely want a different sort of order," different from any of the official sorts on offer. By any name, behavior is the cry of anything that is actual before it reaches the condition of being anything more or other. It is where all the ladders start.

The next stage—next because it has to be represented as coming after our behavior and offering to redeem it or somehow enhance it— marks our aspiration. If the first is behavior, the next is what Blackmur regularly calls manners, or "morals in action." Manners are the ideal insight, so far as it is embodied in society. Ransom associated a code of manners with the formal decency of a poem, and valued it for that association. Blackmur often settled for a phrase from Croce— "theoretic form"—to represent the sense we make of our feelings. "A theoretic form is a way of seeing: no more." No less, either; and what it sees is our feeling or our behavior so far as we want to make sense of it. Theoretic form is what we do to our behavior when we want to convert the actual into the real or momentum into performance. "The great drive is in the craving of the actual to become real." We confront our behavior, and thereafter "our great fear is that our behavior may overwhelm us; our great delight is when we have transformed our aspirations into behavior; our fate is that we shall be mainly incarnations of our behavior." But our delight can't be secured except by an act of the imagination, at once rational, dramatic, and symbolic. In some contexts Blackmur calls this achievement poetry or fiction; or, if he thinks of it in closely linguistic terms, he calls it rhythm, as in what would otherwise be merely the arrangement of syllables. Theoretic form, to try again, is how we construe our behavior when we try to make sense of it by bringing it into relation to different senses already in place: we give it a form and enact it. So, in poetry: the poem is always at a remove from the feelings or the behavior that incited it. Stevens's success "is due largely to his double adherence to words and experience as existing apart from his private sensibility." His great labor has been "to allow the reality of what he felt personally to pass into the superior impersonal reality of words." What is in its natural condition mostly a torment—behavior—is transformed into the poem, "where it may be rehearsed and understood in permanent form." So, too, in criticism: its perennial task is that of "bringing the work of art to the condition of performance." In pursuit of the theoretic form of our behavior, we resort to particular skills, which in a novelist are those of his art and in everyone amount to what Blackmur calls the technical or executive forms.

So much for an ideal conversion of behavior into manners. If it could succeed, all our behaviors would be redeemed, our first steps would arrive, our scribbled first drafts would turn into poems, the words vivid with the life we've given them. But in frequent practice our imaginations are incomplete or otherwise halfhearted. It would be too cynical to represent this condition as the inevitable third phase— inaccurate, too, because sometimes it doesn't obtrude at all and sometimes it has already obtruded before the act of imagination can properly get started. In a diagram it would be set aslant from the sequence of behavior and manners. But in any event it must be regarded as the perversion of manners, or their degraded form. In Blackmur's terms, the perversion involves the ousting of "morals in action" by "morals prescribed"; the congealment of forms as formulae; repetition and rote instead of performance. Here would come the ossification of feelings in the form of ideas.

Blackmur never thought of ideas as having, within the poem or novel, the character they have outside. He always repudiated what he regarded as the cowardice of theory, doctrine, dogma. Or, in a long-established distinction, he could not think of reason as on the same level of value as imagination. He sometimes spoke well of reason— "Reason is in substance all the living memory of the mind," he said in *Anni Mirabiles*. Quoting Maritain, that "art bitten by poetry longs to be freed from reason," Blackmur insisted that reason "is the great reminder of the constant and the grave, what sees the unity, the disparity, the permanent behavior of things." But generally Blackmur sided with Adams's notion in the *Education*, that "the mind resorts to reason for want of training." Words, according to that sentiment, are the behavior of mind which thought, given its way, would domesticate. In any of these versions, reason, habit, and formula would suppress the imagination, and prescribe as order what is mere rote.

But Blackmur has a further set of terms. Assuming that the conversion of behavior into morals takes place, or that we can transform our aspirations into behavior, we haven't come to the end. We have written our poem, perhaps, but there is still poetry itself as more than the sum of poems. We think of Kenneth Burke rather than of Blackmur when we take to the notion of "tracking down the implications" of our vocabularies. Burke, far more determinedly than Blackmur, proposes that we drive our words "to the end of the line." But Blackmur, too, has a sense of ultimacy, though a more occult one than Burke's or Ransom's.

The names we have to invoke to document Blackmur's version of ultimacy are Longinus and, again, Montaigne. Longinus stands for the blow of the sublime, the height of eloquence far beyond any that could have been predicted. In "Between the Numen and the Moha," Blackmur brings Longinus and Montaigne together, on the strength of a passage that he quotes, in Zeitlin's translation, from book 1, chapter 37, of Montaigne:

> Here is a wonder: we have far more poets than judges and inter-
> preters of poetry; it is easier to write it than to understand it. At
> a certain level one may judge it by rules and by art. But the true,
> supreme, and divine poesy is above all rules and reasons. Whoever
> discerns the beauty of it with assured and steady sight, he does
> not see it any more than the splendor of a flash of lightning. It
> does not seduce our judgment; it ravishes and overwhelms it.

Swayed by the last few lines, and sensing in them the tradition of the sublime which Montaigne resumes without having read Longinus, Blackmur posits ultimacy of insight and eloquence under the auspices of imagination and not of reason. Here, he says, "we see the pride of imagination, which is confronted with reality, in the act of breaking down the pride of reason, which manipulates reality in a merely ad-ministrative rather than an understanding sense." The sublime is not the furthest reach of common sense but the ravishing of every sense. In another vocabulary, it is epiphany or revelation; in Shakespeare's vo-cabulary, it is what Ophelia experiences so that she can say "O . . . To have seen what I have seen, see what I see." Blackmur thought he could at least point in its direction by calling it symbol, and saying that "symbol stands for nothing previously known, but for what is 'here' made known and what is about to be made known." But the common understanding of symbol is hardly enough to send it into the abyss or wherever it has to go to register the sublime and the authority beyond prediction which is its blow. At least once, Blackmur called such au-thority God, "who is reality by definition: the reality yet to be." Sometimes he thought its eloquence such that it must be called silence; and he wrote an essay, "The Language of Silence," testifying to it as a ravishing possibility. Or he called it, after Stevens, in every honorific sense, gibberish. Once, Blackmur called the sublime power numen, meaning "that power within us, greater than and other than ourselves, that moves us, sometimes carrying us away, in the end moving us forward unless we drop out, always overwhelming us." Whether the power is in nature or in us hardly matters. If it is in nature, we take it to ourselves or supplicate it by magic or superstition. If it is in ourselves, we recognize it, by preference, in others, and so far as possible reduce its authority in ourselves. Or we come upon it in paintings, music, and literature, or hear it in Myshkin's scream in *The Idiot*—one of Blackmur's instances—of which Dostoevski says that in it "everything human seems obliterated and it is impossible, or very difficult, for an observer to realize and admit that it is the man himself screaming; it seems as though it were someone else screaming from within the man."

Blackmur's figure of the sublime is a phrase: to be beside oneself. To be beside oneself is to be in ecstasy, released from one's demeaning contexts: "obsessed, freed, and beside themselves," as he says of certain animals and men in Marianne Moore's poetry. In "A Burden for Critics," he refers to "those forces that operate in the arts which are greater than ourselves and come from beyond or under ourselves" and, he almost says, drive us beyond ourselves if we attend to them.

How we attend to them is a desperate question. "We have lost," Blackmur believes, "the field of common reference, we have dwindled in our ability to think symbolically, and as we look about us we see all our old unconscious skills at life disappearing without any apparent means of developing new unconscious skills." We have a plethora of new conscious skills, lodged in psychology, anthropology, and sociology, but these are useless for any purpose except that of making trouble for ourselves—they "undermine purpose, blight consciousness, and prevent decision," they promote nothing but "uncertainty, insecurity, anxiety, and incoherence." Besides, so far as they are merely conscious skills, they have no genuine but only mechanical access to the very materials they claim as their own.

Where the old unconscious skills are to be sought is a hard question. With daring and effrontery, Blackmur associates them with bourgeois humanism, but a humanism still in some degree accessible to the sublime. If a political program is implied, it must be bourgeois humanism kept alert and uncomplacent by constant recourse to tory anarchy of spirit, so that what it speaks is a live mixture of common sense and Stevens's "gibberish of the vulgate."

We can now place Blackmur's criticism, taking care not to domesticate it but to bring it into relation to our own concerns and those of his contemporaries. Blackmur's relations to James, Eliot, Ransom, Richards, and Burke are well established but not, I think, well enough rehearsed. It may, however, be more useful to follow Blackmur in considering his relation to a critic with whom he had little in common. Blackmur's review of *The Liberal Imagination*—it is in *The Lion and the Honeycomb*—discloses not only the differences between himself and Trilling but between himself and most of the criticism written in his time. It is clear from the first paragraphs that Blackmur respects Trilling's criticism but regards it as too willingly taking its bearings from a social understanding of literature and criticism. "We see that he cultivates a mind never entirely his own, a mind always deliberately to some extent what he understands to be the mind of society, and also a mind always deliberately to some extent the mind of the old European society taken as corrective and as prophecy." The sentence is excessive; it merely says that Trilling too contentedly thinks he is Matthew Arnold. But it leads to a more telling one. Trilling, according to Blackmur, "has always wanted a pattern, whether a set or a current, a pattern of relevant ideas as a vantage from which to take care of his occasional commitments." This begins to sound as if Trilling's mind were akin to Adams's, needing a pattern in advance of any occasion; the unspoken consequence being that Blackmur himself corresponds to James and gains authority by the comparison. Of Blackmur, as of James, it may truly be said that he cultivates a mind entirely his own, or as nearly his own as its subjection to the syntax of prose allows. Blackmur doesn't want a pattern or a set, because he distrusts anything that offers itself as a formula, and he construes predictive capacity as merely setting limits in advance.

He has a further objection, which he merely implies. Literature best serves society by serving it only in the long run. It is under no obligation to endorse society's official purposes at any moment or to sustain its understanding of itself. "The true business of literature," Blackmur says, "as of all intellect, critical or creative, is to remind the powers that be, simple and corrupt as they are, of the turbulence they have to control." To which he appends this admonition: "There is a disorder vital to the individual which is fatal to society. And the other way round is also true."

If we think of Blackmur's insistence on cultivating a mind entirely his own, we find it easy to be patient with his language even when it runs to exorbitance. "It is only the language we use," he says, "which must abbreviate and truncate our full discourse"—which is not much different from Pater's reference, in the conclusion to *Studies in the History of the Renaissance*, to objects "in the solidity with which language invests them." The impression of stability is a compromise worked out between language and our nerves. The abbreviations and truncations of our discourse are a similar compromise worked out between languages and our biological defensiveness. So Blackmur, insisting on a mind of his own, insists equally on working his language hard, forcing it to the twist and torsion that he calls idiom.

Blackmur's meaning for us is far more active when his style is scandalous than when it is ingratiating. We are reading him at a time of "the new illiteracy" and rampantly self-conscious skills—which he regarded as much the same thing. Criticism's recourse to psychology, politics, anthropology, philosophy, and linguistics is rarely seen for the desperate device it is: what are all or any of these but patterns set in advance, or values having as their sole destiny that they are incessantly applicable? Meanwhile, much of our literature remains, in every sense of the word that matters, unread.

# TRANSLATION IN THEORY AND
# IN A CERTAIN PRACTICE

ഇൟൟൟൟ

I

I choose for commentary an anonymous love-poem written in Irish, probably in the first half of the seventeenth century; it is readily available in *An Duanaire 1600–1900: Poems of the Dispossessed*, edited by Sean O'Tuama and translated into English by Thomas Kinsella (Dolmen Press, 1981) and in *The New Oxford Book of Irish Verse*, edited with translations by Kinsella (Oxford University Press, 1986). In *An Duanaire* it is given as one of a class "of elegant occasional poems in loose syllabic meters dating from the seventeenth century—love poems, satires, religious poems and others." In the *Oxford Book* the date is revised to fifteenth/sixteenth century. As O'Tuama notes in *An Duanaire*, the common form of such poems is syllabic, each stanza of four lines, seven syllables in each line; there are rhyming linkages between the end words of the second and fourth lines, between the final syllable of the first line and an internal syllable in the second, and between the final syllable of the third line and an internal syllable of the fourth. In the second stanza, for instance, internal rhyming in the first two lines links *Créad, d'éag, bhéal*, and *déad*. In the third line, internal rhyming links *míolla* with *aol*, and *crobh* with *t-ucht*; in the fourth, *dáibh* with *bás*.

Here is the poem:

### Ní Bhfuighe Mise Bás Duit

Ní bhfuighe mise bás duit,
 a bhean úd an chuirp mar ghéis;
daoine leamha ar mharbhais riamh,
 ní hionann iad is mé féin.

Créad uma rachainn-se d'éag
 don bhéal dearg, don déad mar bhláth?
An crobh míolla, an t-ucht mar aol,
 an dáibh do-gheabhainn féin bás?

Do mhéin aobhdha, th'aigneadh saor,
 a bhus thana, a thaobh mar chuip,
a rosc gorm, a bhráighe bhán,
 ní bhfuighe mise bás duit.

Do chiocha corra, a chneas úr,
 do ghruaidh chorcra, do chúl fiar—
go deimhin ní bhfuighead bás
 dóibh sin go madh háil le Dia.

Do mhala chaol, i'fholt mar ór,
 do rún geanmnaidh, do ghlór leasc,
do shál chruinn, do cholpa réigh—
 ní mhuirbhfeadh siad acht duine leamh.

A bhean úd an chuirp mar ghéis,
 do hoileadh mé ag duine glic;
aithne dhamh mar bhíd na mná—
 ní bhfuighe mise bás duit!

In the introduction to *An Duanaire* O'Tuama and Kinsella said that their primary aim in the translations was to secure "the greatest possible fidelity of content": the translations "are as close to the original Irish as we could make them." More specifically: "All images and ideas occurring in the Irish are conveyed in translation and images or ideas not occurring in the Irish are not employed."

A few comments on the meaning, emphasis, and tone of Kinsella's translation are called for. Line 1: *mise* is the emphatic form of the first person singular, so it is more insistent than Kinsella's "I will not die for you." Still in line 1: *duit* does not quite mean "for you," if "die for you" is construed as implying sacrifice. Not "for your sake," but "on account of you." I will not, like weaker men, die because of you. Line 2: *úd* means "yonder," a distancing word. *Bhean* means woman in the vocative case, but Kinsella's "lady" is all right, and it gets the distance; the speaker is not talking to her directly but across barriers of caste and class. *An chuirp mar ghéis* is a genitive, therefore more constitutive than Kinsella's merely dative and adjectival rendering. You, yonder woman, of body like a swan. Line 3: *daoine leamha* means empty-headed, foolish people. Line 5: *rachainn-se* is more emphatic again than Kinsella's "me": what would make (a fine fellow like me) go off to die? Line 6: *déad* means the whole tooth-plate, not the individual teeth. Line 7: *an t-ucht mar aol*, the breast like lime. Lime was used in the Big House as whitewash and disinfectant, so it has associations with majesty. Line 8: *féin* keeps the insistence going: I myself. Line 9: *saor* means "free," but Kinsella's "noble" is close enough, since only noble ladies could have free minds. Line 10: *thaobh* means "side." Kinsella's "flank" is a bit Audenesque. Line 13: *úr* means "fresh," alive-looking, not (or not necessarily) Kinsella's "refined." Line 14: Kinsella reverses the phrases: *do ghruaidh chorcra* means "your waving hair," *do chúl fiar* is "your purple cheeks," but Kinsella's "flushed" meets the case pretty well. Line 17: *Do mhala chaol* means "your narrow brow" (singular) or temple, narrow probably because of the veil, hood, or wimple she wears. Line 18: *leasc* means "modest" rather than Kinsella's "languid." Line 19: Kinsella again reverses the phrases. *Do cholpa réigh* means "your ready (or fine) calf." It is a bit livelier than Kinsella's "smooth." Line 22: Kinsella's "hand" is not in the Irish. *Duine* means "person": I was taught by a clever one. Line 23: *aithne* is one of the three forms of knowledge discriminated in Irish: it means what I have learned about people, or about one person, as distinct from *eolas*, which is general information, and from *fios*, which means wisdom. Curiously, *aithne* also means commandment, as in the Ten Commandments, but I do not suppose that comes into the poem.

When the *Oxford Book* came out, I argued that Kinsella was ill-advised in preferring his own translation, in every case, to earlier ones, because this preference suppressed the entire history of the reception of these Irish poems. In the period from about 1885 to 1940, English translations of the Irish sagas and lyrics were the only means by which most of the modern Irish poets and their readers gained access to the lore upon which the ideology of the Irish Literary Revival was based. Yeats and most of his contemporaries did not know enough Irish to read the original poems. Kinsella's decision to use only his own translations had the effect of transcending the experience of several generations. His gifts as a translator are formidable, but it is hardly surprising that every poem he translates sounds as if he had written it. His compacted, laconic style takes charge.

I agree that earlier translations have sinned by taking freedoms. Frank O'Connor's translation of that stanza reads:

> *The devil take the golden hair!*
>   *That maiden look, that voice so gay,*
> *That delicate heel and pillared thigh*
>   *Only some foolish man would slay.*

In the Irish the devil does not take anything, and his intervention not only ignores the woman's narrow brow but ruins the symmetry of the two companionable phrases in each of the first three lines, and therefore the change of tone in the last one.

It may be thought the highest praise to say that Kinsella's translations make the poems sound as if he had written them. But this is a disputed matter, and I want to rehearse a little of the dispute.

## II

There would be no dispute if the translation were offered as a new poem, inspired indeed or at least prompted by the original but now an independent work. The simplest analogies for this procedure come from painting and music. Brahms's *Variations on a Theme by Haydn* pays tribute to an original theme, alludes to it, but does not undertake any representative duty toward it. Nor does Picasso's *Les Demoiselles d'Avignon* propose to speak on behalf of its sources—various *Baigneuses* by Cézanne, bits of Iberian and African sculpture. Allusion is not translation; its relation to the original is opportunistic rather than representative. In one respect, the translator is a modest fellow; he wants to walk by placing his feet in the footprints left by someone else. In another respect, he is a braggart, he claims to carry over—I need a different metaphor—someone else's meaning from that someone's language. Kinsella's translation—I revert to the first metaphor—follows the anonymous Irish poem step by step, and pretends that the differences between Irish and English do not nullify the effort, that the content of the Irish speaker's imagined feeling for the woman may still be recovered. But there is a limit to Kinsella's modesty, and that limit is the settled character of his style: he insists on always sounding like himself.

In *The Sense of an Ending*, Frank Kermode discusses the practice of treating the past as a special case of the present. In translation, we do this when we make the original submit to our modern style, disappearing into it. If we regarded the original as absolutely alien, we would have to deem it untranslatable, an instance of the sentiment in which we regard our "fictions of accord"—to use Kermode's phrase in another context—as specious. In practice, no translator is so severely principled. If a translation is attempted, it is assumed to be at least reasonably possible.

There is a scrupulous device, employed in Stanley Burnshaw's *The Poem Itself*, which is: you do not offer to transpose one structure—say, Mallarmé's *"Don du poème,"* into another, a poem in English. Burnshaw has argued that the only way we can experience the poetry of a language we do not understand is "by learning to hear and pronounce (if only approximately) the sounds of the originals and 'simultaneously' reading literal renditions." In Burnshaw's practice, the reader is held within the sounds and sense of the original language, and is aided by literal rendering and judicious commentary; in the commentary, the translator points to acoustic and semantic properties of the original. The advantage of Burnshaw's method over a crib is that the original poem is not replaced by something else; it is not reduced to a meaning or an action in another language. For the duration of the reading the reader stays in the ambience of the foreign language, an experience so valuable, in Burnshaw's eyes, that even its limitedness is preferable to any English substitute.

There are further possibilities. Pound's theory and practice of translation are predicated on two assumptions: one, that certain foreign poems have perceptions not available in English; two, that these perceptions testify to a road not taken, a development that English should have pursued. In his major essay on Cavalcanti, Pound argues that English poetry since Shakespeare has lost much by resorting to Petrarch rather than to Cavalcanti:

> We appear to have lost the radiant world where one thought cuts through another with clean edge, a world of moving energies *"mezzo oscuro rade,"* *"risplende in sè perpetuale effecto,"* magnetisms that take form, that are seen, or that border the visible, the matter of Dante's *paradiso*, the glass under water, the form that seems a form seen in a mirror, these realities perceptible to the sense. . . .[1]

Pound's way, in his several translations of Cavalcanti—starting with *The Sonnets and Ballate of Guido Cavalcanti* (1911), then the long essay in *The Dial* (1928 and 1929), finally canto 36—is to go back to a pre-Shakespearean English for which Campion and Henry Lawes provide clearest warrant, and to write as if Wyatt, Surrey, and Shakespeare had not dominated English in Petrarchan modes. The results have been examined by many critics, notably by Donald Davie in *Ezra Pound: Poet as Sculptor*, Hugh Kenner in his introduction to *The Translations of Ezra Pound* and in the essay, "Ezra Pound and Modernism," and John Hollander in *Vision and Resonance*.

Some aspects of the procedure are clear, starting with Kenner's insistence that Pound "never translates 'into' something already existing in English." When Pound translates Cavalcanti, he shows what English might have become if it had taken a different tack at a crucial moment, roughly 1600; if it had retained rather than forgotten Chaucer; if it had taken its character from Elizabethan music rather than Elizabethan theater. But Kenner's further argument is more questionable: that Pound "doesn't translate the words," that he goes behind or through the words to "the thing he expresses: desolate seafaring, or the cult of the plum-blossoms, or the structure of sensibility that attended the Tuscan anatomy of love."[2] It follows—or it would follow if Kenner were right—that what Pound is translating is "a modus of thought or feeling" which happened to have been "crystallized," once before, by Cavalcanti or Rihaku or someone else. I do not think anyone would now accept Kenner's easy separation of "the words" from the thoughts and feelings supposedly lying silent behind them. It might be wiser to avoid that problem by holding every issue within language, as Hollander does in his commentary on Pound's deliberate archaism in the Cavalcanti translations and the *Cantos*.

Quoting and analyzing Rossetti's translation of Dante's so-called "Story Sestina"—"A while ago, I saw her dress'd in green"—Hollander shows that there were indeed available to Pound non-Miltonic instances of translation into English, and he goes on to say that "the archaizing element" in Pound's translation of Cavalcanti's "Donna mi Prega"—"In memory's locus taketh he his state"—"may be a rather profound matter, part of a deep attitude toward style and a self-consciousness about it":

> Perhaps it is more like a Chattertonian style of pastiche than we have been able heretofore to think. The matter of Romance was not only an alternative to the mythopoetic world of the American Romantic tradition—the dialectic of landscape and selfhood and their mutual intrusions. An emphatic and intense show of coping with it became for a while as authentic a way to "drink, and be whole again beyond confusion" as, for example, E. A. Robinson's deep draught of English literature, even to the point of his reconsecrating society verse to real poetic purposes.[3]

Romance as an alternative to Emerson, "an emphatic and intense show of coping with it": I take these as indicating Pound's attempt to posit for English a different destiny. The archaism is his insistence that he knows what he is doing, and that it is only because English has taken another road that his translations sound archaic. As Kenner notes in "Ezra Pound and Modernism":

> The radical novelty of "The Seafarer" is that instead of adapting the original to a set of metrical and syntactic conventions we're prepared to recognize as a normal English poem, it adapts the norms of English poetry to the original. That's a Trojan-horse approach to the translator's art; once admitted, some harmless-seeming alien entity proceeds to take possession, modify, conquer.[4]

The analogy is in one respect misleading: whatever combination of syllables, phonemes, words, and syntactical procedures Pound made in "The Seafarer," these were already "there," in English, waiting to be activated. Kenner's references to Victorian poetry make it seem far more circumscribed than it was—it included Hopkins, Whitman,

Clough, and Dickinson—and therefore make Pound's translations seem even more daring than they were. However, he is right to speak up for them. Indeed, there is no reason why we should be more hostile to Pound's deliberate archaism than we are to the efforts of other writers, notably Barnes, Hopkins, and Joyce, to give English a different destiny. In any case, Pound's theory of translation is clear enough: try to recover what we have lost, carry over from earlier poets of a better tradition something of what they have and we need. The process is what Hollander calls "the internalization of other prior models, that they may be incorporated into the new poetic being."

But "internalization" does not quite meet the case: its spatial figure is entirely assimilative, it does not allow sufficiently for one of the richest options available, a translator's resistance to his own process, a scruple darkening the decision. When I said that Kinsella's translations make the original poems sound as if he had written them, I had such resistance in mind. It is not merely an excess of nationalism which prompts me to think that Kinsella might have made the Irish poem offer more recalcitrance, a principled resistance to the destiny he proposed for it. I am not entirely resigned to the implication that an Irish poem goes into the English language so amiably, or, otherwise put, that Kinsella's English, in which one hears not only Kinsella but Eliot and Auden and the Joyce of *Dubliners* and much besides, so winningly smooths over the differences between a seventeenth-century Irish poem and a twentieth-century English one. I would like to find that the Irish poem has retained a mind of its own. So I want to look at two theories of translation, Walter Benjamin's and Paul de Man's, which in their different styles propose a more arduous relation between translation and original.

Benjamin's essay is "The Task of the Translator: An Introduction to the Translation of Baudelaire's *Tableaux parisiens*." It is a difficult work, mainly because it implies a theology of pure *Logos* that may be intuited but only with great inadequacy discussed. So far as the essay may be summarized, it emphasizes that a translation issues from an original, not so much from its life as from its afterlife; it marks a certain stage in the continued life of the original. But the merit of a translation does not consist in transmitting the information, content, or meaning of the original: such an aim would be trivial. Ultimately, the purpose of a translation is to express "the central reciprocal relationship between languages." This relationship is not one of likeness,

but of kinship: the kinship is one of intentionality, "an intention, however, which no single language can attain by itself but which is realized
only by the totality of their intentions supplementing each other: pure
language." Pure language, in Benjamin's context, seems to be the utterance of a primordial *Logos*:

> In this pure language—which no longer means or expresses any-
> thing but is, as expressionless and creative Word, that which is
> meant in all languages—all information, all sense, and all inten-
> tion finally encounter a stratum in which they are destined to be
> extinguished.[5]

It is the translator's task "to release in his own language that pure language which is under the spell of another, to liberate the language
imprisoned in a work in his re-creation of that work."

I repeat that Benjamin's essay is more a tone poem than a para-
phrasable essay. At various points he seems to say that in at least one
respect a translation has a worthier purpose than the original. Every
consideration that causes other translators to despair of their mission—
inevitable failure; disjunction between the connotations of one language and another; the unyieldingness of their own language—is
welcomed by Benjamin. I think the reason is that he welcomes every
occasion on which unity is demonstrably impossible; just as he makes
out a stronger ethical case for allegory than for symbol. He is not dismayed, for instance, to remark that "while content and language form
a certain unity in the original, like a fruit and its skin, the language of
the translation envelops its content like a royal robe with ample folds:
for it signifies a more exalted language than its own and thus remains
unsuited to its content, overpowering and alien." Hence "it is not the
highest praise of a translation to say that it reads as if it had originally
been written in that language." Poet and translator are different beings,
the difference is vested in their different intentions. "The intention of
the poet is spontaneous, primary, graphic"; that is, the poet wants to
write a poem, wants to express something-or-other, wants to incarnate
a feeling, a desire, a passion real or imagined. The intention of the
translator "is derivative, ultimate, ideational"; that is, he makes no
claim upon the original intention or intuition, does not pretend that
it is his own or otherwise accessible beyond words. Benjamin's reason
seems to be that it is the translation, not the original, which points be-

yond itself toward pure language. Evidently, the way up and the way down are the same: down, plunging from abyss to abyss; up, coming to rest in Holy Writ. The particular merit of a translation, Benjamin appears to say, is that it knows it speaks a fallen tongue, it knows that abjection is the condition of its existing at all.

It follows that the relation between a translation and its original, so far as the sense of the original is in question, is comparable to that between a tangent and the circle it touches:

> Just as a tangent touches a circle lightly and at but one point, with this touch rather than with the point setting the law according to which it is to continue on its straight path to infinity, a translation touches the original lightly and only at the infinitely small point of the sense, thereupon pursuing its own course according to the laws of fidelity in the freedom of linguistic flux.[6]

By "fidelity" in that passage Benjamin does not mean the conventional "fidelity to the original"; he means fidelity to the ideal of pure language, and freedom in its pursuit.

The difficulty with Benjamin's essay is that it veers between intuitions of sublime silence, language as Pure Act, and—on occasion—fairly straightforward recommendations, such as the advice offered by Rudolf Pannwitz in *The Crisis of European Culture* that a translator should allow his own language to be powerfully affected by the language of the original, rather than insist on keeping his own language in the state in which he finds it. (This advice, by the way, would support Pound in his dealings with Cavalcanti.) Benjamin's theory of translation is a theory of allegory and at the same time a theory of the sublime; of the linguistic intention of meaning, willing to see itself abject at every point and persisting in its abjection. Translations are precious in this context because they emphasize that the translation, in this sole respect like the original, consists of broken fragments of a once putatively intact vessel. Benjamin's theory is also post-Hegelian, inasmuch as it is a theory of translation as the necessarily fallen recognition of Absolute Spirit.

Paul de Man's essay is almost as difficult to summarize as Benjamin's. It begins by setting aside the messianic or what I might call the "logological" element in Benjamin. Benjamin's *reine Sprache*—pure language—is an embarrassment to de Man, who hastens to declare that there never was such a thing: "There was no vessel in the first place, or we have no knowledge of this vessel, or no awareness, no access to it, so for all intents and purposes there has never been one." The assertion is gruff, indeed positivistic. Benjamin never claimed that a *reine Sprache* exists or has existed as an accessible form of speech, any more than a Christian claims access to the primordial *Logos*, except inasmuch as the imitation of Christ as mediator gives one a partial glimpse of it. The mode of being of *Logos* is in principle, not in particle. But de Man will have none of this talk of *reine Sprache*; if we are exiles, most of all in our native language, we are exiled from a homeland we have never had.

Glossing Benjamin's essay, de Man insists on the differences between poet and translator:

> The poet has some relationship to meaning, to a statement that is not purely within the realm of language. That is the naiveté of the poet, that he has to say something, that he has to convey a meaning which does not necessarily relate to language. The relationship of the translator to the original is the relationship between language and language, wherein the problem of meaning or the desire to say something, the need to make a statement, is entirely absent. Translation is a relation from language to language, not a relation to an extralinguistic meaning that could be copied, paraphrased, or imitated.[7]

Translation, therefore, is concerned with "what in the original belongs to language." It is by definition belated.

Like Benjamin, de Man turns this necessity into a virtue, though not one susceptible to pleasure. The categorical belatedness of a translation allows it to exist in a critical or ironic relation to the original. Like critical theory or, presumably, like Deconstruction, translation acts precisely by not imitating or reproducing the original, and by this refusal it shows in the original "a mobility, an instability, which at first one did not notice." The translation can put the original "in motion" and question its claim to canonical authority by showing that it, too, is merely an afterlife, therefore an absence, a death. De Man values translation—or at least respects it—for the shadow of death it casts upon an original that was naive enough to think itself buoyantly articulate. Translations, de Man takes a certain grim pleasure in reporting, "kill the original, by discovering that the original was already dead."

At the end of his essay, commenting on Benjamin's distinction between *das Gemeinte* and the *Art des Meinen*—between what is meant and the way in which language means—de Man argues that the first is intentional, the second not; or at least that "whereas the meaning-function is certainly intentional, it is not a priori certain at all that the mode of meaning, the way by which I mean, is intentional in any way."

> The way in which I can try to mean is dependent upon linguistic properties that are not only not made by me, because I depend on the language as it exists for the devices which I will be using; it is as such not made by us as historical beings, it is perhaps not even made by humans at all,[8]

Who made the English language seems to me a fairly ascertainable question. Who made language "as such" is not at all interesting, even as a conceit. Paul de Man's version of Deconstruction was always the sinister side of angelism. But in any case he was unduly restrictive in his sense of "the language as it exists." One of the purposes of translation is to show us that the language as it exists is far more diverse than we had thought. Kenner, too, as I have indicated, thinks he knows the lineaments of the language as it exists. Quoting Pound's "Cino,"

> *Lips, words, and you snare them,*
> *Dreams, words, and they are as jewels,*
> *Strange spells of old deity,*
> *Ravens, nights, allurement:*
> *And they are not;*
> *Having become the souls of song*

he remarks, "This isn't the English soul of 1908." Perhaps not, but I do not see how he could know what "the English soul" could possibly be, in 1908 or at any other time. That there are and have been English souls, I am ready to concede, but "the English soul" is a mere notion. Besides, the English language in 1908 contained at least *in potentia* the possibilities enacted by Pound in that year. And more. We may indeed be imprisoned in our language as it exists in our time, but there is no merit in complaining that the space is intolerably restricted.


### III


It is clear that Benjamin and, even more insistently, de Man think of translation not as transmission of meaning but as the exposure of a text to a more explicit stage of its doom. De Man regards the afterlife of a poem as proof not of its continuance but of its death. Translation is a coroner's report: the body is pronounced dead, and the cause of its death is disclosed. The merit de Man claims for translation, as for the deconstructive form of hermeneutics, is the removal of what is deemed to be mystification. The particularly guilty form of mystification is the acquired and reiterated sentiment of unity, unity of apprehension, unity of being.

In common practice, few translators see their job in these terms: the trope of *translatio*, transmission, "bringing over," is still in place. If failure in translation is by definition inevitable, so that the only question is one of degree, most translators put up with this disability, they do not take skeptical pleasure in it.

Kinsella assumes, for instance, that a certain recognizable feeling went into the Irish poem, took that form without visible residue. His aim as translator is to suggest the quality of that feeling, on the assumption that the feeling is common to all, a manifestation of love, desire, need, lack, resentment, barriers of class and station in a particular constellation of sentiment. He shows no serious misgiving about language as such, or the capacity of language to apprehend a certain structure of sentiment. The main problem arises from the structural and other differences between Irish and English. A different translation would testify to a different sense of these factors. If I were to translate the first stanza as

> *I shall not die on your account,*
> *Lady, body of a swan,*
> *Puny men you have ever killed*
> *But not the likes of me*

I would claim, with whatever justice, that my first line comes closer than Kinsella's to the tone, the stance, of the original, the degree of emphasis in the speaker's pride; that my second line is more correctly sensuous than Kinsella's, that it observes the constitutive or genitive intimacy of the description; that my third line is a little more accurate—*riamh* meaning "ever"; that my fourth line is more idiomatically correct—"but" rather than "and"—and that we are both at about the same remove from literalness, the literal translation of the line being, "They are not the same as I." But there are no ideological differences, so far as I can see, between Kinsella's translation and mine. My theory is grumpier than Kinsella's, I suppose, because I want the differences between Irish and English to remain visible, unelided. But my practice, if I had one, would observe what Derrida has called the "twice one" concept of translation, "the operation of passing from one language into another, each of them forming an organism or a system, the rigorous integrity of which remains at the level of supposition, like that of a body proper."

As for Benjamin's theory of translation, and Paul de Man's more lucid version of it: they seem to me to belong, like Deconstruction, to the history of irony. A translator might proceed in that spirit, but most translators continue, like Kinsella, to live among words in the conviction of a more accommodating possibility.

# THE OLD MODERNS

# ON *THE GOLDEN BOWL*

〜〜〜〜〜

I

I propose to come to *The Golden Bowl* somewhat indirectly and to justify my procedure by claiming that this is how the book comes to itself. In my sense of it, there is no moment, no scene, in which the book delivers itself over to us. We never feel, before the end and perhaps not even then, that James has given it to us without reserve and indicated how we are to receive it. We immerse ourselves happily in it, page after page, but we are never allowed to feel sure that we have it right. The relations between what the characters feel and what they say, like the relations between occasions of speech and those of silence, are endlessly to be divined. James leaves us free, gives us more freedom of interpretation than we know what to do with. So I plot my first course of indirection by remarking how *The Golden Bowl* appeared to James before he had written a word of it. On November 28, 1892, he made a note of a situation he had heard of: a father and his daughter marry simultaneously; the daughter marries a young Englishman, the father an American girl of much the same age as his daughter. The father's new wife becomes "much more attractive to the young husband of the girl than the girl herself has remained." The young husband has known his father-in-law's wife before either of their marriages, known her and would have married her if she had had any money. Father and daughter soothe each other by spending as much time together as they can. In turn, the other two are thrown together and resume their intimacy:

> The father marries because he's bereft, but he ceases to be bereft from the moment his daughter returns to him in consequence of the *insuccès* of his marriage. The daughter weeps with him over the *insuccès* of *hers*, but her very alienation in this manner from her husband gives the second wife, the stepmother, her pretext, her opportunity for consoling the other.[1]

On February 14, 1895, James went back to the idea and noted that "the adulterine element in the subject" might make a difficulty for his plan of publishing the story in *Harper's*. In the event, he put it aside for many years; only in 1904 did it become *The Golden Bowl*. But it was then a different story. Father and daughter do not weep together: neither of them gives the other the slightest indication of marital dissatisfaction. The daughter's main object is to protect her father from discovering that his wife has been unfaithful to him. She resorts to every form of humbugging, as she calls it, rather than let him know the truth. In the novel, the father marries not because he is bereft of his daughter but because he wishes to release her from the responsibility of looking after him. There are many other differences, but they are consistent with James's first idea of a "rotary motion" or "vicious circle" consisting in "the reasons which each of the parties gives the other." The title of the novel, which provides the occasion of some of those reasons, James found in the Bible and in Blake. Ecclesiastes 12: "Or ever the silver cord be loosed, or the golden bowl be broken, or the pitcher be broken at the fountain, or the wheel broken at the cistern." Blake's *The Book of Thel* asks:

> *Can Wisdom be put in a silver rod?*
> *Or Love in a golden bowl?*

But Ecclesiastes is enough, the image of a cracked or broken bowl giving James the device of disclosure on which the novel turns.

So much for the germ or first idea. I shall trace one more circuit before coming to the book. *The Golden Bowl* was published in November 1904. James's brother William didn't rush to read it, but he tackled it in the end, a year later. James's late style irritated William, so he was reluctant to subject himself to another dose of it. Fraternal affection drove him on, but put him under no obligation, the deed once done, to conceal his distaste for *The Golden Bowl*. On October 22, 1905, he wrote to Henry about it:

> It put me, as most of your recenter long stories have put me, in a very puzzled state of mind. I don't enjoy the kind of "problem," especially when, as in this case, it is treated as problematic (*viz.*, the adulterous relations between Charlotte and the Prince), and the method of narration by interminable elaboration of suggestive reference (I don't know what to call it, but you know what I mean) goes agin the grain of all my own impulses in writing; and yet in spite of it all, there is a brilliancy and cleanness of effect, and in this book especially a high-toned social atmosphere that are unique and extraordinary. Your methods and my ideals seem the reverse, the one of the other—and yet I have to admit your extreme success in this book. But why won't you, just to please Brother, sit down and write a new book, with no twilight or mustiness in the plot, with great vigor and decisiveness in the ac-tion, no fencing in the dialogue, no psychological commentaries, and absolute straightness in the style? Publish it in my name, I will acknowledge it, and give you half the proceeds. Seriously, I wish you *would*, for you *can*; and I should think it would tempt you, to embark on a "fourth manner." You of course know these feelings of mine without my writing them down, but I'm "noth-ing if not" outspoken. Meanwhile you can despise me and fall back on such opposite emotions as Howells's, who seems to ad-mire you without restriction, as well as on the records of the sale of the book.[2]

There was more to this than William's saying, in effect, "leave the psy-chology to me." Henry can't have been surprised by his brother's at-titude, but he was perturbed by the blankness of its reiteration:

> I mean (in response to what you write me of your having read *The Golden B.*) to try to produce some uncanny form of thing, in fiction, that will gratify you, as Brother—but let me say, dear William, that I shall greatly be humiliated if you *do* like it, and thereby lump it, in your affection, with things, of the current age,

that I have heard you express admiration for and that I would sooner descend to a dishonored grave than have written. Still I *will* write you your book, on that two-and-two-make-four system on which all the awful truck that surrounds us is produced. . . . I'm always sorry when I hear of your reading anything of mine, and always hope you won't—you seem to me so constitutionally unable to "enjoy" it, and so condemned to look at it from a point of view remotely alien to mine in writing it, and to the conditions out of which, *as* mine, it has inevitably sprung—so that all the intentions that have been its main reason for being (with *me*) appear never to have reached you at all—and you appear even to assume that the life, the elements forming its subject-matter, deviate from felicity in not having an impossible analogy with the life of Cambridge. I see nowhere about me done or dreamed of the things that alone for me constitute the *interest* of the doing of the novel—and yet it is in a sacrifice of them on their very own ground that the thing you suggest to me evidently consists.[3]

William had the good grace not to take offense, having given so much of it. On May 4, 1907, writing to congratulate Henry on *The American Scene*, a record of Henry's travels in the East and West of the United States and a book written as nearly as Henry could bring himself to write by the method of two-and-two-make-four, William took yet another occasion to explain his distaste for his brother's late style:

You know how opposed your whole "third manner" of execution is to the literary ideals which animate my crude and Orson-like breast, mine being to say a thing in one sentence as straight and explicit as it can be made, and then to drop it forever; yours being to avoid naming it straight, but by dint of breathing and sighing all round and round it, to arouse in the reader who may have had a similar perception already (Heaven help him if he hasn't!) the illusion of a solid object, made (like the "ghost" at the Polytechnic) wholly out of impalpable materials, air, and the prismatic interferences of light, ingeniously focused by mirrors upon empty space. But you *do* it, that's the queerness! And the complication of innuendo and associative reference on the enormous

scale to which you give way to it does so *build out* the matter for
the reader that the result is to solidify, by the mere bulk of the
process, the like perception from which *he* has to start. As air, by
dint of its volume, will weigh like a corporeal body; so his own
poor little initial perception, swathed in this gigantic envelopment
of suggestive atmosphere, grows like a germ into something vastly
bigger and more substantial. But it's the rummest method for one
to employ systematically as you do nowadays; and you employ it
at your peril. In this crowded and hurried reading age, pages that
require such close attention remain unread and neglected. You
can't skip a word if you are to get the effect, and 19 out of 20
worthy readers grow intolerant. The method seems perverse:
"Say it *out*, for God's sake," they cry, "and have done with it."
And so I say now, give us *one* thing in your older directer manner, just to show that, in spite of your paradoxical success in
this unheard-of method, you *can* still write according to accepted canons. Give us that interlude; and then continue like
the "curiosity of literature" which you have become. For
gleams and innuendoes and felicitous verbal insinuations you
are unapproachable, but the *core* of literature is solid. Give it to
us *once* again! The bare perfume of things will not support existence, and the effect of solidity you reach is but perfume and
simulacrum.[4]

So the matter came to a rest, if not a conclusion. William liked *The
American Scene* because it was not fiction and because it had to acknowledge things in the world which could not have been invented.
The autobiographical books, too, were similarly and happily constrained: the people and places James described existed for other witnesses as well, William among them; they could not be conjured out
of the air.

William's defects as a reader of Henry's last fictions were indeed
constitutional. Urging his brother to call a spade a spade, he required
him further to assume that everything already in the world and everything that might be invented to take its place there resembled a spade
in being an ascertainable object, preferably visible and producible on
demand. It is strange that the author of *Principles of Psychology* and *Varieties of Religious Experience* should put a writer under such constraint.
For whatever reason, William didn't appreciate that the things which

his brother referred to in his late novels did not exist apart from the words he prescribed for them, came into existence only with those words and in that order. In *The Golden Bowl*, James refers to certain things which exist and may be alluded to on that understanding: houses, pagodas, spaniels, silken ropes, carriages, Eaton Square and Portland Place. But the things that matter in the novel can't be named as briskly as these or indeed named at all. They are feelings, desires, intimations that can't otherwise be named than by the conversations that bring them to light or the soliloquies in which they are provoked to appear. In "Little Gidding," T. S. Eliot says of certain words that they "sufficed / To compel the recognition they preceded." So with James in *The Golden Bowl*: it is only by the agitation of words, as in Maggie Verver's case by her agitation among the words, that characters come to learn what it is they feel. It is the friction of word upon word that causes a feeling to reach the state of being recognized as that feeling and not another one. Even then, the feeling can't otherwise be named: the words that have constituted it can't be simplified as mere references.

So if we say that *The Golden Bowl* is a novel about adultery and if we complain, as William did, that James makes the adultery problematic, we are reading the book against its grain in both considerations. It would be only a little better to say that the book is about the exercise of power by means of money—"the power of the rich peoples," as Amerigo muses to himself while window-browsing in Bond Street; it is about power exercised in acquisition, leisure, sex, love, marriage, and lies. Only a little better, because we are still subjecting the book to the conventions of the realistic novel. Realism is a mode of language legitimized by its reference. Like realism, the novel as a genre supposes that there is a world, external to begin with and internal only later and in selected instances, which can be held stable by sufficiently precise acts of reference. Reference, like naming, declares that the world consists of objects sufficiently "there" to be recognized. William James called upon his brother to make this declaration of intent, if not of faith. Henry refused. Most of the things he cared about were not "things" by William's designation but invisible entities, events, relations caught in the act of changing from one sentence to the next. So if *The Golden Bowl* must be called a novel, it is a novel at some far limit of identity where the genre is about to change into symbolism; not because the golden bowl is indeed a symbol of relations gone wrong or categorically defective, but because the world the book intuits is not sufficiently stable to be referred to or described. It would be better to say that James invents a world and then further invents people to live in it. He doesn't allude to the world we think we know. He constitutes an adversary world by finding the words for it; not new words but new relations among them. Indifferent to philosophy, he was still enough of a philosophic idealist to give consciousness every privilege in the constitution of reality. He had no respect for objects as they might be claimed to exist independently of the act of the mind that summoned them to appear. That is what William couldn't bear and thought to deride with talk of perfume, air, gas, and simulacra.

But the issue is difficult. It is well understood that in language a spiritual entity may be said to have a material correlative to which it may be reduced, as Swift in *A Tale of a Tub* reduced the claims of religious transport to breath, belching, and further indignities. There are no words for supernatural or otherwise sublime experiences; there are only ordinary words, to which unusual pressure may be applied in the hope of driving them beyond themselves. That something exalted is "nothing but" something low is an unanswerable charge. This is debunking, an activity richly appealing to ironists and satirists. William James practiced it, in effect, on Henry's innuendoes and associations: he said they were much ado about little. He didn't see that Henry's method was one by which he could advert to the things and values of the common world when they served his purpose; or he could project a spiritual version of them mainly by accumulating qualifications and corrections of their complacency. He could release himself from the vulgarity of references if only by showing how little he respected them. Or he could at any moment revert to their lowly state, as if he witnessed their fall from grace. He could also invent, from the resources of language alone, certain states of feeling and being which he could show but not name.

One consequence of these liberties is that *The Golden Bowl*, as soon as we stop thinking of it as merely and complacently a novel, takes on some of the qualities of an allegory; its characters, even when we accompany them to Eaton Square, Portland Place, Matcham, or Fawns, seem to live chiefly in our moral sense of them and in their moral sense of one another. The main symbols in the book, starting with the bowl that gives it its title, have bearing only in their relation to the ethical drama the Ververs and their associates enact. From time to time we are indeed aware of a common world going about its business and of people who don't even know that the Ververs exist. When Mrs. Rance comes to visit, we are permitted to consider that she comes from somewhere and will return there. But no sense of a common world is allowed to compete, for interest and concern, with the moral situation the novel projects. In much the same way, we may think, while in Adam Verver's presence, of robber barons and of Adam's wealth as having issued, however charmingly, from some ancestor's brigandage. Adam is not a brigand or a robber baron but a connoisseur, a collector of *objets d'art* that he intends giving away to the citizens of American City. Nonetheless, we can think of robber barons, brigands, and other predators when we find Adam, at the beginning of the book, buying the impecunious Prince Amerigo as a gift, a wedding present, for Maggie. When we read that the Prince "was invested with attributes," we are invited to think of the financial transactions which, in late Victorian London as in American City, give point to that investment. How long the thought of Adam's power of purchase stays with us as identifying him depends on our being willing to see him enhanced to the degree of being quite redeemed. When we read that the Prince "was to constitute a possession, yet was to escape being reduced to his component parts," we wonder whether Adam is to be given the same privilege. It is up to James to see us through these transactions. As for the Prince: there is no need to debunk a down-at-heels Italian prince who needs money and finds it by marrying an immensely wealthy man's daughter. The question is how far he may go, how far he may rise above his corruption and the superstition and decay he coolly attributes to his race. "Oh, you deep old Italians!" Fanny Assingham says, taking his point. It is a question, then, how far the Prince may go toward the light, the technology, the modernity embodied in Adam Verver, adept of the American Enlightenment. The force of attraction is Maggie. She, too, may be enhanced. From the beginning, we hear of her as being "little" and "good," her father's loving and loved child. The question in her case is what she will do when she discovers that there is evil in the world. One of the two instances of evil is Charlotte Stant, but she is supposedly wonderful, too, as everyone, including Maggie, keeps telling us. That makes for a further possibility. Where William James wanted Henry to call a spade a spade and an adultery an adultery, Henry insisted on his freedom to move between the accepted names of things and other possible forms of them that he undertook, on authority entirely his own, to imagine.

William was not the only reader of *The Golden Bowl* to find James's treatment of the adultery outrageous. F. R. Leavis thought James a great writer on the strength of *The Europeans, Washington Square, The Bostonians, The Portrait of a Lady, The Awkward Age, What Maisie Knew,* and several of the short stories. But he regarded the late fictions as unsatisfactory; he thought that in these James had "lost touch with concrete life." Of the three last novels, he thought *The Golden Bowl* distinctly the best, but he was dismayed nonetheless, on these grounds:

> What we are not reconciled to by any awareness of intentions is the outraging of our moral sense by the handling of the adultery theme—the triangle, or rather quadrilateral, of personal relations. We remain convinced that when an author, whatever symbolism he intends, presents a drama of men and women, he is committed to dealing in terms of men and women, and mustn't ask us to acquiesce in valuations that contradict our profoundest ethical sensibility. If, of course, he can work a revolutionary change in that sensibility, well and good, but who will contend that James's art in those late novels has that power? In *The Golden Bowl* we continue to find our moral sense outraged.[5]

Why? Leavis doesn't say, precisely. We are to deduce that James, in his last novels—it is William's charge again—indulged himself in obfuscation: having lost contact with concrete life, he let technical elaboration make up for the loss. At this point in his career he suffered from ethical malnutrition. As a result—I am speculating now, wondering exactly what Leavis meant—he allowed himself to imagine that the Prince's adultery could be sublimed away, transfigured by the sighing and breathing of Maggie's consciousness all around it. Speculating further: in "a drama of men and women," presumably, the Prince and Charlotte, finding themselves in love and free of obstacles, would marry and put up with their poverty. Fanny Assingham would never introduce the Prince to Maggie, knowing that he was already involved with Charlotte. Adam Verver would not think of acquiring the Prince and handing him over to Maggie. Charlotte would not turn up, uninvited, at the wedding and station herself beside the Prince to remind him of old times and passion still alive.

Assuming that something like this is entailed both by Leavis's outrage and William James's exasperation, how might one deal with the charge? Surely, as a matter of principle, by allowing the artist the freedom to imagine. More specifically: to imagine that any fact, however gross, such as adultery, might still be altered in someone's sense of it. On one level, the story told in *The Golden Bowl* is a shabby intrigue by which two lovers who are not prepared to live poor-but-honest contrive to maintain their sexual relation by having a wealthy man pay for two marriages. But James asks us to move between that level and another one, hypothetical indeed, on which the story is greatly complicated. In the drama of men and women that Leavis appears to envisage, when the adulterous relation is discovered, there must be a permanent breach in each marriage, and horrors never to be transcended. Or there must be two divorces, and there the matter ends. But James introduces a new factor. Suppose Maggie were to discover the adulterous relation and were to determine that her father must never learn of it. Suppose, further, that she were to decide not to end her marriage but to save it, hold on to her Prince, and merely rid herself of Charlotte. Then the story would have a different emphasis, somewhat as follows. Maggie comes to know that the Prince and Charlotte were once lovers and have resumed their affair despite their marriages. She subsumes the knowledge, makes it clear to the Prince but not at all clear to Charlotte that she knows their secret, and builds a new marriage to the Prince on the basis of the more formidable person she has demonstrably become. No longer merely little, merely good. Suppose, too, that James wanted Maggie to save both marriages, her own and her father's, by talking of them as if they were already secure, the loss of them being a disaster she is not prepared to countenance. Something like this is what happens. James gives the marriages a future by allowing Maggie to pretend that their future is already safe: she has determined to treat them as if they could only be safe.

Otherwise put: the adultery is a fact, but not a fact beyond the reach of Maggie's interpretation, which is hardly to be distinguished from her will. Maggie deals with it to her advantage in the end. She refuses to allow the fact to prevail over her sense of it as a constituent of the new relation between herself and the Prince. In this she differs from her father. According to Fanny Assingham near the end of the

first part of the novel, Adam Verver "has safely and serenely enough
suffered the conditions of his life to pass for those he had sublimely
projected." Maggie insists on making the chief condition of her life,
her husband's infidelity, minister however startlingly to her project.
She forces past and present to become the future—her future, since
she has ordained it.

Does this amount to condoning adultery? Yes, in the sense that
the adultery is not allowed to be the last word or the last deed. A situation is not entirely as it exists but as it is interpreted by the parties
it affects. Maggie interprets it in accordance with the values that define
the future she intends living. She is a princess, a Cinderella who wak-
ens herself to a new life of knowledge, power, and pressure and has to
reckon, at the end, the cost of that achievement. She settles for decorum and, trying to convert her decision into a conviction, feels it
partly as power, partly as dread. Decorum is the form of her victory
and of the punishment she imposes on her husband in achieving it.
Upon the ground of his need of her and of her new authority over
him, she makes a new relation. It can't be as good—or at least as
easy—as the old love that didn't need to know itself. But it is what she
determines to do. Leavis evidently thought it morally repellent, and
that James had died to moral life in projecting it. James evidently felt
confident that he could make his last fictions not as a moralist but as
a prophet; or a moralist in the sense—as we now see his program—in
which Nietzsche and Lawrence were prophets: imagining new forms
of life rather than enforcing old ones.


II


I have been saying that James was somewhat ruefully sensitive to the
common world and to the standard axioms upon which objects in it
were negotiated. But he did not accept that system of valuation, or any
system in which individual acts of consciousness were regarded as playing a merely secondary part. Specifically, he refused to acquiesce in the
cognitive practice that issues in fixities and definitions. Indeed, he was
restless in the presence of images, ideas, and concepts that seem to insist on their being decisive. He makes this clear in the preface to the
New York edition of *The Golden Bowl.* That edition appeared with
decorative illustrations reproducing photographs by Alvin Langdon

Coburn. James felt misgiving not about the quality of the photographs but about their having been used at all. He refers to the question of "the general acceptability of illustrations" as a modern and clearly a regrettable habit. A book that puts forward illustrative claims—"that is producing an effect of illustration"—finds itself elbowed, he says, "by another and a competitive process." The novelist, as a "manipulator of aspects," wants readers to turn his sentences and scenes into images, acting upon the given hallucinations. But James did not want to ordain those images in a reader's mind. Nor was he willing to have pictorial illustrations keep step with the images he evoked in his own medium and terms. Coburn's photographs were acceptable only "through their discreetly disavowing emulation." On that agreement, James was happy to join the photographer in a search for appropriate scenes not merely for *The Golden Bowl* but for the other volumes in the New York edition:

> Nothing in fact could more have amused the author than the opportunity of a hunt for a series of reproducible subjects—such moreover as might best consort with photography—the reference of which to Novel or Tale should exactly be *not* competitive and obvious, should on the contrary plead its case with some shyness, that of images always confessing themselves mere optical symbols or echoes, expressions of no particular thing in the text, but only of the type or idea of this or that thing. They were to remain at the most small pictures of our "set" stage with the actors left out.[6]

It was crucial that the actors be left out. A photograph of Portland Place and one of an antiques store in Bloomsbury or some such district wouldn't do any harm and might offer images cognate with those of the novel while otherwise independent of it. But James would have vetoed any suggestion of including photographs of people who would then be taken for the actors he projected. In the novel, the characters are not described, beyond a few sketches. We know that Adam Verver is small, wears a beard and a monocle, and dresses in a certain style. But we don't know what Maggie looks like. Or Charlotte: the few details we are given through the Prince's eyes in chapter 3 are mainly there to sustain his saying to himself that she looked like a huntress. What the Prince looks like, apart from his blue eyes, we are not told. James is far more interested in having Maggie ask the Prince, now that they are to be married, where he would have been without his inherited archives, annals, infamies. That is a little episode we are invited to make something of, beside which the mere physical appearances of Maggie and her Prince are of little account.

In the matter of photographs, then, as in naming, James shows the same reluctance to "say it *out*, for God's sake, and have done with it." He has no misgiving about the saying, provided he is not called upon to believe in an "it" waiting stolidly to be said. He doesn't despise images—far from it—but he deplores the fixity commonly ascribed to them, their being closed off at this point to any further development they might have had. The formal rhythm of the book is therefore one according to which a possibility, rough or crass as it often is, is recognized—it offers itself as something to be done—but the actor in the case, instead of acting upon it at that moment, holds off till another form of it is divined. Not necessarily a spiritually higher form: often it is lower, abject or desperate by comparison with its first appearance. Lies are among the instruments, the negotiations, by which these developments are achieved. Nearly every character in *The Golden Bowl* lies, apparently for a greater good or a more devious evil and in accordance with the rotary motion of the ensemble. But scruples, too, are allowed to do the work of motion nearly as well as lies: scruples, observances of taste, or simply—as in Maggie's ascendancy—the determination to wait for time to do its best or worst.

## III

We need an occasion, a scene that features some of these scruples, deflections, and lies as agencies in a drama of moral choice. I choose chapter 36, one of the scenes at Fawns. The party is assembled in the smoking-room to play bridge. The Prince partners Charlotte against Adam Verver and Fanny Assingham. Bob Assingham asks to be permitted to write letters at the far end of the room. Maggie, who doesn't play cards, is reading—or pretending to read—a French magazine, but she is mainly watching the players, taking in "the fact of her father's wife's lover facing his mistress; the fact of her father sitting, all

unsounded and unblinking, between them; the fact of Charlotte keeping it up, keeping up everything across the table, with her husband
beside her; the fact of Fanny Assingham, wonderful creature, placed
opposite to the three and knowing more about each, probably, when
one came to think, than either of them knew of either." Maggie puts
aside the magazine, wanders over to the card-table, walks slowly
around, looking at each player in turn, receiving from each a genial
glance. Then she walks out to the terrace. Looking through the window at the bridge-players, she thinks of herself in various roles: an actress waiting off-stage for her cue; one who holds the key to the
mystery of each player; a master card-player with all the cards—
meaning the players—in her hand; a scapegoat required to take upon
himself all the sins of the people and to go forth "into the desert to
sink under his burden and die"; a dramatist who might ordain the play
as she chose:

> Spacious and splendid, like a stage again awaiting a drama, it was
> a scene she might people, by the press of her spring, either with
> serenities and dignities and decencies, or with terrors and shames
> and ruins, things as ugly as those formless fragments of her golden
> bowl she was trying so hard to pick up.

Knowing that "she might sound out their doom in a single sentence," she also knows that she won't. She could create a tragedy,
but her imagining herself doing such a thing is enough to show her
that she won't. Meanwhile, as she walks about, she thinks of Charlotte breaking out of her prison. Charlotte, asking Bob Assingham
to take her place at the bridge-table, comes out to find Maggie and
to accost her with a question: "Have you any ground of complaint
of me?"

James, whom Leavis charged with having lost contact with life,
retained enough sense of life to know that a little instance of it can go
a long way. It is a warm evening, this scene at Fawns, but Maggie has
brought her shawl. When the two women meet and Charlotte starts
leading up to her question, Maggie draws the shawl tight upon her
shoulders:

> Maggie had kept the shawl she had taken out with her, and,
> clutching it tight in her nervousness, drew it round her as if

huddling in it for shelter, covering herself with it for humility.

But when Charlotte perjures herself and Maggie deals with the lie by answering it with another one just as bold, playing her cards just as daringly as Charlotte, she has no further need to appear small or humble:

> And she made a point even, our young woman, of not turning away. Her grip of her shawl had loosened—she had let it fall behind her; but she stood there for anything more and till the weight should be lifted.

Lifted by Charlotte, not by Maggie.

It is the kind of detail an actress would think of or a theater director might suggest: it comes from the tradition of the well-made play. James, a failure in any actual theater, respected the methods of the well-made play and as a novelist developed them further by carrying them into the minds of his characters, where in mere actual theaters they can hardly be shown. But he retained his sense of theater, his respect for the curtain, as here at Fawns he ends the scene by having Charlotte ask Maggie to seal her statement with a kiss—"Will you kiss me on it then?"- and by having the kiss seen by the card-players and especially by the Prince and Adam Verver.


## IV


The ending of the novel has been thought difficult. Conventionally it is a "happy ending." Charlotte and Adam Verver have gone, turned toward the new life of American City, where she will be the splendid hostess and he the wealthy connoisseur. Maggie, the Prince, and their child remain in London; the farewells have been completed. What now? Maggie determines that she will never require of her husband even a word of apology. She turns her attention, and the Prince's, to Charlotte. The novel ends with this passage:

> "Isn't she too splendid?" she simply said, offering it to explain and to finish.

"Oh, splendid!" With which he came over to her.

"That's our help, you see," she added—to point further her moral.

It kept him before her therefore, taking in—or trying to— what she so wonderfully gave. He tried, too clearly, to please her—to meet her in her own way; but with the result only that, close to her, her face kept before him, his hands holding her shoulders, his whole act enclosing her, he presently echoed: " 'See'? I see nothing but *you*." And the truth of it had, with this force, after a moment, so strangely lighted his eyes that, as for pity and dread of them, she buried her own in his breast.

Maggie's "moral," presumably, is that Charlotte's being splendid means that she will have enough splendor left over to make her life in American City the superb thing it should be, for herself and for her husband. Maggie and the Prince will therefore be free to live their lives together without remorse or other embarrassment. "What she so wonderfully gave" is an indication that no apology on the Prince's part will be required. Receiving the casual phrase—"you see"—the Prince returns it to Maggie emphatically and comprehensively: "I see nothing but *you*." But what "the truth of it" comes to is not clear. Is it the truth that Maggie has taken such complete possession of him that he has nothing more to see? Or that his seeing nothing but her epitomizes everything else in the world that he might also see? "So strangely lighted his eyes": why strangely? What is the light? "As for pity and dread of them": the "as" puts a space of analogy between Maggie and the motives otherwise attributed to her. "Pity": for a husband so defeated, so bound. "Dread": of eyes so strangely lighted, the nature of the light unknown and therefore to be dreaded. Is it, as I think, because Maggie's eyes can't meet the Prince's that she buries them in his breast? Can't, because she realizes that she has diminished him, retains him now in his defeat? Or because she doesn't feel the need to answer his light with her own? An actress playing the role would have to decide, and would have difficulty registering pity and dread in one gesture. In the novel we are left free to construe the episode as we choose, within reason; we are given more freedom than we are likely ever to have asked for. It is a matter of accountancy, a reckoning of gain and loss in each case, Maggie and the Prince. The rotary motion has stopped, but it is hard to say how the characters are disposed, now that it has stopped. James leaves us in the position he ascribed to the four principals, in the last chapter, a little before the farewells: "the four of them, in the upper air, united in the firmest abstention from pressure." James likes to leave his characters—or at least those who are up to the experience of it—in that air. His readers, too: how we come to that altitude, breathe that air, is the substance of *The Golden Bowl*.

# WILLIAM WETMORE STORY
## AND HIS FRIENDS:
# THE ENCLOSING FACT OF ROME

ဟၐၐၡၐ

O n December 23, 1903, Henry James wrote to the duchess of
Sutherland, thanking her for liking *William Wetmore Story and
His Friends* well enough to write to him about it. The book
was, he confessed, "the operation of making bricks without straw and
chronicling (sometimes) rather small beer with the effect of opening
champagne":

> Story was the dearest of men, but he wasn't massive, his artistic
> and literary baggage were of the slightest and the materials for a
> biography *nil*. Hence (once I had succumbed to the amiable pres-
> sure of his children), I had really to *invent* a book, patching the
> thing together and eking it out with barefaced irrelevancies—
> starting above all any hare, however small, that might lurk by the
> way. It is very pleasant to get from a discriminating reader the to-
> ken that I have carried the trick through. But the magic is but
> scantly mine—it is really that of the beloved old Italy, who always
> *will* consent to fling a glamour for you, whenever you speak her
> fair.[1]

Not only did James think that Story failed to be massive, he regarded
him as "thinner than thin." There was no subject, he complained to

William Dean Howells (before James had written the book), there was "nothing in the man himself to write about": "There is nothing for me but to do a *tour de force*, or try to—leave poor dear W.W.S. *out*, practically, and make a little volume on the old Roman, Americo-Roman, Hawthornesque and other bygone days."[2]

James regarded Story as a dabbler, something of a clown, and he never forgot the dismal experience of having to listen to him reading, to an audience of four, his five-act tragedy on the history of Nero. As James reported the evening to Charles Eliot Norton, on March 13, 1873, Story "got through three acts in three hours, and the last two were resumed on another evening when I was unavoidably absent." The performance, he continued, "was the result much less of an inward necessity, I surmise, than of a most restless ambition, not un tinged with ——— what an impertinent little word stands for, beginning with *v* and ending with *y*."[3] In *William Wetmore Story and His Friends*, James does not use the word "vanity," but he refers to "talkative emphasis" when he quotes one of Story's early letters to James Russell Lowell.

The *tour de force* to which James referred showed itself as a possibility when he realized that under the excuse of writing a biography of Story he could paint a group portrait of the American and English friends whom Story and his wife entertained at their apartment in the Palazzo Barberini—the Brownings, Margaret Fuller, William Page, Landor, Hawthorne, and many more. James could also draw upon his own experience of Rome when he first visited it in 1869. The book, as Leon Edel has noted, is judiciously titled: *William Wetmore Story and His Friends: From Letters, Diaries, and Recollections*; it was written as a chore and to keep a promise exacted from James by Story's son Waldo.

In the event, the book was a commercial success, especially in America, and some readers took it more seriously than James intended. I think James was embarrassed, as much as pleased, when Henry Adams wrote to say that the book was the life not only of Story but of every such American of his generation, including Charles Sumner, Emerson, Lowell, Longfellow, Adams, and indeed James himself, each of whom was an ignorant, bourgeois Bostonian trying to make himself something else. James's reply evaded the large issue and pleaded that the biographical form itself made its subjects seem thin, "throws a chill upon the scene, the time, the subject, the small mapped-out facts."[4]

The book started under the worst possible auspices: a thin subject and an unwilling biographer who had better and more urgent things to be doing, including a novel called *The Golden Bowl*. It is true that some of James's pages are barefaced fillers of space, and that other pages, more agreeably written, are merely workmanlike. I have in view, as an example of professionally respectable but otherwise unexciting work, James's account of the episode in *The Marble Faun* where Hawthorne sends Miriam to visit the sculptor in his studio and to see the statue of Cleopatra; as Hawthorne acknowledged in his preface to the book, the statue was Story's work, and one of his most successful. James's allusion to *The Marble Faun* is charming so far as it goes, but he demands far less of the book than he did in his early biography of Hawthorne, published in 1879, where he takes the book seriously enough to find it a faulty production. He still likes "its laxities of insistence, its timidities of indication, its felicities of suggestion, its sincerities of simplicity and, most of all, its total vague intensity, so curiously composed of all these,"[5] but he no longer cares enough about it to pursue the questions that troubled him in the biography, even though these included questions about an American imagination trying to cope with a Roman scene.

These pages in *William Wetmore Story and His Friends* are, then, professionally adequate, but unexacting. Indeed, the book came alive only under one form of pressure, that of remembrance, especially the act of remembrance incited by James's thoughts of Rome. In that aspect, the book is of a piece with the affectionate record of Italy, of Florence, which James spoke of again in his preface to the New York edition of *Roderick Hudson*. The principle of remembrance is often intimated and at least once in the book on Story it is described: "the value of the pleasure derived from the act itself, the act of remembrance lively almost to indiscretion."[6]

But the pleasure was nothing unless it consisted in renewed relations, personal and social, in the immediately recalled instance, and, at a further remove, the sense of one's general relatedness to lives otherwise gone. It was this general sense that prompted James, in *The Portrait of a Lady*, to let Isabel drive out to the Campagna and there drop her sadness into the silence of lonely places—an attempted release James had already come upon, as Q. D. Leavis has shown, in *Little Dorrit* and *Middlemarch*.

The principle of remembrance was simple enough. As James gave it in the book on Story: "To live other people's lives is nothing unless we live over their perceptions, live over the growth, the change, the varying intensity of the same—since it was *by* these things they themselves lived."[7] But it would not answer if one merely lived over these perceptions in any sequence that came to one's mind, a procedure no better than random: the "living over" had somehow to bespeak the mutual relation of parts, a sense of the whole, for which the best analogy was spatial, as in the felt unity of a great house. In recalling the Palazzo Barberini, James pondered again, as he reported, "the old mystery of the strong effect that resides in simplicity and that yet is so far from merely consisting of it."[8] Simplicity is the form in which mutually acknowledged relations are recognized, and it is the work of remembrance to produce them under that sense of responsibility.

What is remembered need not be a great thing in itself. Some of the liveliest recollections in the book on Story are incited by recalling Mrs. Procter, "mother of Adelaide Procter the poetess, the ornament of anthologies when anthologies are not, as we may say, pedantic."[9] The liveliness is of the kind which enabled James, having reported that Mrs. Procter had had a falling-out with Kinglake to the extent of not speaking to him thereafter for a quarter of a century, immediately to add: "She was magnificent."

But it is unnecessary to draw a sharp line between James's remembrance of minor people and of the Rome in which they figured. He makes this clear again when he comes to refer to *Roba di Roma* in 1863. In 1909, James assembled his own early essays on Venice, Rome, Florence, Siena, Ravenna, and other Italian places, and published them as *Italian Hours*. In this context, *Roba di Roma* is hardly a book to make James feel jealous—it is a rambling, garrulous work—except that it disclosed on Story's part a degree of intimacy with Italy that James could not claim. His reference to *Roba di Roma* is characteristically generous:

> The golden air, as I look over its pages, makes a mist; I read them again in the light of old personal perceptions and emotions; I read, as we say, too much into them, too many associations, pictures, *other* ineffaceable passages. . . . [The book] summed up, with an extraordinary wealth of statement, with perpetual illustration and image, the incomparable *entertainment* of Rome, where almost everything alike, manners, customs, practices, pro-

cesses, states of feeling, no less than objects, treasures, relics, ruins, partook of the special museum-quality.[10]

In James's memory of Rome, revived now by *Roba di Roma*, virtually everything was at least interesting. "To read these passages over," he says, "is to taste and feel again the very air of early rambles, when one was always agaze; to hear the sounds, to smell the dust, to give one's self up once more as to the thing that was ancient and noble even when homely or sordid, the thing that might be mean but that yet couldn't be vulgar."[11]

The act of remembrance had a further, and this time a more painful, responsibility: to evoke places and manners that in 1903 were chiefly to be recognized as having been destroyed. When James recalls the artist's life, whether the particular artist was Story, or Page, or Browning, or lesser men like Eugene Benson and Rollin Tilton, he has to report that the blissful conditions in which they first saw Rome were now largely defaced. The artist's life, he said, "in the romantic conditions and with the romantic good faith, is a thing of the past; the Campagna, near the walls of Rome, has been for the most part cruelly curtailed and cockneyfied; the hotels, huge and overflowing, the paradise now of the polyglot element, much more copious than of old and more strident, outface the palaces and entertain, gloriously, themselves and each other."[12] James found still more acute reason for his sense of loss when he made his final visit to Italy in 1907, just as he discovered in 1904 that America was no longer the place he had known. All the more reason, in both cases, for the renewed act of remembrance, because only by its ministry could he find, as he said in the book on Story, that "the softer tone lives still, on the spot, in a fond memory here and there, and echoes of the old evenings in especial, of the Roman balls, say, before the days of mourning, even yet fall upon the ear."[13]

In fact, the work of James's last years is best understood not as an intermittently indulged "backward glance" but as an elaborate reconsideration and recovery of old experience; he is endlessly engaged in circling back upon former places and intimations, the poignancy in most cases issuing from a sense of difference and change, the mitigating advantage being the consideration that at least he, the mindful artist, is still here to bear witness and tribute to what other people have forgotten or never known. In the only note we have for *William*

*Wetmore Story and His Friends*, long before James had written a line of it, he jotted this down:

> For W. W. Story. Beginning. "The writer of these pages—(the scribe of this pleasant history?) is well aware of coming late in the day ... BUT the very gain by what we see, *now*, in the contrasted conditions, of happiness of old Rome of the old days."[14]

The book became a balancing of that loss and this gain. The conditions of the old Rome have changed in nearly every respect for the worse; the former state of things must be recovered by documents, such as Story's letters to his friends, but more strenuously by one's own remembrance. The modern artist who has known Rome in both sets of conditions sees it the more clearly, and makes a finer picture.

It follows that James's technique is one of survey and distantiation. He is writing, in 1902, of the Roman atmosphere from about 1849, when Story and his wife started going to Italy, and concentrating on the years from 1856, when they settled permanently in Rome. The conditions, as James construes them, remained much as they were till 1869, when he himself started going to Italy, and he considers that the changes became decisive in 1870 with the Franco-Prussian War. At the beginning of the book, and on several occasions thereafter, he speaks of Story and his generation as precursors, "the *éclaireurs*, who have gone before." They were the ones, "the tentative generation," American artists for the most part, or at least men and women who aspired to the practice of art, who first tried the experiment of living a certain form of life in Rome. They made it easier for their successors, men and women of James's generation, to maintain, as Americans, a relation to Italy, and to know what such a relation would entail. An American relation to Rome, which would involve residence there or at least periodic visits of some duration, was a paradigm, a possible way of living, and there was every need to understand it. It might be taken as the type of any and every American relation to Europe, though of course James recognized that residence in England or France or Germany would entail, at least, different nuances. In *William Wetmore Story and His Friends*, as elsewhere, James thought of it as a bristling situation, that of a consciousness, American by birth and fate and in varying degrees by choice, encountering a more complicated world in Europe, with whatever consequence. His interest in the sit-

uation coincided with his wonder at the sight of a mind somehow becoming more perceptive, but he thought it made for a still richer mixture if the mind continued to be, in some sense, what it always was.
When he refers to Story and his friends as precursors, he means to distinguish this mixture of conditions and motives, and to imply that his
own mixture is bound to be different. The precursive situation is well
enough outlined by this passage near the beginning of the book:

> The dawn of the American consciousness of the complicated
> world it was so persistently to annex is the more touching the
> more primitive we make that consciousness; but we must recog-
> nize that the latter can scarcely be interesting to us in proportion
> as we make it purely primitive. The interest is in its becoming
> perceptive and responsive, and the charming, the amusing, the
> pathetic, the romantic drama is exactly that process. The process,
> in our view, must have begun, in order to determine the psycho-
> logical moment, but there is a fine bewilderment it must have
> kept in order not to anticipate the age of satiety.[15]

James does not bother to say what is obvious enough: that the psychological moment corresponded to a certain historical, social, and economic moment; it coincided with particular conditions—the relative
inexpensiveness of Italy in relation to the American dollar, the extensive development of European railways, the weather of Rome, and the
ease of escaping from it to any of the charming hill towns surrounding
it or farther afield—conditions which made the psychological moment
feasible.

The mixture of trial and error, perceptiveness and bewilderment,
in the American mind of Story's generation made it a matter of peculiar interest to James. These men and women colonized Rome, and
made it easier for James's generation to enjoy the satisfactions of being
"settled partakers of the greater extension." The advantage of the
earlier generation was that everything for them was a surprise; the fate
of the later was that many things were found to be matters chiefly of
regret.

The precursive relation is what concerns James in the first several
chapters of the book, and his metaphors of annexation and coloniza-
tion imply that the enterprise is continuous. Story and his friends ran
ahead, set up field stations, made the rudimentary domestic arrange-

ments; the main body of the army then followed and enjoyed the comforts of a settled perceptiveness. But as the book goes on, the precursors seem to lose their standing; they became echoes, ghosts, and shades. The act of remembrance is still performed, but what is recovered is a sequence of traces. It is as if the forerunners had died off, which they mainly had, leaving behind them at most a certain defunct music. A letter from Mrs. Gaskell about Hawthorne starts up an echo. Trying to recapture what James does not scruple to call the "Arcadian" time, he speaks of his "impulse to recover any echo of an echo (as I might have held a sea-shell to my ear)."[16] Changing the metaphor but not the impulse, he speaks of Story and his friends as "the hovering ghosts." One of Story's references to General McClellan is described as having "a spectral actuality," renewing the feeling of that moment in the middle of the Civil War, "that feeling of the time which so often makes itself intense as from the sense of its only chance, of foreknowing that it will scarce be the feeling of any other time."[17]

In yet another version of the impulse, what James recovers is called a shade, and I cannot be sure that he distinguishes at all between shades and ghosts. Referring to Siena, where Story and his wife spent the summer of 1857 and several other summers, James says that the town "is peopled for us to-day with wandering shades—impalpable phantoms of lightly-dressed precursors that melt, for every sense, into the splendid summer light."[18] Presumably he calls them shades rather than ghosts because for the moment he is content to see them casting a shadow or otherwise darkening the light of summer before yielding to it. Later in the book, referring to himself as "the chronicler with a sense of shades," he describes the congenial years in England, before the dreaded year 1870, when it was still possible to remain "unconscious of the emphasised rule of the mob." In that case, the shades are distinguishable from ghosts by knowing that they have been defeated by rough force, rather than by merely having died. But James sometimes uses the word "shade" in a more genial sense, as if he meant merely some figure that arrests one's memory without striking fear in it. "We wander here still among shades," he says at one point, as if wandering were an easy stroll. And there is at least one reference in which James, requiring us to make a distinction between shades and ghosts, apparently thinks of ghosts as the more terrible of the species. Alluding to Colonel Hamley, who introduced Story to the Blackwoods, he remarks that "his name meets me, as it comes up, with that imputed recognition to which we have responded for every figure in our dim procession, he too being, in his degree, one of the friendly, the less ghostly, shades."[19]

I try to distinguish between echoes, ghosts, and shades, if only because James's first word, "precursor," seems to be neutral; it leaves open the question of the precise relation between precursors and successors, even though in a military or imperial vocabulary those who are sent ahead are deemed to be expendable in an emergency. The important people are those who come later. But James is not so bound by this figure as to confine himself to such a discrimination.

It is true that in one version of the precursive relation, the precursors are patronized. James tended to give pioneers the kind of honor that is compatible with their being naifs. He writes of his predecessors in the art of the novel as if they deserved the greater respect, considering that they did not know what they were about and had no standards by which they might be guided. He condescended to Fielding and Jane Austen and Hawthorne in much the same way as to Emerson and Thoreau and Margaret Fuller; they did well, given that there was little they thought of doing. When Story first comes to Europe, he exhibits what James calls "the good faith of the young American for whom Europe meant, even more than now, culture, and for whom culture meant, very much more than now, romantic sentiment."[20] As a sculptor, Story was naive and quite untrained; he did not know what good sculpture was or where he might go to discover it; he was "the victim, all innocent at first, and unconscious, of an order of things from which standards were absent."[21] As a poet, Story loved the lyric and dramatic forms, and never discovered why such love was not enough to produce great poems. As an expatriate, Story never understood the price he paid for the felicity of that condition, though James is evidently willing to believe that Story at least knew that some price was in question. He concedes, without producing much evidence for the concession, that Story was alert to the matter:

> He therefore never failed of any plenitude in feeling—in the fulness of time and on due occasion—that a man always pays, in one way or another, for expatriation, for detachment from his plain primary heritage, and that this tax is levied in an amusing diversity of ways. . . . He could suspect, on plenty of evidence, the definite, the homely proof of the pudding—the show, as to *value*,

of the general heterogeneous production to which the general
charmed life could point. He could suspect it—which was all that
was necessary for the prime lucidity—at the same time that he
could do it justice and feel how things happen and how the case
stood and how, if Boston had never been Rome, so Rome could
never be Boston; and also how, in a word, they had all danced to
good music and in the noblest ballroom in the world.²²

James does not measure, in this passage, the extent to which Boston
failed to be Rome, or the extent to which Rome declined to be Boston. He seems to think the question sufficiently answered by its having
been mentioned, and he assumes that Story at least gave it occasional
thought in the intervals of the Roman dance. But it is hard to be sure,
in this part of the book, whether he is reporting what Story thought
or thinking on Story's behalf on an issue—the question of expatriation—crucial to both of them.

 The question arises because it is a variant of the other question
that pervades the book: how may an American, specifically an American artist, "take" Europe—in the particular case, "take" Rome? On
the whole, James felt that Story's way of taking Rome was charming,
and would have been splendid if only there had been more to the
taker. Other ways of taking it were variously exemplified by
Longfellow, Lowell, and Hawthorne, men who resorted to Rome be-
times but not for long enough to think of weighing it in a balance
against Boston. In the book on Story, James found Longfellow "interesting for nothing so much as for the secret of his harmony (harmony
of situation and sense I of course mean) and for the way in which his
'European' culture and his native kept house together." They kept
house together, James speculates, perhaps because Longfellow had
"worked up his American consciousness to that mystic point . . . at
which it could feel nothing but continuity and congruity with his European."²³ Hawthorne was in a more difficult state: as James presents
him, he was too simple, too provincial to make anything of Rome, too
untutored even to divine that others might make a lot of it. Notoriously, James patronized Hawthorne, and thought him in the end a
lightweight, but he admitted that Hawthorne had made himself an artist by just being American enough: there were possibilities in such re-
silience. As for Lowell, "his theory," as James said, "was that of the
American for whom his Americanism filled up the measure of the

needful; his practice was that of freely finding room for any useful contribution to the quantity from without." Put like that, it seems a nearly perfect formula, and it allows for smiling occasions of dispro- portion, on which the theory is put into question by some extraordi- nary catching practice.

But it is not precisely James's theory. In the book on Story, as elsewhere, James held to a riskier program; he assumed not that his Americanism would fill up the measure of the needful, but that it ev- idently would not. The measure would have to be filled, in his case, by whatever in addition we find issuing from England, France, and Italy. It was T. S. Eliot, not James, who made the extraordinary state- ment that "it is the final perfection, the consummation of an Ameri- can to become, not an Englishman, but a European—something which no born European, no person of any European nationality, can become."[24] But Eliot said this in a memorial essay on James. I assume that he was not recommending any such "becoming" as a general pro- gram for Americans, but merely pointing to a certain possibility, a par- adigm which a particular American might pursue. I do not think James pursued it, even in Rye, but he opened his being an Ameri- can to every risk entailed by the quantity and the quality of expe- rience from without. When he considered the price exacted from Story for the blessing of expatriation, he must have reckoned that his own theory and his far more telling practice raised the same question.

James recognized differences of theory, as of one's general stance toward the question of America and Europe, or Boston and Rome. But I think he saw, at least for himself, two possibilities, either of which would keep him safe. The first was a matter of concentration, and in the context of Story and his friends he saw the lack of it in Elizabeth Barrett Browning and in Story himself, just as he saw the force of it in Robert Browning, who testified to the possibility of a double identity: one could be a man of the world and at the same time one could be fully at home to the demands of an exacting art. While Story was distracted and diverted from his main task by everything he saw and heard in Rome, Florence, and Siena, so that he never fully became any of the several things he sought to become—sculptor, poet, dramatist—Browning never allowed anything, even the experience of living in Florence, to become too much for him:

That weight of the whole mind which we have also speculatively invoked was a pressure that he easily enough, at any point, that he in fact almost extravagantly, brought to bear. And then he was neither divided nor dispersed.[25]

By comparison, and James tries to avoid saying it bluntly, Mrs. Browning could never sufficiently mind her own business; she could never keep any of her mind intact above its engrossments. The cause of Italy, its daily ramifications, so preoccupied her that she quite let down "her inspiration and her poetic pitch." We are "less edified than we ought to be," as James concluded.[26] Similarly with Story. He "was not with the last intensity a sculptor":

Had he been this he would not, in all probability, have been also with such intensity (so far as impulse and eagerness were concerned) so many other things; a man of ideas—of *other* ideas, of other curiosities. . . . He was as addicted to poetry as if he had never dreamed of a statue, and as addicted to statues as if he were unable to turn a verse.[27]

James does not commit the indelicacy of saying that Story and Mrs. Browning were alike, but he leaves it to the reader to observe that they were alike in having not enough indifferences; they did not have enough objects of interest toward which, on particular occasions, their tenderness was a matter of choice. With Mrs. Browning, it was always Italy; with Story it might be anything. Clearly, James had the contrast with Robert Browning especially in view when he said of Story:

How could he be, our friend, we sometimes find ourselves wondering, so restlessly, so sincerely aesthetic, and yet, constitutionally, so little insistent? We mean by insistence, in an artist, the act of throwing the whole weight of the mind, and of gathering it at the particular point (when the particular point is worth it) in order to do so.[28]

Story irritated James and was most of all a scandal in his eyes because he allowed himself to become in Italy "the prey to mere beguilement." He was, in the end, merely an amateur, a tourist, even though he spent many years among compelling reasons for being something much more.

James's clear implication in *William Wetmore Story and His Friends* is that so long as an artist throws the full weight of his mind upon the work in hand, and does not allow himself to be promiscuously beguiled, he is secure anywhere. Browning was the supreme type of that capacity, and his being English did not alter his suggestive case: he showed the best way of being a foreigner in Italy. What James, in his essay on *The Ring and the Book*, called "Browning's own particular matchless Italy" was something Story could never have possessed, because he was not with sufficient intensity an artist. But there were still further possibilities, which James divined as if they lay beyond Browning. It is for us to say that they were Jamesian, and I find the most complete indication of them, as a matter of theory, in a passage of *William Wetmore Story and His Friends* and again in the preface to *The Aspern Papers*.

In the preface, recalling that he got wind of his tale in Florence, he says:

> It was in Florence years ago; which is precisely, of the whole matter, what I like most to remember. The air of the old-time Italy invests it, a mixture that on the faintest invitation I rejoice again to inhale—and this in spite of the mere cold renewal, ever, of the infirm side of that felicity, the sense, in the whole element, of things too numerous, too deep, too obscure, too strange, or even simply too beautiful, for any ease of intellectual relation. One must pay one's self largely with words, I think, one must induce almost any "Italian subject" to *make believe* it gives up its secret, in order to keep at all on working—or call them perhaps rather playing—terms with the general impression.[29]

James does not further explain what the relation should be between the Italian subject and the mind that responds to it, apart from saying a few sentences later:

> So, right and left, in Italy—before the great historic complexity at least—penetration fails; we scratch at the extensive surface, we meet the perfunctory smile, we hang about in the golden air. But we exaggerate our gathered values only if we are eminently wit-

less. It is fortunately the exhibition in all the world before which, as admirers, we can most remain superficial without feeling silly.[30]

James does not say how one might, as an American artist in Italy, avoid being superficial, as Story, for instance, was bound to be superficial and was regularly silly. But the notion of paying one's self largely with words, in default of complete possession of the Italian subject, is elaborated in the book on Story. What James intuits is that a decent response to Rome might take one of two forms. In one, the passionate pilgrim would see himself condemned to be superficial, indeed, but would not be appalled by that discovery. He would feel somewhat as Roderick Hudson felt, in the chapter called "Rome" and while he is still in possession of himself. He is for the moment one of those spirits, as James describes them, "with a deep relish for the artificial element in life and the infinite superpositions of history."[31] Roderick does not pretend to understand these matters, but he is still good enough to bring his curiosity to attend upon them. In *William Wetmore Story and His Friends*, James cannot help giving his own sense of Rome, under the guise of attributing some of it to Story, but he is usually vigilant in indicating where his own responsibility for such perceptions begins and ends. "The Roman air, for us," he said, "insistently pervades and tinges; so that—to make my own confession at least complete— I see no circumstance too trite, no image too slight, to be bathed by it in interest and in beauty."[32] To what extent Story felt what James felt, we have to guess for ourselves, but in any event the city is there, and the responsibility it imposes must at least be acknowledged. If one pays one's respect in words, the words are bound to fall ridiculously short.

That is the first form, in which if we compare the object with our expression of it, the relation is humiliating. But there is a second possibility, in which the comparative question can be evaded. It is as if James were saying, to testify to this possibility in the experience of Rome, "only recognize the spirit of the place, surrender yourself to that, and it won't matter that your sense of anything in particular is puny." If the pilgrim obeys this instruction, he finds every inequality removed. In this connection, James recalls meeting Matthew Arnold at the Palazzo Barberini:

> He had been, in prose and verse, the idol of my previous years, and nothing could have seemed in advance less doubtful than that

to encounter him face to face, and under an influence so noble, would have made one fairly stagger with a sense of privilege. What actually happened, however, was that the sense of privilege found itself positively postponed; when I met him again, later on, in London, *then* it had free play. It was, on the Roman evening, as if, for all the world, we were *equally* great and happy, or still more, perhaps, equally nothing and nobody; we were related only to the enclosing fact of Rome, before which every one, it was easy to feel, bore himself with the same good manners.[33]

James goes on to explain that this sense of equality, of equal submission to the spirit of Rome, would not have been possible in London, Paris, or New York—cities, he says, in which the spirit of the place has long since lost any advantage it may ever have practiced over the spirit of the person:

So, at any rate, fanciful as my plea may appear, I recover the old sense—brave even the imputation of making a mere Rome of words, talking of a Rome of my own which was no Rome of reality. That comes up as exactly the point—that no Rome of reality was concerned in our experience, that the whole thing was a rare state of the imagination, dosed and drugged . . . by the effectual Borgia cup, for the taste of which the simplest as well as the subtlest had a palate.[34]

I derive from this passage, and from other passages of similar bearing, that there are indeed two ways of proceeding, faced with the Rome of reality. The first is to try to be responsive at every point and to every particular, even while discovering that one's response is trivial in comparison with its object. It is to try, given a subject, as James told Mrs. Humphry Ward in another connection, to "work one's self in the presence of it." And of course to fail: the city will not give up its secret. The second way is by not competing, by assenting so wholeheartedly to the spirit of the place that the mere details, momentous and historic as they are, may be taken for granted. This relation, then, may be expressed without humiliating oneself in the process, by paying oneself largely with words; by creating in one's mind and demeanor a Rome of words, and by not worrying at all about their adequacy or their applicable force. The value of the words as making reference to a city or as somehow describing it is alternative to this second response, by which the chosen words pay tribute to the object by not even offering to emulate it.

It is clear, too, that this second form of responsiveness can indeed be regarded as barefaced irrelevancy, but James was not prepared to give up the privilege of what he called "subjective amplification." Coming to the end of the book on Story, he leads himself into a theme of the prefaces: the question of a subject. He has referred to "our conviction of the puerility of any pretended estimate of property in *subject*." Then he drives the conviction further:

> A subject is never anything but his who can make something of it, and it is the thing made that becomes the property. But as between the thing made and the making the distinction is not to be seized, it is to the treatment alone that the fact of possession attaches—from which it is superfluous to warn us off.[35]

But to go back to James's starting point: what if the subject, Story's life in this case, is not worth the treatment, the spirit expended upon it? The glib answer is that in that case we have a new subject, the result of James's determination to take responsibility for every occasion, however slight, and to work it for more than, on any ordinary valuation, it was worth. But James took an artist's pride, even when a subject was apparently thin, in seeing what he could make of it, how ample it might appear to become under his treatment.

When James went back to Rome in 1907, he found—as I have mentioned—much changed. But all was not lost, and James's act of remembrance had the effect of making the recalled and recovered thing nearly as satisfying as if it were still actual, still present. "The city of his first unpremeditated rapture shines to memory, on the other hand," he reported of the mature visit in *Italian Hours*, "in the manner of a lost paradise the rustle of whose gardens is still just audible enough in the air to make him wonder if some sudden turn, some recovered vista, mayn't lead him back to the thing itself."[36] In a remarkable chapter called "A Few Other Roman Neighbourhoods" in *Italian Hours*, James, strolling through the Villa d'Este, fancies that the ruined fountains are themselves waiting to be remembered in their first play and movement:

> The ruined fountains seemed strangely to wait, in the stillness and under cover of the approaching dusk, not to begin ever again to play, also, but just only to be tenderly imagined to do so; quite as everything held its breath, at the mystic moment, for the drop of the cruel and garish exposure, for the Spirit of the place to steal forth and go his round.[37]

James is writing in "the spirit of the postscript," making last-minute additions to documents of an otherwise lost time. He recalls not only Rome but the first agitated consciousness that, as a young man, he brought to it. He sees himself as precursor to the mature visitor he is now, a shade among shades:

> No one who has ever loved Rome as Rome could be loved in youth and before her poised basketful of the finer appeals to fond fancy was actually upset, wants to stop loving her; so that our bleeding and wounded, though perhaps not wholly moribund, loyalty attends us as a hovering admonitory, anticipatory ghost, one of those magnanimous life-companions who before complete extinction designate to the other member of the union their approved successor.[38]

James is writing in 1909, looking back nearly forty years to his first sight of Rome. He is thinking of earliness and lateness, of himself as *éclaireur* and now as successor to himself. The idiom is that of *William Wetmore Story and His Friends*, but with a difference: James is not inclined to patronize the young man he was. Indeed, the figure of the magnanimous life-companion has the opposite effect. The thing itself is Rome, loved as the young James loved her: the nuptial relation signified as much. The designated successor cannot be supposed entirely to fill the place left by the young man: he cannot be more than a worthy substitute. His worth, indeed, consists in the degree and force of his remembrance: without that, he would be a usurper or, at best, merely posthumous to the only consciousness that matters.

# THE MODERN YEATS

"I too have tried to be modern," W. B. Yeats confesses, or claims, in his introduction to *The Oxford Book of Modern Verse 1892–1935* (1936). It is not clear what he means: his context doesn't help. He has merely been saying that such contemporary poets as Cecil Day Lewis, Charles Madge, and Louis MacNeice "are modern through the character of their intellectual passion." In the next sentence he says that "we have been gradually approaching this art through the cult of sincerity, that refusal to multiply personality which is characteristic of our time." The allusion to Wilde's epigram—"What people call insincerity is simply a method by which we can multiply our personalities"—is clear enough. Yeats means that the poets of the thirties, Auden's generation, have decided that they must speak directly, sincerely, each in his own voice; they have given up the device, in high repute from Browning, Wilde, and Nietzsche to Yeats and Eliot, of speaking through a mask. Still referring to Auden's generation, Yeats says: "I can seldom find more than half a dozen lyrics that I like, yet in this moment of sympathy I prefer them to Eliot, to myself—I too have tried to be modern." Can he mean: "I too, much as I love the doctrine of the mask and much as I have managed to say by using it, now feel inclined to speak directly in my own voice"? If so, it suggests that Yeats was at any moment willing to be modern, but that he was not sure what being so would entail.

At the beginning of his career, he let Arthur Symons convince him that modernity was French. From the autumn of 1895 to the following spring, Yeats shared a flat with Symons at 2 Fountain Court in London, and received from him the news of Paris. The new method was Symbolism, the procedures of Baudelaire and Rimbaud culminating in Mallarmé. Symbolism produced, according to Symons, "a literature in which the visible world is no longer a reality, and the unseen world no longer a dream." The aim of such literature was not to denote things but to suggest essences. Words would be used to prohibit a quick translation into meanings; instead, words would imply a divination, a tone escaping from the things that ostensibly provoked it. A certain rhythm would be sustained among words summoned mainly to sustain that rhythm. Being modern, in that sense, meant turning away from realism—mere mimicry of the surfaces of life—and cultivating a brooding reverie, an inward gaze. The supreme emblem of this reverie is Mallarmé's Hérodiade, a force as if self-begotten, purified of character and circumstance: pure being, pure action. Many years later Yeats wrote:

> Yet I am certain that there was something in myself compelling me to attempt creation of an art as separate from everything heterogeneous and casual, from all character and circumstance as some Hérodiade of our theatre, dancing seemingly alone in her narrow moving luminous circle.

Symons's *The Symbolist Movement in Literature* (1895) convinced Yeats that a truly modern poet would seek such purity, at whatever cost to companionship and communication. The lesson was easy to learn, since it accorded with Yeats's earlier affiliations; it allowed him to find his visionary company in Shelley and Blake rather than in Wordsworth and Keats, in the neo-Platonism of Henry More and Thomas Taylor, in the spirituality of occult lore at once Celtic and universal.

It is clear from Yeats's early poems that he was a neo-French Symbolist before he ever heard of such a designation; long before he met Symons, he was writing world-weary poems, yearning for rarefied states of being, poems in which texture so predominates over structure that, reading them, one rarely feels inclined to specify either their syntax or their bearing. It is enough that each poem envelops the reader in an aura from which, for the duration of the experience, he feels no impulse to escape:

> *Rose of all Roses, Rose of all the World!*
> *You, too, have come where the dim tides are hurled*
> *Upon the wharves of sorrow, and heard ring*
> *The bell that calls us on; the sweet far thing.*
> *Beauty grown sad with its eternity*
> *Made you of us, and of the dim grey sea.*

This is not obscure, if we take "Rose" as Yeats's symbol of intellectual beauty, and if we construe the last two lines as saying that beauty, the abstract quality or power, created intellectual beauty as a projection of human desire—"us"—and the condition—"the dim grey sea"—in which those who desire have to live. Intellectual beauty is not, as abstract beauty is, entirely separate from those who pursue it: it is made "of us." But Yeats's language discourages the reader from inquiring further, from asking, for instance, whether the two constituents of intellectual beauty have equal status or whether the repetition of "dim" has more than acoustic force. If we find such questions arising, we are reading the poem against its spirit; it is not that kind of poem.

Yeats soon realized that his neo-French version of Symbolism made every poem written according to its principles sound the same. He interested himself in Irish ballads with the hope of giving his poems a greater range of rhythms. But he couldn't see his way out of the impasse until he started reading Nietzsche seriously (in September 1902) and sensed that a Nietzschean aesthetic of conflict might release him from vague yearnings and equivocations. When readers of Yeats's *Collected Poems* respond to "Adam's Curse" as to a new and stronger tone, they recognize not only that Yeats is acknowledging time and loss in a specifically contingent setting—women worrying about getting old and losing their looks, a poet weary of the labor of writing poems—but that he is steadying his nerve in the face of such considerations. Reading Nietzsche, Yeats saw that he could gain continuous energy for his poems by setting each constituent of his desire against its opposite.

An instance of this device is "A Dialogue of Self and Soul," in which self means the values that arise from the body and return to it, and soul speaks for transcendence and the desire to be released from earth and time. Nietzsche and Wilde enabled Yeats to develop a doctrine of the mask, translating into theatrical terms the general theory that supposes that the human imagination is the power by which we may project states of being other than our own.

Not that Yeats's middle poems are really dialogical: in each case, and depending upon the mood of the occasion, one of the values in conflict is allowed to "win." But in the supreme poems, such as "Sailing to Byzantium" and "Among School Children," equipoise is achieved; the rival claims of reality and justice are finely adjudicated.

These poems have a distinctly modern character, even though the clearest precedents for them are in certain English seventeenth-century poems like Marvell's "A Dialogue between the Resolved Soul and Created Pleasure" and "A Dialogue between the Soul and Body." The reason is that Yeats was peculiarly resourceful in giving his conflicting values—Hic and Ille in "Ego Dominus Tuus," as a case in point—rhetorical capacity equal to the causes they serve. When Ille says

> By the help of an image
> I call to my own opposite, summon all
> That I have handled least, least looked upon

we hear the distinctive Yeatsian music, the post-Miltonic emphasis on "all," the calling answered in rhyme as in sufficient reason, the breaking of the third line on the stressed "least," with the word repeated at once in the unstressed metrical position but carried forward by the alliteration "least . . . looked." The conflict between self and image doesn't humiliate either party, even though the balance of the argument goes at last in Ille's favor.

I am not claiming that Yeats's reading of Nietzsche made him a modern poet, or that the intellectual companionship of Nietzsche and Wilde was enough to turn him into a Modernist. But these rhetoricians of the mask prepared him to recognize one version of Modernism when he met it in Pound. Especially in the years 1909 to 1915, Yeats learned from Pound that there was a Modernist project, even though he disappointed Pound by retaining his old affiliations with Symbolism. As late as December 1912, Pound was still asserting that Yeats was the greatest living poet, but he was also recognizing that Ford Madox Ford represented a better way of being intelligent. "Mr.

Yeats has been subjective," Pound wrote. "[He] believes in the glamour and associations which hang near words." Pound had little interest in such glamour; by temper and conviction, he sought the virtues of French prose, not those of Mallarméan verse. Ford "believes in an exact rendering of things." In the end, Pound gave up on Yeats. Just as he came to believe that what Ford was trying to do was done more successfully by Joyce in *Dubliners* and *A Portrait of the Artist as a Young Man*, so he decided that what Yeats was doing in the mode of Symbolism was better done in Eliot's early poems. Still, Pound had much to do with Yeats's development of an elaborate theory of history. *Per Amica Silentia Lunae*, which Yeats wrote when he was close to Pound, was a trial run for the theory of historical gyres and cycles he developed in *A Vision*.

It is not self-evident that *A Vision* is a work of Modernism, so I should say a few words of explanation. There are as many versions of Modernism as there are critics who take an interest in propounding such things. According to the version of Modernism that I deduce from Simmel's *The Philosophy of Money*, one's interiority is real but vulnerable: to become valid, it must be bodied forth in relation to something else, something potentially alien to itself. There must be some other value at large so that the fluid and mobile character of one's interiority may be stabilized, measured, questioned by appeal to an independent set of criteria. Modernism is the project of construing one's interior life in relation to everything that has come to be the case: the city, distress of nations, sheer necessity. History, the taking possession of the past in some sense, provides the criteria by which the force of one's inner life, the "violence within," may be steadied and its value judged.

In Eliot, the crucial part of the past that is to be acknowledged is "the mind of Europe," the significant achievements—he called them "monuments" in a regrettable passage of his "Tradition and the Individual Talent"—from Homer to the twentieth century. The value Eliot placed upon these works was chiefly disciplinary: the individual talent should submit itself to the intellectual and moral pressure exerted by the works that constitute tradition, and should curb the excesses of its subjectivity by that submission. Pound's *Cantos* enforce another version; they claim to show what is entailed by taking possession of the past, or rather of those instances, "luminous moments," in which intelligence was exerted in a particular relation to power.

Confucius's writings, Malatesta's *Tempio* at Rimini, the correspondence of John Adams and Thomas Jefferson—these are samples of intelligence in a certain relation to public life. They show the necessary ambience within which any subjectivity worth talking about could be authenticated. "How is it far if you think of it?" In Yeats's *A Vision*, the past is distinguished from mere chronology and invoked by way of instances hardly less arbitrary than Pound's, with this difference—Yeats's criteria are aesthetic rather than cognitive or administrative. The *Cantos* demand that society be so ordained as to constitute a place fit for artists to live in, but Pound's criteria are based not only upon art but upon the bearing of intelligence in economic life. Yeats's evidence, especially in the later essays and poems, is drawn from the history of art, from aesthetic achievements he admired in Byzantium and Renaissance Italy. He then turned a prejudice into a theory: "History is necessity till it takes fire in someone's mind and becomes freedom or virtue."

Yeats convinced himself, led toward this conviction by his wife's dreams and her automatic writing, that the current historical period would end in 1927, having lasted for the two thousand years that he supposed an age to run. The new age would be as unlike the Christian one as Yeats could imagine. The force necessary to whirl old into new would probably be war; in any case, the apocalypse would be violent, surgical, harsh. The differences between the old age and the new would correspond to Yeats's basic polarities: subjective/objective, primary/antithetical, solar/lunar, and so forth, as *A Vision* deployed them. In Joyce, the "other criteria" are provided not by historical acts and monuments, as in Eliot, Pound, and Yeats, but by interpreting history as language: the English language, to begin with, and in *Finnegans Wake* a multiplicity of languages, diversely invoked and compromised.

In this sense, Yeats was a Modernist: the true task of intelligence was deemed to be a determination of the relation—whatever relation seemed best—between past, present, and future so that one's inner life might proceed without humiliation. The vastly enlarged stock of historical images that nineteenth-century archaeologists discovered in many diverse cultures offered the mind a particular challenge: how could anyone cope with such a plethora? Any competent archaeologist was liable to uncover new images, new artifacts. Since one's historical sense is necessarily a matter of choosing certain images and ignoring a thousand for every one observed, is historical understanding a fiction like any other? What form should a serious engagement with the past take, granted that one can draw a historical fact or event into any number of structures, each showing a different disposition toward the world? The moral sense of Modernism was provoked by this consideration.

I have been implying that Yeats is a Modernist only in one respect, his sense of history. The clearest indication of his resistance to Modernism, in the sense in which the canonical Modernists are Eliot and Joyce, is that he was never tempted to reject the vernacular character of the English language. In his early poems he tried to thwart the march of English syntax, but he soon made common cause with it. The "juxtaposition without copula" that Marshall McLuhan presented as the distinguishing device of literary Modernism, the neo-Cubist clash of surfaces, the dislocation of perspective, capitulation to the random contents of one's mind; none of these procedures appealed to Yeats. This is not to say that he took dictation from Standard English, or that he accepted the current state of an English language besotted with positivism and empiricism. Yeats's early poems are attempts to make fellowship between Celtic and French intimations, set off against the enforcements of Standard English. But he never thought of abandoning the civic vernacular. Indeed, his progress as a poet, from "Adam's Curse" to the middle poems, is marked by the development of a style at once colloquial and majestic—colloquial in its main character but ready to be "raised" to Yeatsian hauteur and splendor, given any warrant:

> But all is changed, that high horse riderless,
> Though mounted in that saddle Homer rode
> Where the swan drifts upon a darkening flood.

It doesn't sound like Standard English, but we can readily imagine Yeats speaking like that on a formal occasion. His speeches in the Senate are as enhanced as these verses. But nothing in the verses threatens the privilege of Standard English and its normative sequences. We have no more difficulty in deciphering Yeats's middle style than we have in negotiating, patiently indeed, one of Henry James's elaborately postponed later sentences. Yeats never complained about the language, except for the corruption it couldn't guard against.

Perhaps this explains why, in the introduction to the *Oxford Book,*

Yeats distanced himself from Eliot, Pound, Joyce, and Lewis. Especially from Eliot. He had no ear for Eliot's poems, couldn't work up much interest in *The Waste Land*, thought Eliot a satirist rather than a poet, and admired him only on the rare occasions when his poetry sounded like Yeats's own:

> *And sang within the bloody wood*
> *When Agamemnon cried aloud,*
> *And let their liquid siftings fall*
> *To stain the stiff dishonoured shroud.*

Yeats would not have remarked the siftings, but otherwise the stanza is one he would have been willing and able to write.

# ON A LATE POEM BY YEATS

∿∿∿∿∿

In Washington about a year ago, Seamus Heaney gave a reading of poems, his choice among his own, and some by other poets that for one reason or another meant much to him. Among the latter group was Yeats's "Man and the Echo." I forget whether Heaney called it, as many editors do, "The Man and the Echo." There is manuscript justification, too, for calling it "Man and Echo," according to the version Yeats transcribed for Dorothy Wellesley. So the title isn't a hanging matter. I wondered, listening to Heaney's reading, why "Man and the Echo" spoke so intimately to him and why in turn he recited it so vigorously to us, emphasizing the rhymes more resolutely than in any other reading I had heard. The poem had to make its way that evening with other poems in even higher standing. Heaney put it close to Keats's "To Autumn" and the first part of Hopkins's "The Wreck of the Deutschland." Yet I found it among the most telling poems, and now when I recall the reading it is Yeats's poem more than any other that recurs to me. The notes that follow are my tribute to the poem and to Heaney's grace in choosing it.

When I started out reading poems and paying some attention to the critical lore that attended them, I found myself admonished to distinguish between the poet and the person who lived a domestic or civic life under the same name. It was easy to observe this rule when

[177]

the poem was clearly a dramatic monologue; to distinguish between the implied speaker of "The Love Song of J. Alfred Prufrock," for instance, and the public figure one heard of from time to time as T. S. Eliot. Gradually I accustomed myself to keeping the distinction in mind even when it was not emphasized by such a title. I schooled myself to believe that the "I" of a poem did not mean the poet in his biographically constituted person but a personage invented for the occasion. There were difficult cases. I could not believe that the words of *The Waste Land* supposedly issued from one voice or articulated the experience of one hypothetical person, male or female; or of Tiresias, male and female. The notion of a voice independent of a personality supposedly stable enough to authorize it made a difficulty, and still does. But for the most part I found it possible to read a poem as a dramatic monologue and to separate the implied speaker from the putative author. It was worthwhile to keep up the attempt, because I had a prejudice according to which the imagination is the mind in the aspect of its freedom, and the main consideration is its freedom to invent, to posit, to summon new experience to the reader's presence. The imagination, I often assured myself, isn't a photocopying machine; it doesn't take dictation from what has merely occurred: it wants to have a future independent of the supposed logic of past and present.

I was also admonished to drive a wedge between the poem as it appeared formally on the page and the vernacular forms of English as I couldn't help knowing them. Poems might imitate colloquial behavior, as *The Waste Land* does in one section, but the imitation is not thought to undermine a fundamental difference between demotic and formally disciplined speech. To enforce a sense of this difference, a poet resorts to artifice, to diction he probably wouldn't speak if he were ordering a meal in a restaurant, and to the meters, all the better because no one speaks in verse even on high occasions. The meters make for delay and scruple in the otherwise too swift replacement of words by the meanings we assign to them. "A formal meter impresses us," Ransom said in *The World's Body*, "as a way of regulating very drastically the material, and we do not stop to remark (that is, as readers) that it has no particular aim except some nominal sort of regimentation." Meter exerts gentle violence upon the things to be expressed or negotiated. In that sense, it emphasizes the invented or fictive character of the poem. Ransom said in the same book that art "always sets

out to create an 'aesthetic distance' between the object and the subject, and art takes pains to announce that it is not history."[1] If Ransom
were writing now, he would have to strengthen that word "history"
and establish a convincing distinction between history and fiction. On
all sides we hear that history is merely the particular fiction that has
won, political power having enforced it.

I submitted myself to these admonitions and trusted that they
would keep me secure. So, in reading "Man and the Echo," I recited
to myself such maxims as these: the speaker is not Yeats biographically
ascertained; the poem may allude to historical events, but even if it
does, the meters and other devices are designed to remove consideration of these matters to an aesthetic distance and to hold them there
for the duration of the reading. The formality of the poem protects it
from the indignity of yielding to the matter, more or less formless,
from which it notionally began; protects it, too, from the predatory
motive in readers, who are likely to lay violent hands upon it and seize
it for their own purposes, political, religious, or otherwise ideological.

As a young reader of poems, I received some such instruction
from my elders, and I suppose it has remained to guide or inhibit me.
But it is not clear how the general lesson helps me in reading "Man
and the Echo." I am not even sure how to begin. Heaney began by
announcing the title and naming the speakers as "Man" and "Echo"
when these were indicated on the page. I wondered about that. In
reading "Ego Dominus Tuus" aloud, should I announce "Hic" and
"Ille" at the points assigned to them; "My Soul" and "My Self" when
these phrases appear on the pages of the "Dialogue"; split up the sev‐
enth section of "Vacillation" to introduce "The Soul" and "The
Heart" as the figures engaged in debate? I'm not sure. But I recall that
Heaney lowered his voice and announced "Man" and "Echo" when it
was the turn of one or the other to speak. Perhaps he construed them
as characters in a play, as in a sense they are, and thought that each
should be named on every occasion. I suppose he was right, if only
because the changes of tone marked the formality of the proceedings
and the decorum it entailed. But it could also be argued that these in‐
dications are meant for the reader's eyes and are not supposed to be
heard. The poem begins with Man:

> *In a cleft that's christened Alt*
> *Under broken stone I halt*

> *At the bottom of a pit*
> *That broad noon has never lit,*
> *And shout a secret to the stone.*

Who is speaking? The matters in hand are close to those we have come to recognize as Yeats's, and the lines might easily be taken as autobiographical. But even if they were, it would still be possible to keep the wedge driven between the speaker, "I, the poet William Yeats," and William Butler Yeats, son, brother, and husband. To ascribe certain words to Man is to claim for them a character nearly anonymous. These five lines make complete sense but leave the sound in suspense: we are waiting for a companionable rhyme in reply to "stone," according to the pattern established in the first four lines. The meter is tetrameter, trochaic to begin with: it is the meter of Milton's "L'Allegro":

> *Come, and trip it as you go*
> *On the light fantastic toe*

and of such childhood pieties as

> *Gentle Jesus meek and mild,*
> *Look on me, a little child.*

For the moment, the speaker, "I," is in the shadow of the dominants, "Alt" and "halt." Scholars of Yeats agree that Alt is a glen on the side of Knocknarea or Ben Bulben, mountains near Sligo, but there is no need to have that in mind. They also agree, more to the point, that poems which rhyme as closely as this one does—*aabbcc*, and so forth—should rhyme on different parts of speech, as here noun rhymes with verb, "Alt . . . halt," "pit . . . lit." I am not sure why this is preferred, though I remember an essay in which W. K. Wimsatt studied the rhymes in Pope and thought them feeble when noun answered noun or verb verb. In *Rhyme's Reason*, John Hollander observes the rule, too:

> *When meaning makes a gap which sound can span, it's*
> *As if the rhyme words came from different planets;*

> *Or when a final verb, perhaps, will reach*
> *Out to rhyme with some different part of speech.*[2]

Yeats breaks the rule, if rule it is, in a few places: "strain . . . brain,"
"checked . . . wrecked," "release . . . disease," "theme . . . dream,"
"sight . . . night." Sometimes, as in "sight . . . night," there is a semantic difference. "Sight" here means an abstract capacity, and "night" a
state so far from abstraction that they nearly have the force of different
parts of speech.

  "Done," the rhyming answer to "stone," maintains continuity
across the gap of syntax, tells the secret:

> *All that I have said and done,*
> *Now that I am old and ill,*
> *Turns into a question till*
> *I lie awake night after night*
> *And never get the answers right.*
> *Did that play of mine send out*
> *Certain men the English shot?*
> *Did words of mine put too great strain*
> *On that woman's reeling brain?*
> *Could my spoken words have checked*
> *That whereby a house lay wrecked?*
> *And all seems evil until I*
> *Sleepless would lie down and die.*

It is difficult here to maintain the fiction that the speaker and the biographical Yeats are two, not one. It is hard to rinse your mind clean
of the information, once you have heard it, that the first performance
of *Cathleen ni Houlihan* on April 2, 1902, roused some members of the
audience to nationalist fervor; that Margot Ruddock was a crazed girl
in love with Yeats; that in Yeats's lifetime Lady Gregory's house at
Coole Park was allowed to fall into decay. Readers innocent of this
lore are fortunate: they don't have to see the poem reduced to footnotes. All the better if they take the lines merely as indicating any episodes in the speaker's life for which he feels guilt or remorse.
Informed readers have to remind themselves that the speaker is a constituted fiction, a *factum*, not a *datum*, even if lore and the newspapers

declare that some of the constituents of the fiction are also factual. Yeats as biographically projected is also a fiction, but a different one.

In the version of the poem as given to Dorothy Wellesley, Yeats is harder on himself than in the printed versions; he confesses to the several mischiefs, doesn't let them merely turn into a question:

> All that I have said or done,
> Now that I am old and ill
> Seems to have done but harm, until
> I lie awake night after night.
> I never get the answer right.[3]

The singular "answer" is more demanding than "answers," the plural spreading the risk as it allows the corresponding questions to be diverse. Revising the Wellesley version, too, Yeats got rid of a bad rhyme—"perplex . . . wreck"—and turned "wreck" into "wrecked," making a rhyming "checked" indicate what his intervention at the right time might have achieved.

But the dominant feature of this first part of the poem is the rhyming. Monosyllabic rhymes are commonly thought to be naive, their simplicity that of a rhyming child. Helen Vendler's study of the early poems shows that Yeats soon tired of these monosyllables.[4] Why, then, did he go back to them in "Man and the Echo," a poem written in July 1938, lightly revised till October, and published the following January? All the rhymes are monosyllabic, except for "release . . . disease," "he . . . stupidity," "view . . . pursue," and "voice . . . rejoice." There are no rhymes on plural nouns. I think Yeats associated monosyllabic rhymes not only with a child's directness but with the moral simplicity appropriate to an old man's taking stock of his life. In an old man's winter night there is no time to equivocate. Let him ask himself the question, and let him answer it.

Yeats has only a few poems in this metrical form, the trochaic or iambic tetrameter with couplet rhymes. Unless I err, he associates the form with accusation, as in "Man and the Echo," or a moral claim, as in "To Ireland in the Coming Times":

> Nor may I less be counted one
> With Davis, Mangan, Ferguson,
> Because, to him who ponders well,

> *My rhymes more than their rhyming tell*
> *Of things discovered in the deep,*
> *Where only body's laid asleep.*

I take it that "Man and the Echo" is a poem in which an aging man talks himself back into life when many considerations urge him to give up and die. The considerations are diversely moral and aesthetic, and they take a dismissive form. Instead of "would lie down and die," Echo says only "lie down and die" and finds no reason to speak against that counsel; the subjunctive becomes an imperative.

The big dictionaries remind us that in Greek mythology Echo was deemed to be an Oread or mountain nymph who caused the acoustic phenomenon alluded to in the word; and in *Romeo and Juliet* Shakespeare has Juliet say:

> *Bondage is hoarse, and may not speak aloud,*
> *Else would I tear the cave where Echo lies. . . .*

"Man and the Echo" observes this decorum and doubles it by arranging, as in many earlier poems, that a line will repeat the concluding syllables of the preceding line, so as to supply an answer to the notion contained in it. Yeats's Echo is, as Hollander has remarked in *The Figure of Echo*, "voice's self."[5] I suppose that Hollander means: voice as if it were personified, as the Greeks personified Echo, and given every attribute proper to its name and none adhering to another. There are many echoing poems in English, including Swift's "A Gentle Echo upon Woman" and George Herbert's "Heaven"—in this latter, "high" is echoed in "I," "know" in "no," "delight" in "light," "enjoy" in "joy," and "persever" in "ever." Man hears the echo and argues against it:

> *That were to shirk*
> *The spiritual intellect's great work*
> *And shirk it in vain. There is no release*
> *In a bodkin or disease,*
> *Nor can there be work so great*
> *As that which cleans man's dirty slate.*
> *While man can still his body keep*
> *Wine or love drug him to sleep,*

> *Waking he thanks the Lord that he*
> *Has body and its stupidity,*
> *But body gone he sleeps no more,*
> *And till his intellect grows sure*
> *That all's arranged in one clear view,*
> *Pursues the thoughts that I pursue,*
> *Then stands in judgment on his soul,*
> *And, all work done, dismisses all*
> *Out of intellect and sight*
> *And sinks at last into the night.*

"Spiritual intellect" is the mind as an eternal capacity, freed by death to a state without B.C. or A.D. It is Blake's "vision" or "imagination," a power innate to human life and not at all indebted to natural life. In "Are you Content?" Yeats says that "Eyes spiritualised by death can judge . . ." and in the last stanza of "All Souls' Night" he has talked himself into a state in which the mind knows both Hell and Heaven, a mummy–state:

> *Such thought, that in it bound*
> *I need no other thing,*
> *Wound in mind's wandering*
> *As mummies in the mummy-cloth are bound.*

"Man and the Echo" is familiar with the imaginings of *Purgatory* and the last plays, with the revised version of *A Vision* and Yeats's various attempts to work out the logic of reincarnation and the cyclic character of experience. But it is even more clearly a revision of the "Dialogue of Self and Soul," in which "My Soul" claims access to a form of darkness indistinguishable from the soul; to "ancestral night," which can "deliver from the crime of death and birth"; and to "that quarter where all thought is done." The poem glances back, too, toward the stanza in "All Souls' Night" in which Florence Emery is credited with having learned from an Indian sage much about the soul's journey:

> *How it is whirled about,*
> *Wherever the orbit of the moon can reach,*
> *Until it plunge into the sun;*
> *And there, free and yet fast,*

*Being both Chance and Choice,*
*Forget its broken toys*
*And sink into its own delight at last.*

The sinking at last into the night of "Man and the Echo" is more rueful than Florence Emery's discovery: in the earlier version Yeats is still
in the purging, self-delighting dance of Mallarmé's Hérodiade and of
his own dance-plays, in which the sublime is achieved as the extremity
of self-possession. Echo, repeating "Into the night," retains chiefly its
ironic finality rather than its sublimity. No matter: it is only there as
a willed obstacle, as if nature were speaking from the cleft or, as in another poem, from the shell held close to one's ear. The obstacle is
there so that Man's achievement in overcoming it may appear to have
been won. Man seems to ignore Echo's intervention and ends the
poem in terms congenial to himself:

*O Rocky Voice,*
*Shall we in that great night rejoice?*
*What do we know but that we face*
*One another in this place?*
*But hush, for I have lost the theme,*
*Its joy or night seem but a dream;*
*Up there some hawk or owl has struck,*
*Dropping out of sky or rock,*
*A stricken rabbit is crying out,*
*And its cry distracts my thought.*

Dorothy Wellesley transcribed the first line as "O rocky void," but this
must be her mistake in deciphering Yeats's hand. The rhyme for "rejoice" must be "voice." Some editions have "Rocky Voice," superior
case; some, including Finneran's, lower. If superior, the connection
with "The Gyres" is emphasized: "Old Rocky Face look forth." Old
Rocky Face is often taken to be Shelley's Ahasuerus in *Hellas*, who
tells Mahmud to think not of past or future but of the One, "the un-
born and the undying." But Ahasuerus doesn't rejoice in that knowledge. I have read comparisons, too, with passages in Dante and in Ben
Jonson. My co-editor in *An Honoured Guest*, J. R. Mulryne, thinks
that Yeats is addressing mainly himself, a self now virtually become an
image. As an image, it would be impersonal enough to be addressed

as if it were already consubstantial with the immortality of spiritual life. Perhaps there is no need to be more specific than Hollander is in deeming the one addressed or summoned to be the figure of Echo: "The 'Rocky Voice' which plays no verbal tricks in its answers comes at the end of the tradition of the echo scheme: its irony is that it is not expectedly ironic."[6] But there is no harm, while reading "The Gyres," "Lapis Lazuli," and "Man and the Echo," in hearing Nietzsche's exultant, tragic joy, which is energy delighting in itself, regardless of the dire conditions in which it lives. Irony would admit an equivocation. The rocky voice should speak with the authority of Nietzsche's German, or of Yeats's Nietzschean English, as in the letter to Dorothy Wellesley (July 26, 1935) in which he tells her:

> To me the supreme aim is an act of faith and reason to make one rejoice in the midst of tragedy. An impossible aim; yet I think it true that nothing can injure us.[7]

Nothing can injure us because we believe in reincarnation and in the law of change. The poem is itself an echo of the last stanza of "The Apparitions":

> When a man grows old his joy
> Grows more deep day after day,
> His empty heart is full at length,
> But he has need of all that strength
> Because of the increasing Night
> That opens her mystery and fright.
> Fifteen apparitions have I seen;
> The worst a coat upon a coat-hanger.

But this calls upon a more familiar range of feelings; panic at the approach of death, justly rhyming "Night" with "fright." A belief in reincarnation is not necessary for such dread. When Echo says "Into the night," we have no cause to anticipate that Man will take up the word again and make it far more portentous than it has appeared to be; will make it virtually one of Yeats's technical terms. "Shall we in that great night rejoice?" "Great" transumes the common meaning, night as the state of dread, into distinctly Yeatsian grandeur; no wonder it goes on to "rejoice."

But I must now add to what I said a while ago: in the poem the speaker talks, keeping himself alive in the face of death. He summons, as Echo, another form or mood of himself, according to a procedure well established in "Vacillation" and the other dialogues: one mood thwarts another, and victory may go either way. What Man says is preparation of his soul for the Day of Judgment, when the soul will stand in judgment on itself according to criteria resolutely Nietzschean. God is not dead; he is alive, if not well, and his name is Nietzsche.

But the poem doesn't end upon that conceit. Two rhetorical questions make more difficulty than I can well explain. Let us have them again:

> *O Rocky Voice*
> *Shall we in that great night rejoice?*
> *What do we know but that we face*
> *One another in this place?*

In the first question the "in" is difficult: does it go with "rejoice," as in "rejoice in" one's good fortune, rejoice here in the ultimacy of the transformation by which the spiritual intellect accomplishes its great work? Or rejoice, immersed in the state of soul, mummy-knowledge, for which "that great night" is Yeats's chosen analogue? What about "this" in the second question? Is this place Alt, as distinct from some other place; is it the place where Yeats imagines himself summoning Rocky Voice to come forth, face-to-face, as judge of a lifetime's works and days? Before Rocky Voice can answer, the speaker hushes him:

> *But hush, for I have lost the theme,*
> *Its joy or night seem but a dream;*

There is no evidence that he has lost the theme, but we take his word for it. The internal and external rhyming of "theme," "seem," and "dream" is a sign of displacement: one mode of speech is about to be displaced by another. We note that Echo is not allowed to have the last word, though it would have been easy enough to find a conclusive echo, as in "ought." One style of discourse yields to another. The first style has been discursive, and authoritative in that mode. Man has drawn the discourse to himself as its center, briefly impeded by two echoing and echoed phrases. But the poem ends when this mode has been displaced by another one: an image, imagined and not claimed as having happened, a pure hypothesis, a hawk or owl swooping down on a rabbit. What status can this have except as that of the otherwise silenced Echo, allowed now to intervene in the antithetical form of an image? The image is imperative in the sense that it does not ask to be completed in other terms, as by further elucidation or discourse: it is merely itself, pure act. "And its cry distracts my thought." "Cry" is beneath thought or beyond it, *hysterica passio* or sublimity beyond discourse. Either way it is a scandal to syntax, because syntax always wants the discourse to continue as it has begun.

The poem ends, then, when it has allowed the dominant form of itself to be deflected. Nothing unusual in that: several of Yeats's poems end by reaching an accepted limit in the particular form of speech they have practiced. "In Memory of Major Robert Gregory" ends when there seems no point in continuing; "Friends" when the feelings recovered from memory have taken possession of the speaker's body and left nothing more to be said; "What Then?" when a metaphysical impasse is reached; "The People" when the speaker sinks his head abashed; the first part of the "Dialogue" when the speaker's tongue has turned to stone.

I recall from Heaney's reading of the poem his emphasis on the word "all" and the other words in its acoustic vicinity. In *The Structure of Complex Words*, William Empson has a chapter on "all" in *Paradise Lost*, making the point that the word is peculiarly suited to Milton's temper "because he is an absolutist, an all-or-none man":

> All else is unimportant beside one thing, he is continually deciding; he delights in the harshness of a theme which makes all human history turn on an absolutely trivial action. The generosity of the proud man also requires the word; when he gives he gives all. It is as suited to absolute love and self-sacrifice as to insane self-assertion. The self-centred man, in his turn, is not much interested in the variety of the world, and readily lumps it together as "all."[8]

This is as true of Yeats as of Milton, even though I want to keep the description separate from the old argument, diversely maintained by Robert Lowell and Donald Davie, that Yeats was so self-regarding that he was virtually blind to the variety of the world. The stilted water-hen of "Meditations in Time of Civil War" refutes the charge, but it is hard to claim that Yeats regularly suppresses himself in favor of a world he celebrates as given and independent of the mind that celebrates it. "All" is one of his favorite words: it takes up twelve pages of the *Concordance*. Listening to Heaney, I started thinking that the whole poem was a set of variations on the sound of "all," the dominant sound, if we allow for its minor repetition as the middle syllables of "intellect" and such words. Here is a list of its forms and variants as I find them or their first cousins line by line: "Alt," "halt," "all," "till," "all seems evil," "spiritual intellect's," "While," "still," "till," "intellect," "all's," "soul," "all work done, dismisses all," "intellect," "Shall." I don't find it in the last eight lines, and I wonder why. Maybe it's because "all" belongs to discourse, argument, claim and counterclaim. When the unannounced imager in the last lines put a stop to this, there is no call for the sound.

But even by saying as little as this about "all," I raise a question about the form of the poem. It is counted as one of Yeats's dialogues, but is it really? These days we have to use the word "dialogue" in a fairly stringent sense: a work of literature isn't dialogical, Bakhtin warns us, merely because two voices are audible. It is dialogical only when the author gives each voice complete independence. I can't do justice to Bakhtin's argument, especially as it exists in several versions and contexts, but it is enough to recall his analysis, in *Problems of Dostoevsky's Poetics*, of Tolstoy's story "Three Deaths." Bakhtin maintains that Dostoevski's novels are polyphonic in the sense that the several characters, several voices, are allowed to speak and act for themselves: it is as if Dostoevski were to postpone indefinitely the expression of his own attitude or sense of life. René Wellek has disputed Bakhtin's account of Dostoevski's novels in that respect, but I can't adjudicate the matter. In "Three Deaths," according to Bakhtin's interpretation, there are several characters, "but only one cognitive subject, all else being merely objects of its cognition."[9]

Yeats's sensibility thrives upon conflict. His art does not aspire toward the condition of music, in which discords are at last resolved, but to the condition of drama, in which the meaning is not found at any point but in the process it enacts, the trajectory of its force. But it remains a question whether, in a particular poem, the conflicting values are given their independence or merely allowed to express Yeats him-

self in two or more of his recurrent moods. I have never troubled myself with the question, but recently I have adverted to it not through
Bakhtin's vocabulary but through Levinas's. Levinas is even more stringent than Bakhtin, his distinctions more invidious. His most compelling distinction is between the "I" that insists on recovering its identity
through all that happens to it and the "I" that gives itself gratuitously
to others and does not call upon their goodwill or even their acknowledgment. Levinas contrasts Ulysses with Abraham in that respect. In
"La Trace de l'autre" he writes:

> The God of the philosophers from Aristotle to Leibniz by way of
> the God of the scholastics is a god adequate to reason, a compre-
> hended god who could not trouble the autonomy of conscious-
> ness, which finds itself again in all its adventures, returning home
> to itself like Odysseus, who through all his peregrinations is only
> on the way to his native land. . . . To the myth of Odysseus re-
> turning to Ithaca, we would like to oppose the story of Abraham
> leaving forever his homeland for a land yet unknown and forbid-
> ding his servant to bring even his son to this point of depar-
> ture."[10]

I may be asked: why are you bringing these big philosophic guns
to bear upon a poem of Yeats's which is merely one of many and not
his most demanding? Why are you implying that the conflict in this
poem, and perhaps in other poems by Yeats, is mere shadow-boxing,
one mood of a subjective mind challenging another of its moods,
merely for the show of it? I'm not sure that I can answer those questions or even fend them off. But I don't apologize for bringing in
Bakhtin and Levinas. More and more, I realize that when I read a
poem, I read it subject to the interests and emphases which obtain in
my mind at that time. This procedure is not as capricious as it appears:
at least the most blatant irrelevancies drop away or are put in parentheses. One motif tells upon another when I allow myself to attend upon
them. That, I assume, is how a state of mind comes into being. So I
read "Man and the Echo": it calls attention to itself as a dialogue, an
echo-poem. I can't ignore the questions that arise from this form. It
is embarrassing to have to confess that I haven't given adequate
thought to this aspect of Yeats's poems, or questioned (for instance) the
bearing of the rhetorical question at the end of "Man and the Echo,"

a question addressed to Rocky Voice, a force that can't answer. What is the status of "we" (three times) in the two questions that follow:

> O Rocky Voice,
> Shall we in that great night rejoice?
> What do we know but that we face
> One another in this place?

A rhetorical question is a question designed to produce an effect rather than to draw an answer. If that is so, can "Rocky Voice" be independent of the mind that calls to it; or must it be merely—but why do I say "merely"?—yet another form of that mind? "Our moods do not believe in one another," Emerson says in "Circles." Perhaps it is enough, then, that Yeats allows the figure of Echo to speak at all. Enough, I mean, for the purpose of a Bakhtinian or Dostoevskian dialogue. But if I think of Levinas's books, which are ethically more radical than Bakhtin's, I have to find that the peregrinations of "Man and the Echo" are Odyssean rather than Abrahamic. Echo is not even allowed to change the words, as George Herbert allows him or her to turn "abide" into "bide," a turning that makes a difference, if not all the difference in the world.

Bringing these notions together and adding a few comments: the poem now seems to me to arise from the conceit of shouting a secret to one who by definition will keep it; a cleft, a stone, like a shell that echoes one's last sounds without adding any of its own. The motif is predicated not upon music or drama but upon sculpture or landscape, the experience of addressing something that is already completely formed, keeping its mind and force to itself. Mulryne has noted the provenance of sculpted forms in Yeats's last poems, as if any other forms were liable to equivocate. Yeats's refusal to equivocate is embodied in several linguistic and phonetic features of the poem: most of its verbs are verbs of action, rather than verbs of process or of state—to use Jespersen's distinction in *The Philosophy of Grammar*. There is also a distinctive Yeatsian rhetoric in the juxtaposition of interrogatives—three in Man's first speech, none in his second, two in his third and last; the rest is indicative. Finally, the dominant feature of the poem is its "poetry of grammar"—Jakobson's phrase: it is metonymic rather than metaphorical, the progression from one unit of discourse to the next justified by contiguity rather than by similarity or difference.

There are few images after the first one, the cleft: all is discursive, grammatical, polemical, till the discourse is resolved at the end, in the cry of the stricken rabbit. One mode of cognition yields to another, about which much may be said—by Blake, Darwin, Hopkins—but not, for now, by Yeats.

Am I yielding my argument to Lowell and Davie? No; or not yet. But I am warning myself that the mere admission of two voices in a poem by Yeats, even in the "Dialogue of Self and Soul," does not guarantee the independence of either. If the entire story of philosophy from Plato to Husserl and Heidegger is, as Levinas claims, a philosophy of being in which consciousness insists on returning every object of its experience to itself—if all roads lead back to Ithaca—then I have to admit that Yeats's poetry is written, on the whole, in that spirit. The apparent dialogues are dialogues of the mind with itself. The plays embody, I think, Yeats's scruple, his misgiving about the imperiousness of his genius. That is to say, the character of his genius is visionary, not dramatic—to call upon a distinction proposed in Pater's essay on Botticelli. The genius "of which Botticelli is the type," according to Pater, "usurps the data before it as the exponent of ideas, moods, visions of its own; in this interest it plays fast and loose with those data, rejecting some and isolating others, and always combining them anew."[11] To Botticelli, as to Dante in Pater's account of both, "the scene, the colour, the outward image or gesture, comes with all its incisive and importunate reality; but awakes in him, moreover, by some subtle law of his own structure, a mood which it awakes in no one else, of which it is the double or repetition, and which it clothes, that all may share it, with visible circumstance." Reading that sentence, I am inclined to suspect a misprint, that "his" structure should be "its," but there is no misprint: by "his own structure" Pater means the particular type of genius that asserts itself in giving apparent objects a character chiefly subjective. "Usurps" is severe, and strange, when we consider that Pater shares the type of genius he ascribes to Botticelli, as distinct from the type he ascribes to Giotto, Masaccio, and Ghirlandaio. I take it that "usurps" conveys Pater's misgiving, as Echo conveys Yeats's.

# T. S. ELIOT:
# THE COMMUNICATION OF THE DEAD

ၒၒၯၐၑၯၒ

I

Two lines from the last of Eliot's *Four Quartets*, "Little Gidding,"
are carved on the headstone of his grave at East Coker:

*the communication*
*Of the dead is tongued with fire beyond the language of the living.*

I propose to comment on those lines. But I approach them indirectly.
There is a passage in the first version of *A Vision* in which Yeats
is trying to find evidence in favor of his philosophy of history. He
thinks of certain artists whom he regarded with a mixture of admiration and dismay. The condition he found exemplified in Eliot, Pound,
Joyce, and Pirandello was one in which the mind, recoiling from abstraction, turns upon itself. These writers, Yeats said, either "eliminate
from metaphor the poet's fantasy and substitute a strangeness discovered by historical or contemporary research" or they "break up the
logical processes of thought by flooding them with associated ideas or
words that seem to drift into the mind by chance." As in Pirandello's
*Henry IV*, Eliot's *The Waste Land*, the early *Cantos* of Pound, and
Joyce's *Ulysses*, the mind sets side by side "the *physical primary*—a luna-
tic among his keepers, a man fishing behind a gas works, the vulgarity
of a single Dublin day prolonged through 700 pages—and the *spiritual*

*primary*, delirium, the Fisher King, Ulysses' wandering." Yeats's explanation for these wild conjunctions was that myth and fact, "united until the exhaustion of the Renaissance, have now fallen so far apart that man understands for the first time the rigidity of fact, and calls up, by that very recognition, myth—the Mask—which now but gropes its way out of the mind's dark but will shortly pursue and terrify."[1]

In that passage Yeats appears to mean that a fact is rigid when it presents itself as if by its own will, indifferent to the mind that witnesses it. I think he had in view the world according to realism and naturalism, in which the mind capitulates to whatever it happens to know. Myth, in turn, becomes monstrous when it is separated from every fact that would make it humanly available—monstrous, like the Furies pursuing and terrifying their victim.

To prevent the separation of fact and myth, Yeats resorted to symbols; because a symbol is at once fact and the halo of value that surrounds it, it is an object in the world inseparable from its natural or ancestral associations. But in January 1925, when he wrote the paragraph I have quoted, he was in one of his recurrent apocalyptic moods, sensing that a great historical era was coming to an end, and troubling himself with visions of its successor, some rough beast slouching towards Bethlehem to be born. He had reason to fear that such a thing would ignore a poet's symbols and the desires they embodied.

I propose to start from Yeats's comments on *The Waste Land* and the separation of fact and myth, and to reach a point where Eliot, too, invokes the symbol in a spirit both like and unlike Yeats's. But I should say at once what I understand by a myth. I take it as a story always already told, a communication of the dead for the benefit of the living; a story recited over and over as a communal interpretation of life, and offered for the instruction and the cohesion of the community that receives it. It tells the members of a community what it is good for them to hear and to believe. The myth aims to be true, as we say of a story that it is true to life. It is designated to make sense of the human experience and to protect the community that receives it from being enslaved to time and process. In that respect, a myth turns what has merely occurred into a narrative of repetitions, and its grammar becomes the continuous present tense: it gives point to anniversaries, recurrences, religious ceremonies, occasions on which people wish to assure themselves that they are members of a community. Like Yeats, we distinguish between a myth and a fiction. A fiction is a story that we claim not to be true but to be in some other way useful or diverting. We make such fictions, and we hold some of them in our minds, but we do not act on them or give them any special privilege. A myth, on the other hand, is, as Yeats said, "one of those statements our nature is compelled to make and employ as a truth though there cannot be sufficient evidence."[2] If a fact and a myth were to coincide, it would mean that the fact participated in the universal story and embodied its truth. The myth would be, for its society, the one story worth telling. A myth does not merely report what happened but what, having happened, is re-enacted as an archetype every time it is performed. When a fact lacks its myth, it is merely what it is—rigid, as Yeats sees it. When a myth fails to find its proper communal embodiment, it seeks and finds, as in fascism, a monstrous incarnation.

We can guess, I think, the attributes of *The Waste Land* that Yeats saw with whatever degree of dismay. He saw that its few intimations of happiness—the hyacinth girl, the "inexplicable splendour of Ionian white and gold" of Magnus Martyr—are uncanny because autonomous; they have no before or after, no story completes them. He saw, too, that while no single myth makes sense of the experiences that Eliot intuits in the poem, there are several myths from different cultures, and they imply several moral perspectives, each of them superior to the events it is called upon to judge. What each perspective lacks is completeness: one myth is merely succeeded by another. So the problem of authority is not resolved.

Eliot provided the theory of these several perspectives when he remarked, in his Harvard dissertation on F. H. Bradley, that "the life of a soul does not consist in the contemplation of one consistent world but in the painful task of unifying . . . incompatible ones, and passing, when possible, from two or more discordant viewpoints to a higher which shall somehow include and transmute them."[3] He repeated the theory, in effect, when he reviewed *Ulysses* in November 1923 and distinguished between the narrative method of fiction—which is the common procedure of realism—and the mythical method, which Joyce invented upon a hint, it appears, from Yeats's middle poems. By using Homer's *Odyssey* as the frame of *Ulysses*, by maintaining a continuous parallel between contemporaneity and antiquity, Joyce arrived at a method, as Eliot said, "a way of controlling, of ordering, of giving a shape and a significance to the immense panorama of futility and anarchy which is contemporary history." Eliot's way of reading *Ulysses* may or may not be useful: it is still contentious. I remark only that he found in the early chapters of the book, as he read them between 1919 and 1921, hints of the method he needed and, with Pound's editorial help, found in completing *The Waste Land*. The extent of the influence of *Ulysses* upon *The Waste Land* is still in mild dispute. The chief difference of form between the two works is that Joyce used the mythic perspective of one story, the *Odyssey*, while Eliot employed several provisional perspectives.

The moral bearing of these perspectives is clarified by Eliot's argument in "Tradition and the Individual Talent" that writers should submit themselves to a historical myth which he called tradition; it was far more valuable than the talent that addressed it. The self-discipline of a writer who is willing to surrender himself to tradition is "the historical sense." Tradition is the force that Eliot, on becoming a Christian, chose to call orthodoxy; the force not oneself to which a properly disposed mind submits. In *The Waste Land*, the higher perspectives have mainly punitive intent, as Yeats and Pound recognized in thinking Eliot chiefly a satirist. Sometimes the judgment is imposed by voices that have every right to impose it; the Buddha in "The Fire Sermon," Ezekiel and Dante in "The Burial of the Dead," the divine voice of the Upanishads in "What the Thunder Said." But the most formidable if also the most disturbingly repellent perspective is the one imposed by Tiresias, who foresees more than is good for him—the seduction of the bored typist—and foresuffers less than he might. In any event, Tiresias can see the world only as one alienated from it, he does not "give" or "sympathize," he does not participate in the suffering and transformation of "What the Thunder Said." When all is accounted, he merely enforces one of several discontinuous myths, charged with diminishing further the things to be looked down upon.

In Eliot's early poems, the main things looked down upon are instances of vanity, meaningless sexuality, the sundry masquerades that time resumes, the consciousness pathetically adrift from any valid purpose it might find for itself. But there are also things looked up to, including—in the "Preludes"—

> *The notion of some infinitely gentle*
> *Infinitely suffering thing . . .*

and the girl in "La Figlia che Piange," "her hair over her arms and her arms full of flowers." These images are preserved from any punitive perspective, or they are held as if in parentheses, waiting for the redemptive perspective in which they will be completed.

It is a commonplace that in Pound and Wyndham Lewis and in the Yeats of "On the Boiler" and the last poems, the separated and deracinated myth found a dreadful form for itself: for several years the rough beast turned out to be Hitler and Mussolini, the nearest likenesses to an Italian Renaissance prince the twentieth century could produce. In Eliot, the myth took no contemporaneous form but the narrative form of Christ, his birth, death, and resurrection. On his conversion to the Anglican communion in 1927, Eliot disposed his will to construe the facts of his entire experience in a Christian light. He submitted himself to a structure of belief that had as one of its great merits the fact that he had not invented it. Some readers regard his conversion as a scandal, and complain that for a whiff of incense a great poet abandoned them. There are readers, too, who think the conversion further proof, if proof beyond that of the early poems is required, of a pervasive debility beneath the surface of his work. I hold that Eliot, far from being a man of little energy and will, knew himself to be a man of dangerously extreme passion; he put phrases together and somehow made poems of them in the desperate hope of keeping himself from falling apart. What he chiefly wanted, in writing poems, was the experience of exhaustion, of good riddance, that he found in releasing himself from certain intolerable feelings. As he moved toward the Christian communion, I think he felt the exhausting satisfaction of submitting violent and morbid imageries to the discipline of impersonal doctrines and dogmas. When he said, in "Tradition and the Individual Talent," that "poetry is not a turning loose of emotion, but an escape from emotion; it is not the expression of personality, but an escape from personality," he went on immediately to remark that "only those who have personality and emotions know what it means to want to escape from these things."[4]

In referring to Eliot's religious beliefs, one risks being impertinent. But the conversion has been the object of such intemperate comment that I think it worth saying that Eliot's right to become a Christian is as clear as anyone else's right not to. I don't understand why Eliot's becoming a Christian attracts more aggressive comment than any other poet's agnosticism. If it could be shown that his conversion resulted in the impoverishment of his poetry, that would be a different matter, but it hasn't been shown. There are readers who think *The Waste Land* Eliot's greatest poem, and the poetry of his Christian years a falling off from that achievement. But that, too, is a difficult case to make. A list of Eliot's most achieved poems that did not find places for "Marina," "Ash-Wednesday," and at least three of the four *Quartets*—I have doubts about "The Dry Salvages"—would be an eccentric show.

But it is reasonable to ask, within the context of Christianity, not what precisely did Eliot believe and practice but rather what particular tradition, or traditions, within Christianity did he avow, since there is a certain latitude in that communion? The question is worth asking, because until we try to answer it we can't be sure where, in reading Eliot's later poems, the emphasis should fall.

When he rejected the Unitarianism in which he was brought up, Eliot moved toward the most stringent theology he could find. Within Christianity, two traditions engaged him. One was Augustinian: it involved the theological exactitudes extending from Augustine to Pascal. The other was the mystical tradition, which Eliot understood mainly from Evelyn Underhill's book on mysticism—and it took the particular emphasis, for Eliot, of his reverence for the English medieval mystics and especially for Juliana of Norwich. He found enough scholasticism, Aristotle, and Aquinas in the *Divine Comedy* and the *Vita Nuova* to reconcile every theological tradition he valued. Those affiliations might with equal force have led Eliot into the Roman Catholic rather than the Anglican Church. He submitted to Canterbury rather than to Rome, I think, because he wanted to pay tribute to England, both the England in which he chose to live and the England of the early seventeenth century, from which his ancestors had set out to make a new life in America. He revered the English church of Lancelot Andrewes, Donne, Herbert, and Nicholas Ferrar. Besides, he did not regard the differences between Canterbury and Rome as at all comparable to those that distinguished Christianity from paganism.

For Eliot, as for any Christian, the founding event of the Christian myth is the Incarnation, the birth of Christ as Son of God. The chief purpose of human life, seen in the light of the Incarnation, is "to glorify God and enjoy Him for ever."[5] In that pilgrimage, the crucial force is faith, which takes precedence even over morals: religion "is not, and can never survive as, simply a code of morals." Morals are a consequence of one's faith, not a cause of it. Faith is never as secure as a believer would wish it to be, but doubt and uncertainty "are merely a variety of belief."[6] Genuine blasphemy, as in Baudelaire, depends upon the belief it affronts. Like any other Christian, but with unusually reiterated emphasis, Eliot believed in Original Sin, and he insisted that without a conviction of that categorical guilt, human life becomes trivial or brutal. In *After Strange Gods*, he claimed that the diabolic element in modern literature was related to the loss of the idea of Original Sin: with its disappearance, and "with the disappearance of the idea of intense moral struggle, the human beings presented to us both in poetry and in prose fiction today . . . tend to become less and less real." It is, Eliot said, "in moments of moral and spiritual struggle depending upon spiritual sanctions, rather than in those 'bewildering minutes' in which we are all very much alike, that men and women came nearest to being real."[7] The bewildering minutes—a phrase Eliot found in *The Revenger's Tragedy*—are those in which, through lust or other violence, we merely lose ourselves.

Eliot's most emphatic statements on sin are in his essays on Dante, Pascal, and Baudelaire. In the essay on Baudelaire he says that "in the middle nineteenth century, the age which (at its best) Goethe had prefigured, an age of bustle, programmes, platforms, scientific progress, humanitarianism and revolutions which improved nothing, an age of progressive degradation, Baudelaire perceived that what really matters is Sin and Redemption." To such a mind, the "recognition of the reality of Sin is a New Life; and the possibility of damnation is so immense a relief in a world of electoral reform, plebiscites, sex reform and dress reform, that damnation itself is an immediate form of salvation—of salvation from the ennui of modern life, because it at last gives some significance to living."[8]

It follows that Eliot insists on the letter of Christian doctrine that refers to Hell, Purgatory, Limbo, and Heaven, and construes its spirit in Augustinian terms. Of the *Inferno* Eliot says, "the torment issues from the very nature of the damned themselves, expresses their essence; they writhe in the torment of their own perpetually perverted nature."[9] It is clear that Eliot regarded Hell, Purgatory, and Heaven as states of being, eternal conditions that, even on earth and in time, we could at least imagine. One could begin in this life to suffer the eternity of Hell. In a letter to Paul Elmer More, Eliot said:

In this life one makes, now and then, important decisions; or at least allows circumstances to decide; and some of these decisions are such as have consequences for all the rest of our mortal life. Some people find themselves consequently in circumstances such that the whole of their mortal life *must* be a torment to them. And if there is no future life then Hell is, for such people, here and now.[10]

Eliot took the idea of Purgatory with corresponding gravity. He was shocked that Yeats, writing *Purgatory*, did not recognize a purgatorial process. In the section of "Little Gidding" where Eliot refers to the re-fining fire by which the soul may be restored, he took the theology of Purgatory so seriously that he scolded his friend John Hayward for questioning the diction of the passage. In one of the drafts of that sec-tion, Eliot had the soul learning to swim in that fire, and when Hay-ward demurred over the swimming, Eliot reminded him that in canto 26 of the *Purgatorio* the people who talk to Dante "are represented as not wanting to waste time in conversation but wishing to dive back into the fire to accomplish their expiation."[11] Hayward should have re-membered that Eliot put the relevant line into *The Waste Land*—"*Poi s'ascose nel foco che gli affina*"—and quoted it again in his major essay on Dante, remarking that "in purgatory the torment of flames is deliber-ately and consciously accepted by the penitent." The souls in Purga-tory, Eliot said, suffer "because they *wish to suffer*, for purgation":

> And observe that they suffer more actively and keenly, being souls preparing for blessedness, than Virgil suffers in eternal limbo. In their suffering is hope, in the anaesthesia of Virgil is hopelessness; that is the difference.[12]

Blessedness, which Eliot usually called beatitude, is the soul's eternal gift, received from God, of His presence.

I risk indelicacy in suggesting that Eliot's reflections on Hell, Pur-gatory, Limbo, and Heaven come with particular force from a man who felt himself to suffer and prayed that his suffering would turn out to have been purgatorial and not meaningless. It is clear, in any case, that Eliot's early poems issue from an acutely personal context in which the predominant emotions are those of guilt, self-disgust, and revulsion. A religious faith that offered to make sense of guilt and suffering by extending the hope that these emotions could be turned to spiritual purpose would have special provenance for such a soul.

The awkward side of this is the question of human relations in such a world. Eliot's satiric gift was propelled by what he regarded as inescapable cause. He felt that much of human life was disgusting. In his Christian years he believed that his best practice, in addition to daily prayer, was to regard human relations as provisional and ancillary to some relation beyond them. In his essay on Baudelaire, Eliot presents that poet "reaching out towards something which cannot be had *in*, but which may be had partly *through*, personal relations":

> Indeed, in much romantic poetry the sadness is due to the exploitation of the fact that no human relations are adequate to human desires, but also to the disbelief in any further object for human desires than that which, being human, fails to satisfy them. . . . Baudelaire has perceived that what distinguishes the relations of man and woman from the copulation of beasts is the knowledge of Good and Evil (of *moral* Good and Evil which are not natural Good and Bad or Puritan Right and Wrong).[13]

The force of this position in Eliot is as if to say: love God, then you may do as you wish. Or: act on the understanding that what we do must be either good or evil; we live in the choice—so far as we make it—between salvation and damnation.

But if we are afflicted with Original Sin, and if the blessedness of Heaven cannot be enjoyed in this life, what is the status of personal relations? Eliot argues that we must be willing to postpone our demand upon happiness and enjoy it in the eternal company of God. In the essay on Dante, he speaks of not expecting more from life than it can give, or more from human beings than they can offer, and of looking "to death for what life cannot give."[14] But sometimes in his poems, early and late, he allows the reader to feel that intimations of beatitude occur and that one's experience of them is not necessarily a delusion.

The question is complicated by the fact that in Eliot's poems an event and its significance rarely coincide: the fact and the myth are discontinuous. The meaning of an event becomes available only when it is recalled; or when it rushes back into one's mind, by grace of memory; or when it is reconsidered in relation to something else, on another level of being, by an act of hope. It is only by the force of a perspective other than the immediate or punctual one that an event takes on meaning. It follows that Eliot's poems—and his plays and essays—are always displacing a conventional account of some event in favor of another one, from an apparently higher and more exacting perspective, a structure of final causes.

Eliot's way of displacing the low dream in favor of the high dream (as he calls these practices in relation to Dante's poetry), is to commit himself first to the higher perspective, the higher dream, and to convey that by a myth, if he can find an adequate one, and then to let the ordinary human fact establish itself, if it can, in relation to the myth. In poems from "Marina" to "Little Gidding," he invokes spiritual reality first, the vision, the high dream of Christianity, and waits to discover whether it can be embodied to any extent. The paradigm of such an action is the meeting of Lear and Cordelia, in act 4, scene 7, when Lear says to her, "You are a spirit, I know; when did you die?" The sequence begins with Lear's recognition of Cordelia as spirit: she must have died to one life before gaining a new life. The gradual, bewildered perception of her being at once spirit and body recovers Lear from his spiritual death.

But this order of precedence in the structure of Eliot's interests entailed grave moral risk. The priority of the pattern, the form "laid up in heaven," over the claims of any of its particles, led to a dangerous disjunction in him. One form of the danger was a moral instinct in favor of those people whom he deemed capable of consciousness, against the many he regarded as spiritually null. So far as biographical evidence is available, it strongly suggests that Eliot located his spirituality far above his mere deeds, and set a pattern in place before there was any particular need of it. I cannot otherwise explain, and can't explain away, his apparently heartless treatment of some people who cared for him and devoted many years to that care. I am thinking of Emily Hale, Mary Trevelyan, and John Hayward, people whose lives, in one degree or another, Eliot appropriated; it was as if they had nothing better to do than to facilitate the pattern he prescribed for himself. In the end, it becomes difficult to exonerate Eliot from a charge of moral obtuseness; and the matter is not resolved by quoting his too well known distinction between "the man who suffers" and "the mind which creates."

The necessary distinction is between Eliot's prose and his poetry. They served different motives. In his prose, as perhaps in his personal life, the myth takes precedence over the fact, and imposes stringent criteria in determining the facts to be recognized. Bakhtin and other critics have argued, though not with Eliot especially in mind, that a myth exercises hegemony over language, just as language exercises hegemony over the perception and conceptualization of reality. But the argument can be met, I think. Suppose we were to regard a particular myth as the narrative basis of the moral principles by which members of the community to which it is addressed are urged to live. Everyone wishes to live a principled life rather than remain at the mercy of every fact one happens to come upon. A myth is a story upon which, in a certain community, certain moral principles are defined and maintained. In Eliot's prose, the myth determines the principles to be applied, and in turn the facts to be recognized. Failures in this regard are then subjected to doctrines of sin and purgation. that one does not always commit sin is ascribed to divine grace. But in the poetry, experiences that are authenticated by being remembered, by emerging irresistibly from Eliot's past life or from a buried life of images, are never disowned. The myth by which they will be tested is held at arm's length until the experiences are acknowledged.

The pattern of this acknowledgment in the poetry is one of emergence: its most compelling paradigm is that of features gradually forming themselves into a face. So, in reading the poems, the misgiving we feel about the polemical prose becomes far more honorably a matter of degree and emphasis as we act upon the elusive movements of tone that establish themselves with extraordinary delicacy. The poems to offer in evidence of this emergence, with an implication of an achievement on Eliot's part at once poetic and moral, are "Marina" and "Little Gidding."

## II

"Marina" begins with an epigraph from Seneca's *Hercules Furens*, Hercules' first words on coming to himself from the madness—imposed by Juno—in which he has killed his wife and children. He looks about, bewildered, and asks, "What is this place, this region, this shore?": "*Quis hic locus, quae regio, quae mundi plaga?*" Eliot admired the passage, and quoted it again in the essay "Seneca in Elizabethan Translation." The title of the poem recalls the scene of recognition in

Shakespeare's *Pericles* in which the lost daughter, Marina, is restored to her father. Her words to Pericles, and his to her, suffice to compel the recognition they precede. "I will believe thee," Pericles says,

> *And make my senses credit thy relation*
> *To points that seem impossible. . . .*

Like Lear, Pericles knows that she is a spirit: he has still to convince himself that she is also flesh and blood. "Have you a working pulse?" he asks her.

Some aspects of Eliot's poem are clear enough. In the first lines the speaker awakes to the plenitude of restored images, and to a not yet secure relation they bear to his daughter. Since a soul must die to the old life before putting on a new one, the next lines record the process by which the old life, identified as Death, becomes unsubstantial. The emerging face does not present itself of a sudden, but as if intermittently, forming and fading as in a dream. Memory, bewilderment, intuitions of dissolving and merging turn for the next lines on the building of ships. But the difficult lines come later:

> *This form, this face, this life*
> *Living to live in a world of time beyond me; let me*
> *Resign my life for this life, my speech for that unspoken,*
> *The awakened, lips parted, the hope, the new ships.*

It is a poem about the new life we may be granted upon resigning the old one, leaving "the stye of contentment"—the more lavishly granted for its realization in someone else, as here a daughter. Empson once remarked of the poem that living "in a world of time beyond me" can scarcely be a description of Heaven: "The daughter in the story at any rate was really alive and in the world, and he was glad to find her precisely because his stock would now live beyond him in a world of time." So the poem makes sense in an ordinary paternal reading: new ships are what one hopes for in this life, especially for one's children. The poem also makes sense as a poem about waking up to find yourself a Christian, not knowing quite what to make of it all. The notion of redeeming one's life by giving it away is available, too, in this world: the self-sacrifice may feel like death, but it may be a better life in the long run. The poem invites us to conceive of a state of beatitude, as the face forms and the father's desires are fulfilled. The movement from "O my daughter" at the beginning to "My daughter" at the end corresponds to the difference between a questioning invocation, coming to oneself in bewilderment, and a decisive vision, finding one's true life in the recognition of another's. It is Eliot's version of Pericles's saying to Marina:

> *O, come hither,*
> *Thou that beget'st him that did thee beget.*

But this giving and receiving of lives are marked, in Eliot's poem, not by a bold syntax moving from one achieved perception to the next but by the tentative emergence of phrases, hauntingly intuited possibilities, divinations of a life for which one's ordinary experience gives little warrant. The warrant is provided, in Eliot's later poems, by the ascetic and mystical traditions of Christianity. The ultimate perspective is death, identified with the possibility of new life in the enjoyment of God.

## III

In May 1936, Eliot made a visit to Little Gidding, site of an Anglican community of about forty members, which Nicolas Ferrar and his family established in 1625; it is between Huntingdon and Oundle in Huntingdonshire. The community was of some historic significance: it sheltered King Charles I after his defeat at Naseby, it was ransacked by Cromwellian soldiers in the winter of 1646, it was destroyed by fire, the chapel was rebuilt in the eighteenth century and added to in the nineteenth. Five years after his visit, Eliot started drafting a poem of that name, the last of the *Quartets*, this one having not earth, air, or water, but fire as its element, appropriately, since its setting was the London of the war, German bombing raids, and the Battle of Britain. It is clear from the manuscripts that the governing theme of the poem was the return of the dead, a summoning of spirits from the past. The past in question was English history, and it culminated in Eliot's own struggles as a poet in the English language. Beyond those considerations, there was the Christian theme, the communion of saints—according to the Catholic catechism, "the union that exists between the members of the true Church on earth with one another, with the saints in Heaven, and the suffering souls in Purgatory." Eliot's first scribbled notes for the poem include this program: "They vanish, the individuals, and our feeling for them sinks into the flame which refines. They emerge in another pattern & recreated & reconciled redeemed, having their meaning together not apart, in a union which is of beams from the central fire. . . . Invocation to the Holy Spirit."[15] In the final version, published on October 15, 1942, this note became the lines:

> And what the dead had no speech for, when living,
> They can tell you, being dead: the communication
> Of the dead is tongued with fire beyond the language of the living.

Here we have another "beyond," a further perspective upon the complacencies of communication.

The most admired passage in the poem is the most elaborate summoning of the dead, a familiar compound ghost. The immediate source is Dante's encounter with his dead master Brunetto Latini in canto 15 of the *Inferno*. There are also continuities between Eliot's early poems and this passage of "Little Gidding," notably the face of the compound ghost "still forming" and the recognition the spoken words precede. The passage is Eliot's most achieved scene of recognition. Gradually it emerges that the ghost is compounded of Yeats, Mallarmé, Swift, and perhaps one or more of Eliot's earlier selves. The dead master is encountered as if on a London street on the morning after an air raid. The words the master speaks come from the dead; from that perspective, there is no obstacle between life and death:

> But, as the passage now presents no hindrance
> To the spirit unappeased and peregrine
> Between two worlds become much like each other. . . .

The two worlds seem to be our own and Purgatory, much like each other because the world of war and fire is much like the purgatorial process. The word "peregrine" comes, as R. P. Blackmur noted in *Language as Gesture*, from canto 13 of the *Purgatorio*:

*O frate mio, ciascuna è cittadina*
*d'una vera città; ma tu vuo' dire*
*che vivesse in Italia peregrina.*

*O my brother, each one here is a citizen*
*of a true city; but you mean*
*one who lived in Italy while a pilgrim.*

*Peregrina* means a foreigner, lacking the rights of a Roman citizen, or a pilgrim not yet arrived at the place of pilgrimage. Dante has been asking the souls in Purgatory if there is any soul among them who is Italian. The reply, as C. S. Singleton has noted, marks "a striking change of outlook":

> These souls, being already elect and inside the gate of Purgatory proper now, have their conversation in Heaven and no longer indulge in those lingering attachments to the world of the living that were characteristic of souls in Antepurgatory, outside the gate, who were as pilgrims.[16]

So "the spirit unappeased and peregrine/Between two worlds become much like each other" is still in this world, still in London, but with evidence of fire and death all around him is ready to go through the fires of Purgatory. Dante met Brunetto Latini in Hell, but the encounter in "Little Gidding" is with Eliot's literary masters, who can't decently be sent to Hell. So the first consequence of "peregrine" is to displace the meeting from Hell to Purgatory and to interpret transition as the possibility of purgation and eventually of beatitude. The first sign of that progress is that the ghost finds "words I never thought to speak." The next is that what is shared by Eliot and the ghost is the common pursuit of true judgment, another achievement of perspective, a compound act of aftersight and foresight. This perspective offers a revision of standard axioms about growing wise by growing old:

*Let me disclose the gifts reserved for age*
*To set a crown upon your lifetime's effort.*
*First, the cold friction of expiring sense*
*Without enchantment, offering no promise*

> But bitter tastelessness of shadow fruit
> As body and soul begin to fall asunder.
> Second, the conscious impotence of rage
> At human folly, and the laceration
> Of laughter at what ceases to amuse.
> And last, the rending pain of re-enactment
> Of all that you have done, and been; the shame
> Of motives late revealed, and the awareness
> Of things ill done and done to others' harm
> Which once you took for exercise of virtue.

This is Eliot's redaction of many lives and experiences besides his own. I hear in it much of the Anglican morality of the early seventeenth century. The rage at human folly is Swift's, "laceration" a word John Hayward suggested. The "re-enactment/Of all that you have done, and been" is Yeats's, in *A Vision*, *Purgatory*, and other late plays, and the poem "Vacillation." The "things ill done" that "once you took for exercise of virtue" strike close to home and speak, I imagine, of Eliot's sense of his own actions, or of some of them. There is also, later on, the sense of the mug's game of having spent one's life as a poet, wrestling with words and meanings. Stevens reported that "Ariel was glad he had written his poems." Eliot was not so sure. His doubt on that score was expressed by alluding to several writers as partial myths of the life of literature.

Of the writers implied in "Little Gidding," Yeats is the one most emphatically summoned. This is strange. For much of Eliot's early life as a poet, he did not take Yeats seriously; he was put off by the elder poet's dealings with magic and spooks, and he strongly criticized Yeats's attempt to make a religion for himself out of folklore, superstition, and table-rapping. Eliot regarded Yeats as a heretic, though not as dangerous as D. H. Lawrence in that respect. So he held back from appreciating Yeats for many years—until April 1916, if we may settle upon a date, when Ezra Pound brought Eliot to see a performance of *At the Hawk's Well* in London. Thereafter, Eliot knew that Yeats was a major poet, and he read the middle poems in a much more respectful light. But Yeats had to die before Eliot gave him full recognition as the greatest poet of his time, a tribute he paid in his memorial lecture in Dublin. Praising Yeats as "pre-eminently the poet of middle age," Eliot quoted "The Spur":

> You think it horrible that lust and rage
> Should dance attendance upon my old age;
> They were not such a plague when I was young;
> What else have I to spur me into song?

On that poem, Eliot commented:

> These lines are very impressive and not very pleasant, and the
> sentiment has recently been criticized by an English critic whom
> I generally respect. But I think he misread them. I do not read
> them as a personal confession of a man who differed from other
> men, but of a man who was essentially the same as most other
> men; the only difference is in the greater clarity, honesty, and vig-
> our. To what honest man, old enough, can these sentiments be
> entirely alien? They can be subdued and disciplined by religion,
> but who can say that they are dead? Only those to whom the
> maxim of La Rochefoucauld applies: "Quand les vices nous
> quittent, nous nous flattons de la créance que c'est nous qui les
> quittons." The tragedy of Yeats's epigram is all in the last line.[17]

The Yeats of "The Spur" is the poet who comes most powerfully into
"Little Gidding." The perspective from which the ghost speaks is
chiefly that of Yeats's last poems: "The Spur" was written in December 1936, a little more than two years before his death. It is especially
appropriate that in "Little Gidding" the hope of the purgatorial experience and of passing through it to paradise is suggested in figurative
terms common to Yeats and Dante:

> From wrong to wrong the exasperated spirit
> Proceeds, unless restored by that refining fire
> Where you must move in measure, like a dancer.

The refining fire is a translation, as we have seen, from Dante. It is also
an allusion to the spiritual fire of Yeats's "Sailing to Byzantium" and
"Byzantium." In the third stanza of "Sailing to Byzantium" Yeats summons the "sages standing in God's holy fire" to be "the singing-
masters of my soul." The passage in "Little Gidding" is Eliot's version
of the same summoning, just as the words of the ghost are his judgment upon the condition of being "caught in that sensual music." The

moving in measure like a dancer is pure Yeats, not only the poet of "Among School Children"—

> *Labour is blossoming or dancing where*
> *The body is not bruised to pleasure soul—*

but the dramatist of the *Plays for Dancers*. Measure or dance is movement according to the highest perspective of form.

The rest of "Little Gidding" is inhabited by four interrelated concerns: memory, the past, love, and language. Each is adduced in the light of the end of all merely temporal things, and each shows an aspect different from the one disclosed by its common provenance.

Memory includes its voluntary and its involuntary characters. Why, Eliot wondered in *The Use of Poetry and the Use of Criticism*, out of all the experiences that one has had, do a certain few assert themselves, keep coming back: like his own experience, as a boy on summer vacation in Gloucester, peering through sea water in a rock pool and finding for the first time a sea anemone? Voluntary memory is the act of summoning the otherwise gone figures from his past, not in the hope of recovering them as they were but of finding one's apprehension of them becoming a new thing in the later light:

> *See, now they vanish,*
> *The faces and places, with the self which, as it could, loved them,*
> *To become renewed, transfigured, in another pattern.*

Here the process of revision, which corresponds to a Jamesian scruple, is conveyed through the elaborately suspended syntax, as if no noun could reach its verb, no past participle settled upon, till every possible form of it had been considered.

But memory, in Eliot, is a morally complicated act. It was crucial to him not because he needed to retain sensitive continuity with gone occasions but because he felt impelled to release himself from their importunity. They could not make a claim upon him while he brooded upon their significance. Like certain mystics, he enriched his spirituality by detaching himself from every object that might claim his desire. There is a passage in Rilke's *The Notebooks of Malte Laurids Brigge* that might usefully be brought into Eliot's context:

And still it is not yet enough to have memories. One must be able to forget them when they are many and one must have the great patience to wait until they come again. For it is not yet the memories themselves. Not till they have turned to blood within us, to glance and gesture, nameless and no longer to be distinguished from ourselves—not till then can it happen that in a most rare hour the first word of a verse arises in their midst and goes forth from them.[18]

In Eliot's case, the memories no longer to be distinguished from him-self must not bring with them any intimation of desire; they must minister to his vision, not to his appetitive zest:

> *This is the use of memory:*
> *For liberation—not less of love but expanding*
> *Of love beyond desire, and so liberation*
> *From the future as well as the past.*

The possibility of achieving love beyond desire has been well under-stood in the history of ethics, and especially in those ethical principles that are based upon aesthetic appreciation. It is a harder possibility when the object of love is a person. It is difficult, where human rela tions are concerned, to appeal to a perspective beyond desire: the ap-peal casts doubt on the reality of the feelings engaged. What Eliot speaks of as liberation is hard to distinguish from indifference; only the misgiving revealed in the poems keeps the distinction alive.

As for the past, it has been the subject of much rumination in "Burnt Norton." The third section of "Little Gidding" seems to dis-avow nostalgia: let the dead bury their dead. Again the admonition is the same: consider the end, the idea, the ideal form of whatever claims your attention. In this passage Eliot distinguishes, among the dead, be-tween the fortunate, those who have won, and the defeated, who in some sense have not—or not merely—lost. Walter Benjamin main-tained, in his "Theses on the Philosophy of History," that history is al-ways recited in favor of those who have won: there has never been a history of the defeated. But in the perspective of "Little Gidding,"

> *Whatever we inherit from the fortunate*
> *We have taken from the defeated*

> *What they had to leave us—a symbol:*
> *A symbol perfected in death.*

This symbol differs from Yeats's, which is always in nature and shared life even when he longs to find it, or to project himself, "out of nature." Eliot is unwilling to recognize a symbol as such until he has seen or imagined its force in the light of death; according to that vision, time is no longer mere *tempus*, one-thing-after-another, but *aevum*, time redeemed in the end and meanwhile lived in the light of that end.

And there is language. In *The Waste Land*, Eliot was much concerned with the question of authority in language, with the different sources and kinds and degrees of authority that sustain our words or fail to sustain them. In "Little Gidding," released now from the familiar compound ghost, he speaks of language no longer in the apocalyptic or demotic terms of *The Waste Land* but by appeal to the idea of a decently composed sentence:

> *And every phrase*
> *And sentence that is right (where every word is at home,*
> *Taking its place to support the others,*
> *The word neither diffident nor ostentatious,*
> *An easy commerce of the old and the new,*
> *The common word exact without vulgarity,*
> *The formal word precise but not pedantic,*
> *The complete consort dancing together)*
> *Every phrase and every sentence is an end and a beginning,*
> *Every poem an epitaph.*

Every poem is an epitaph in the sense that it commemorates feelings otherwise formless if not defunct. Wordsworth, another poet sensitive to memory and the decencies of our important occasions, wrote essays upon epitaphs that are among the finest considerations of the question: what should one say, given that occasions call for something to be said? "Little Gidding" continues:

> *And any action*
> *Is a step to the block, to the fire, down the sea's throat*

Or to an illegible stone: and that is where we start.
We die with the dying:
See, they depart, and we go with them.
We are born with the dead:
See, they return, and bring us with them.


IV


"See, they return" is an allusion to a poem by Pound about the return
of the gods: the gods, figures of an otherwise lost time, are seen returning, wavering, but they are still unmistakably gods. I take Eliot's
allusion to Pound's poem as indicating how we are to read this one,
"Little Gidding": it, too, is a poem about the return, the survival, of
the gods. There is a well-established history of this motif, to be con-
sulted in Jean Seznec's *The Survival of the Pagan Gods: The Mythological
Tradition and Its Place in Renaissance Humanism and Art*. Variations on
the theme are to be found in Heine's "The Gods in Exile" (1853), in
Gautier's essay on Leonardo (1864), the chapter on Pico della
Mirandola in Pater's *Studies in the History of the Renaissance* (1873), and
his "Apollo in Picardy" (1893). Heine describes, in a passage that Pater
quotes, how the gods of the older world, at the time of the triumph
of Christianity, hid themselves among us here on earth under all sorts
of disguises. That Apollo should be imagined turning up in Picardy is
only one such instance of survival.

If we read "Little Gidding" as a poem about the survival of the
gods, it is hardly necessary to say that Eliot's gods are not Pound's or
Pater's or Gautier's or Heine's. He finds his God according to the theology of the Christian church, and therefore can freely summon as if
they were lesser gods those men and women who were important to
him in the respects he cared about; figures from his personal history,
his family, the history of literature—mainly in English, French, and
Dante's Italian. The allusion to Pound's poem is Eliot's way of paying
tribute to one of his masters, and at the same time of separating himself from Pound in the consideration that mattered more. Pound took
his gods where he found them, just as he took his myths opportunely
if not opportunistically from Confucius, Ovid, Jefferson, and anyone
else he admired. Remember that I have remembered, Pound said. It
was far more important to Eliot that he believed and that he subordi-

nated to belief every other consideration. The communication of the
dead is tongued with fire beyond the language of the living because
the dead are now, as we are not yet, complete, perfected in death.
"Tongued with fire": an allusion, first and foremost, to the episode in
the Acts of the Apostles when the apostles, gathered in a room, suddenly heard what sounded like a great wind from Heaven, and something appeared to them that seemed like tongues of fire; the tongues
separated and came to rest on the head of each of them. The shape of
the flame as in Isaiah 6 is associated with prophecy, the gift of tongues.
A further explication is given in the last lines of "Little Gidding":

> *And all shall be well and*
> *All manner of thing shall be well*
> *When the tongues of flame are in-folded*
> *Into the crowned knot of fire*
> *And the fire and the rose are one.*

The immediate allusion is to the consolation offered in a vision to
Lady Juliana; then to the passage in *The Dark Night of the Soul* in
which St. John of the Cross says that love is like fire, which always
rises up with the desire to be absorbed in the center of its sphere. A
further reference is to the passage in the *Paradiso*, canto 33, where
Dante sees the divine vision as scattered leaves of the universe, in-
gathered now by love in one mass: substance and accident and their
relations ("sustanzia ed accidenti, e lor costume") as though fused together, "so that what I speak of is one simple flame" ("che cio ch' io
dico e un semplice lume").

   At the end of "Little Gidding," Eliot has reconciled, more completely than anywhere else in his poetry, myth and fact, mitigating the
abstraction of the one, the rigidity of the other. That he saw his poetic
aim in these terms, one can hardly doubt, especially in view of the admiration he expressed in his essay on Dante for "the power of the
master who could thus at every moment realize the inapprehensible in
visual images." Referring to the lines in the *Paradiso* in which Neptune
is imagined full of wonder at the passage of the Arno over his head,
Eliot said that he did not know anywhere in poetry "a more authentic
sign of greatness" than the power of association that could introduce
the river and the god of the waves into a presentation of the divine
vision.

## V

Eliot has again become a controversial poet. But the grounds of the dispute are not those on which readers of *Prufrock and Other Observations* and *The Waste Land* quarrelled. The poetry, as evidenced in "The Love Song of J. Alfred Prufrock," "Portrait of a Lady," "Gerontion," "La Figlia Che Piange," "Marina," "Ash-Wednesday," "Burnt Norton," "East Coker," and "Little Gidding," is the work of a major poet. I can't see how it could be thought to be anything less. But the current exacerbations, in Eliot's vicinity, touch the poetry hardly at all; they have to do with the image of Eliot as an authoritarian social critic, allegedly a sinister figure concealing himself behind an urbane style. There is much talk of Eliot's anti-Semitism, especially by critics who have no scruple in presenting themselves as hating Christianity. Some readers are affronted that Eliot, even more successfully than Pound, appropriated Modernism, and established his version of a Symbolist and Modernist program as the only one worth pursuing. Most of this complaint issues from critics who advance the claims of an alternative ideology, American pragmatism in the service of populism. But there is a far larger issue, arising from the question with which I began: the Yeatsian issue of fact and myth. The only reason for seeking a myth or accepting one is that you want to submit to something other than your own will, either because you regard your will as dubious or because you want to surrender it to a force of greater explanatory power. Many readers who resent Eliot's conversion to Christianity claim that what they resent is his submission to any authority; it merely happened to be Christianity. They believe that after the Holocaust, no institution has the right to claim moral privilege.

Poets since Yeats and Eliot haven't given up looking for a source of order other than their own charisma. Olson's *Maximus* poems are just as dependent as Yeats's upon a philosophy of history. Robert Duncan turns toward myths as resolutely as Eliot does or the Joyce of *Ulysses* and *Finnegans Wake*. But most of the poems one reads in magazines seem to trust in the power or the idiosyncrasy of their particular voices; they recite experiences, often local and domestic, and let the myths recede. Frost and Stevens, rather than Eliot or Yeats, are their masters: Frost, who got much from Emerson and more from Darwin but deemed the power of his individual will sufficient for any poetic purpose; Stevens, who wrote, in *Notes Toward a Supreme Fiction*:

> *Phoebus is dead, ephebe. But Phoebus was*
> *A name for something that never could be named.*
> *There was a project for the sun and is.*
>
> *There is a project for the sun. The sun*
> *Must bear no name, gold flourisher, but be*
> *In the difficulty of what it is to be.*

Where Eliot named the project in Christian terms—Pentecostal fire, Ash Wednesday, the Annunciation—Stevens retained the gods of an old world only as sites of a project that may or may not be pursued but must in any case live without the names. The pagan gods survive in Stevens hardly better than the Christian one, and only because they make no demands upon belief or practice. Much as I love *Notes Toward a Supreme Fiction*, I have never understood how Stevens's relation to the fictions he composes upon his sole authority can be accounted belief.

Nor do I understand why it is necessary to choose, as here between Eliot and Stevens. I see no difficulty in acting upon the program that Empson recommended—more in theory than in his subsequent practice, I admit—in *Milton's God*. "The central function of imaginative literature," he maintained, "is to make you realize that other people act on moral convictions different from your own."[19] I applaud the sentiment and only wish it were more generously practised. I assume that Empson's "other people" include Christians, in which case we should not be hearing a prejudicial word against their beliefs, and Eliot should be celebrated for the eloquence, the distinctly creative force of his poems.

# ON "BURNT NORTON"

For even when hours and days go by in silence and the
   phone
Never rings, and widely spaced drops of water
Fall from the eaves, nothing is any longer a secret
And one can live alone rejoicing in this:
That the years of war are far off in the past or the future,
That memory contains everything. And you see slipping
   down a hallway
The past self you decided not to have anything to do with
   any more
And it is a more comfortable you, dishonest perhaps,
But alive.
                                        —John Ashbery, "A Wave"

The first readers of "Burnt Norton" did not know that they were rehearsing a quartet or that it might be useful to think of certain works by Bartók and by Beethoven. Or that the poem was the first of a sequence rather than what it appeared to be, the last poem of the book in hand, *Collected Poems 1909–1935*. Residents of Gloucestershire might have known that Burnt Norton was an old manor house, no longer occupied, near Chipping Campden, and perhaps that the house had a garden, neglected now, and pools now dry. Many readers thought that Eliot's career as a poet was finished and that he had committed himself to literary, social, political, and religious criticism. "Burnt Norton" had an air of finality about it: the end of a book of poems collected, not selected.

Readers who knew Greek probably assumed that Eliot, a poet much given to epigraphs, had left two fragments from Heraclitus untranslated because no translation into English could encompass the diverse meanings of the Greek *Logos*. Readers who did not know Greek probably assumed that Eliot's English would give the gist of the Greek matter in due time. A few readers may have gone to the bother of translating the Greek somewhat in these terms: (1) Although the Word is common to all, most people live as if each had a private intelligence of his own, and (2) The way up and the way down are one and the same. A rebuke, followed by an opacity, directed those readers into a poem that begins with its own opacity, four unforthcoming sentences about time.

In 1936, readers could not know that those statements in the first fourteen lines of the poem were originally written for the Second Priest in *Murder in the Cathedral*, to follow Thomas's speech after the departure of the Second Tempter. The passage was cut before the first performance, but Eliot liked it well enough to use it as the opening meditation of a poem he took more seriously than anything else in *Collected Poems 1909–1935*.

No reader in 1936 knew that Burnt Norton was a special place for Eliot, that sometime between late August and early September 1935 he had wandered about the garden there in the company of Emily Hale, a woman he might have married if he had not married Vivien Haigh-Wood. By the late summer of 1934, Eliot had started a legal process of separation, but in every spiritual sense he was still married. The emotions he felt in the company of Emily Hale may have included regret for years mainly wasted and remorse for things ill done, but there was no question of seeking a divorce and starting a new life with Emily Hale or any other woman.

The only advantage we have over the first readers of "Burnt Norton" is our sense of the significance of the poem's coming between *Murder in the Cathedral* and *The Family Reunion*, plays in which many feelings barely disclosed in "Burnt Norton" are more explicitly expressed: notably self-disgust, a conviction of the meaninglessness of any life closed against divine grace, a sense that the important consideration is not our feelings but the pattern we may make of them. The plays feature the same imagery as "Burnt Norton": enchanted gardens, sudden illuminations, gates opened or closed, clouds concealing the sun, children in foliage, the still point of a turning world; these, and motifs of loss, revulsion, temptation, inner and outer compulsion, and in the end achieved patience, assent to the will of God.

The first readers of "Burnt Norton" knew as much as they needed to know about Eliot's beliefs, or at least about the beliefs that inhabit the poem: they were clearly stated, for instance, in Eliot's introduction to the *Pensées* of Pascal:

> We cannot quite understand any of the parts, fragmentary as they are, without some understanding of the whole. Capital, for instance, is his analysis of the *three orders*: the order of nature, the order of mind, and the order of charity. These three are *discontinuous*; the higher is not implicit in the lower as in an evolutionary doctrine it would be. In this distinction Pascal offers much about which the modern world would do well to think. And indeed, because of his unique combination and balance of qualities, I know of no religious writer more pertinent to our time. The great mystics, like St. John of the Cross, are primarily for readers with a special determination of purpose; the devotional writers, such as St. François de Sales, are primarily for those who already feel consciously desirous of the love of God; the great theologians are for those interested in theology. But I can think of no Christian writer, not Newman even, more to be commended than Pascal to those who doubt, but who have the mind to conceive, and the sensibility to feel, the disorder, the futility, the meaninglessness, the mystery of life and suffering, and who can only find peace through a satisfaction of the whole being.

That passage, available since 1931, gives as much of Eliot's belief, and of his insistence on it, as a reader of "Burnt Norton" needs to know. Not that even as much as this is necessary, because something approaching it can be deduced from the poem or divined within it. The merit of knowing the nature of Eliot's belief and its particular vocabularies—sufficiently indicated by reference to Augustine, St. John of the Cross, Donne, Andrewes, Hooker, Pascal, and the English medieval mystics—is that we know what not to expect, the concessions and felicities in the absence of which F. R. Leavis and other readers of "Burnt Norton" have been affronted to the point of rejecting the main thrust of the poem. There is no need to feel affronted: the poetry does not depend upon a doctrine held but upon a doctrine felt. To read "Burnt Norton," it is necessary only to conceive a form of feeling, different from one's own if it has to be, and to imagine what that form means to a mind that holds it or is possessed by it.

The four statements about time with which the poem begins can't have won many readers; they sound like a bewildered seminar. Their value consists not in what they say about time but in starting a form of discourse in which the nature of the speaker is the least germane consideration. These sentences are propelled not by a speaker in charge of them but by solemn, impersonal agitations maintained as if without human intervention. Progress from one phrase to the next is made chiefly by repetitions of the emphasized words—"time," "past," "present," "future"—and the discrimination of conditions in their vicinity: what might have been, what has been. Not that the sentences are trivial. The first one—"Time present and time past/Are both perhaps present in time future,/And time future contained in time past"—implies determinism, since every aspect of time is already inscribed in a future we can't know. The second—"If all time is eternally present/All time is unredeemable"—moves the determinism to the present continuous tense but doesn't otherwise improve the situation: "unredeemable" because not open to change. In *The Family Reunion*, Harry tries to tell Charles and Gerald how he feels:

> *I am the old house*
> *With the noxious smell and the sorrow before morning,*
> *In which all past is present, all degradation*
> *Is unredeemable.*

Later, he says to Dr. Warburton:

> *Your ordinary murderer*
> *Regards himself as an innocent victim.*
> *To himself he is still what he used to be*
> *Or what he would be. He cannot realise*
> *That everything is irrevocable,*
> *The past unredeemable.*

The poem's third statement—"What might have been is an abstraction/Remaining a perpetual possibility/Only in a world of speculation"—posits a world such as Stephen Dedalus's in *Ulysses*, where Stephen diverts himself with Aristotelian notions of potentiality and actuality: "Or was that only possible which came to pass?" In the fourth sentence, not a moment too soon, determinism seems to be set aside—"What might have been and what has been/Point to one end, which is always present"—a release effected by letting several possibilities, including hopeful ones, hover upon the hospitably ambiguous "end." We read this "end" as purpose, the ultimate aim, as well as the conclusion. Nothing in the sentence makes forgiveness impossible, or the reception of divine grace, or the reconstitution of one's past life in another pattern.

The direction of this passage, its abstracting style, maintains a distanced relation to events. No impression of immediacy, of an irresistibly punctual convergence of deed and word, experience and the words for it, is allowed to enforce itself. Events will intrude, but only at the one remove of memory. Even then, they are events that didn't happen but might have happened. So while the governing style seems to change from abstract to concrete, from generalizing to narrative, the change is only ostensible, at the double remove of "memory" and "echo."

In Eliot's poetry, birds, not people, urge one to seize the day, and often the listener lives to regret the urging. Or in the presence of birds one is willing to risk immediacies of sense, as in "Cape Ann": "O quick quick quick, quick hear the song-sparrow." Now in "Burnt Norton": "Quick, said the bird, find them, find them,/Round the corner"—and even then, if a human intelligence is present, it warns of the "deception of the thrush."

Many sources or analogues have been suggested for Eliot's rose-garden: *Alice in Wonderland,* Kipling's "They," Elizabeth Barrett Browning's "The Lost Bower," Frances Hodgson Burnett's *The Secret Garden,* and a recollection of Eliot's own "New Hampshire" with its "Children's voices in the orchard." All that is required (and nearly any *Kinderscenen* would intimate it) is a sudden, momentary sense of the sublime, of unity sufficient to put one beside oneself or beyond oneself, an otherwise impossible conviction of unity among the constituents of the occasion; human, natural, botanic, meteorological—the complete consort implying perfection of being, its brevity of no damaging account:

*Into our first world.*
*There they were, dignified, invisible,*
*Moving without pressure, over the dead leaves,*
*In the autumn heat, through the vibrant air,*
*And the bird called, in response to*
*The unheard music hidden in the shrubbery,*
*And the unseen eyebeam crossed, for the roses*
*Had the look of flowers that are looked at.*

The movement of the verse is such as to discourage our asking who "they" were—perhaps the quiet-voiced elders who emerge more clearly in the second part of "East Coker." Here they are figures in a ballet of childhood, called upon to be nothing more than present. The main direction of the passage gives another instance of the disjunction between existence and essence, between the actual and the real, between temporal enchainment and time redeemable. The bird's song is in response to unheard music. As in Keats's distinction between heard melodies and those unheard, unheard music is absolute, the essence of sound as distinct from its sensible existence. The essence of sound, as Kenneth Burke has remarked, would be soundless, by definition removed from the experience of sound, just as the unseen eyebeam testifies to the essence of seeing rather than to mere seeing. That the bird, rather than the children or the elders, should respond to it is entirely appropriate—they have fewer distractions—just as the roses seem to be looked at. The status of these looks and responses is notional, only to be stabilized—and even then not in mere existence—by memory.

Appropriate, too, that the bird should convey the admonition—"human kind/cannot bear very much reality"—which Thomas has given to the terrified Chorus in *Murder in the Cathedral.* We can't bear very much reality unless and until we see it fulfilled as the figure of God's purpose:

*Peace, and be at peace with your thoughts and visions.*
*These things had to come to you and you to accept them.*
*This is your share of the eternal burden,*
*The perpetual glory. This is one moment,*
*But know that another*

*Shall pierce you with a sudden painful joy*
*When the figure of God's purpose is made complete.*
*You shall forget these things, toiling in the household,*
*You shall remember them, droning by the fire,*
*When age and forgetfulness sweeten memory*
*Only like a dream that has often been told*
*And often been changed in the telling. They will seem unreal.*
*Human kind cannot bear very much reality.*

In "Burnt Norton" the sublime moment—"And the lotus rose, quietly, quietly,/The surface glittered out of heart of light"—is one in which existence and essence seem to be one and the same. That is what the experience of the sublime comes to, an epiphany, an intuition of divine grace, given lest we despair. In "Burnt Norton," as in *The Family Reunion*, a black cloud occludes the sun almost before we have apprehended its dazzle and the heart of light from which it issues. In one sense, the brevity of the experience doesn't matter; it is an epitome, a sample of the ultimate experience, beatitude, the Heaven of God's presence. In another, nothing matters more, because the disjunction between existence and essence makes existence appalling unless we live it in the demanding light of eternity.

It would be absurd to repeat the canard that Eliot hated life and longed only to be rid of it. The poet who wrote, here in "Burnt Norton," "Dry the pool, dry concrete, brown edged,/And the pool was filled with water out of sunlight," felt the ravishments of sense just as keenly as those poets who advertise their possession of such opulence. Asceticism did not come to Eliot more naturally or more easily than to anyone else who practices it. We may wonder why he felt impelled to live among such imageries, but the speculation is null: that was the form his spiritual genius took. It is my prejudice that Eliot was a man of emotional and spiritual violence, living for the most part upon the edge of the rational imagination, compelled by imageries of pain—think of his infatuation with the martyrdom of St. Sebastian—and irregularly but irresistibly coming upon the other sublimity, of exaltation and joy.

In the second part of "Burnt Norton," we see the poetic as well as the spiritual form of Eliot's genius. When he read, in 1908, Arthur Symons's *The Symbolist Movement in Literature*, he saw that the modern

French form of Symbolism effected yet another disjunction between existence and essence. The motives were secular, chiefly a refusal of the conventions, the positivist syntax, of everyday life. But the otherwise diverse procedures of Baudelaire, Mallarmé, Corbière, and Laforgue could serve a religious end by repudiating current axioms of complacency. The notion that reality could be verified merely by describing its constituents was just as trivial as the commonplace assumptions of evolution and progress.

The first lines of this second part of the poem indicate Eliot's kinship for the time being with Mallarmé: "Garlic and sapphires in the mud/Clot the bedded axle-tree." A manuscript of "Lines for an Old Man" has "Thunder and sapphires . . ." with the thunder scored out and replaced by "Garlic," a change in the direction of Mallarmé's "M'introduire dans ton histoire"—"Tonnerre et rubis aux moyeux." There is a recollection of Mallarmé's "Le Tombeau de Charles Baudelaire": "Sépulcrale d'égout bavant boue et rubis." How garlic got into the line I have no idea, but it causes among the words "the shock of their inequality" to an even greater degree than Mallarmé's "thunder" does. The axle-tree stayed in Eliot's mind from an early reading of Chapman's *Bussy D'Ambois*: "fly where men feel the cunning axle-tree." In the typed draft of "Burnt Norton" and in the American *Complete Poems and Plays 1909–1950*, the last line of "The trilling wire in the blood/Sings below inveterate scars/Appeasing long forgotten wars" appears as "And reconciles forgotten wars," a worse line if only because the repeated "reconciles/reconciled" is a rough nudge to an apparently drowsy reader. But in either version we are in the poetic world of Poe, Baudelaire, and Mallarmé, sufficiently glossed by Eliot's "Note sur Mallarmé et Poe" in its reference to "un élément d'*incantation*." With "Ulalume" and "Un Coup de Dès" in view, Eliot refers to "cette incantation, qui insiste sur la puissance primitive du Mot (Fatum)."[1] The first meaning of *fatum* is a divine utterance, the expressed will of a god, as in Cicero's *fata Sibyllina*. Eliot is claiming for "la puissance primitive du Mot" in poetry what he has claimed for *Logos* in theology, by way of the epigraph from Heraclitus: the force we can't put into our words but may find already there. Such force is primitive and for that reason irrefutable, as Eliot recognized more fully than any other modern poet. In *The Use of Poetry and the Use of Criticism* he says:

What I call the "auditory imagination" is the feeling for syllable and rhythm, penetrating far below the conscious levels of thought and feeling, invigorating every word; sinking to the most primitive and forgotten, returning to the origin and bringing something back, seeking the beginning and the end. It works through meanings, certainly, or not without meanings in the ordinary sense, and fuses the old and obliterated and the trite, the current and the new and surprising, the most ancient and the most civilised mentality.

The one thing the auditory imagination does not do, apparently, is settle for the swift conversion of syllables into a tangible meaning. Lest we think that Eliot is merely talking gorgeous nonsense, he reverts to the same emphasis in the conclusion to *The Use of Poetry and the Use of Criticism*, where the context has to do with mysticism, pure poetry, and the Abbé Brémond. Eliot speaks of inspiration, but only to go further and refer to "this disturbance of our quotidian character which results in an incantation, an outburst of words which we hardly recognise as our own"—a very different thing, he maintains, from mystical illumination:

> The latter is a vision which may be accompanied by the realisation that you will never be able to communicate it to anyone else, or even by the realisation that when it is past you will not be able to recall it to yourself; the former is not a vision but a motion terminating in an arrangement of words on paper.

The opening passage of the second section of "Burnt Norton" is a motion terminating in words available mostly, if not solely, to divination:

> *Garlic and sapphires in the mud*
> *Clot the bedded axle-tree.*
> *The trilling wire in the blood*
> *Sings below inveterate scars*
> *Appeasing long forgotten wars.*
> *The dance along the artery*
> *The circulation of the lymph*

*Are figured in the drift of stars*
*Ascend to summer in the tree*
*We move above the moving tree*
*In light upon the figured leaf*
*And hear upon the sodden floor*
*Below, the boarhound and the boar*
*Pursue their pattern as before*
*But reconciled among the stars.*

R. P. Blackmur found in these lines the effect of behavior rising into belief, and made much of the two reconciliations, one as something that happens in the blood under scars, the other as something that happens among the stars; made much, too, of the superior drift not only of stars but of the universal course of things. The drift is figured in the rhymed formality of the lines, and in the murmuring of a language that appeases itself in the repetition of "stars" and "figured," the rhyme of "tree" with itself, the drift from "move" to "moving." In this style of incantation, "Ascend to summer in the tree" is joined grammatically to "Are figured in the drift of stars," but it is mobile enough to anticipate the "We" of the line that follows. If the passage shows behavior rising into belief, the behavior is a force at work in life, and the belief is as if congenital, given by the gods. So it is useless to ask who is speaking these words: they issue from an impersonal source and are heard as if overheard.

A phrase repeated from "Coriolan," "At the still point of the turning world," alters the rhythm of "Burnt Norton" at this point, but not the belief. What follows clears or cures the ground by removing the commonplace possibilities of description. The pattern (neither this nor that) becomes the structural figure of the third section of the poem. As in the remaining *Quartets*, when a personal voice is heard, it is heard confessing its inability to say exactly what it means or to make enough sense to satisfy the desires it has recognized: "I can only say, *there* we have been: but I cannot say where./And I cannot say, how long, for that is to place it in time."

The first consequence of these inabilities, in the next passage, is that the language deploys nine lines and sixty-three words without completing a sentence; intoned phrases explicate one another without sending their vibrations in one direction rather than another. The whole passage sounds as if it were spoken by Thomas à Becket, explaining yet again why humankind cannot bear very much reality:

> *Yet the enchainment of past and future*
> *Woven in the weakness of the changing body,*
> *Protects mankind from heaven and damnation*
> *Which flesh cannot endure.*

Heaven and damnation are both belief, the one above the moving tree and among the stars, the other beneath the inveterate scars. Each involves a scale of values terrifyingly different from those which are gratified by the convergence of our interests upon the daily events that appease them. Because Baudelaire recognized as much, he knew, according to Eliot, that what really matters is Sin and Redemption, and therefore "he walked secure in this high vocation, that he was capable of a damnation denied to the politicians and the newspaper editors of Paris."

The second movement of the poem ends with a resumption of its first style—brooding on time—and with a crucial appeal to the higher perspective of memory. The merit of memory is not otherwise self-evident. Why we remember one episode rather than another is, of course, interesting and Eliot often wondered about it, as in *The Use of Poetry and the Use of Criticism*, but the memory he invokes in "Burnt Norton" is mainly valuable because it is another disjunction between the actual and the real; between the immediacy of an event and the saving grace of distance in which we consider its meaning:

> *Time past and time future*
> *Allow but a little consciousness.*
> *To be conscious is not to be in time*
> *But only in time can the moment in the rose-garden,*
> *The moment in the arbour where the rain beat,*
> *The moment in the draughty church at smokefall*
> *Be remembered; involved with past and future.*
> *Only through time time is conquered.*

This smokefall got itself into the *Supplement* to the *O.E.D.* ("after 'nightfall' ") with an explication by Helen Gardner: "the moment when the wind drops and smoke that had ascended descends." The smoke of incense, presumably. In *The Family Reunion*, Eliot indulged himself in snobbery by separating Harry so far from the company at Wishwood—"You are all people/To whom nothing has happened"— even to the extent of saying that an accident followed by concussion can't make much difference to brother John. In "Burnt Norton" the distinction between those who are conscious and those who aren't isn't drawn: memory is available to anyone who doesn't capitulate to every passing moment. At least the "strained time-ridden faces" aren't named, though only a brave reader would claim to be exempt from the condition. "Conquered" is a gruff word—"Only through time time is conquered"—when there has been so much talk, in Eliot's early poems and in his essay on Dante, about the redemption of time. It is conquered, presumably, because in the perspective of memory an event can't be peremptory, as it was when it occurred.

It is not necessary to say much about the third section of the poem. Hugh Kenner's version of the pattern in process is convincing: opposite values, falsely reconciled, and at last truly reconciled. I might add: truly reconciled not by any Hegelian synthesis but by giving a more demanding sense to one of the values. As here: light and darkness are the opposing values, falsely reconciled in the "flicker" of the third movement, the London Underground episode, then truly reconciled by giving darkness a more profound sense, by recourse to the Dark Night of the Soul in St. John of the Cross. The motif of the second movement (neither this nor that) is repeated: neither daylight nor darkness; neither plenitude nor vacancy. But the vacated space is now filled with the flicker of distraction. St. John's distinction between the "night of sense" (available to ordinary penitents) and the "night of soul" (only to adepts of sanctity)—"This is the one way, and the other/Is the same, not in movement/But abstention from movement"—seems to have suggested itself to Eliot by his remarking the two ways (the stairs and the lift) of getting to the tube at Gloucester Road.

The fundamental motive of "Burnt Norton" is to void the claim of spontaneity; to represent as vulgar any immediate response to an event; to imply a form of life in which the meaning of an event comes long after its occurrence and in a light which is not that of punctuality. According to the rhetoric of Eliot's Christian poetry, the only event in which meaning coincides with the act is the Incarnation.

In the fourth movement of "Burnt Norton," a brief lyric trans-
acts events of the past—"Time and the bell have buried the day"; the
present continuous—"The black cloud carries the sun away"—lingers
upon an entirely hypothetical future—

> *Will the sunflower turn to us, will the clematis*
> *Stray down, bend to us; tendril and spray*
> *Clutch and cling?*
> *Chill*
> *Fingers of yew be curled*
> *Down on us?*

—and reverts to a present indicative steadied by the repeated "still":
"After the kingfisher's wing/Has answered light to light, and is silent,
the light is still/At the still point of the turning world." Again the effect of the four questions—about sunflower, clematis, tendril and
spray, and yew—is to keep the phrases hovering indeterminately above
the ground of our beseeching. The whole passage, one of Eliot's con-
summate achievements, is at once impersonal, as if the words were ut-
tering themselves in a ritual to make sense of man's presence in the
natural world, and irresistibly personal in the turns and trillings of the
phrases. The sunflower turns to the sun, but we do not feel obliged to
ask who is the "us" to whom it may also turn. An extraordinarily personal presence inhabits the phrases, but in such a way, and with such
unaggressive emphasis, as to remain within the weavings of word and
word; the rhyme of "turn to us," "bend to us," and "curled/Down on
us"; the imperative "Chill" occupying a whole line of verse without
our knowing, at first reading, whether it is a noun (like the beginnings
of its companion-questions: sunflower, clematis, tendril and spray) or
the adjective it turns out to be. The word stays in the air of our minds
till it finds its rhyme, three lines later, in "still," another word we can't
construe—adjective or adverb?—till the last line makes it clear.
Hopkins's kingfisher ("As kingfishers catch fire . . .") made a parable of
selving, the flame of face testifying to the type of individuality. Eliot's
kingfisher speaks of answering light to light, of the silence into which
words after speech reach, and the stillness poised upon the axle of the
turning world.

The fifth and last movement of the poem is its most contentious
part, for reasons I'll try to explain. Much depends on the value we

give the first three lines: "Words move, music moves/Only in time; but that which is only living/Can only die." The sentence recapitulates the statement about being conscious and remembering; as if to say that while of course we have to live in time, we are not obliged to live according to its chronometer or in deference to its "metalled ways." The distinction between Chronos (Yeats: "the cracked tune that Chronos sings") and Kairos, the time of meaning and value, is much to the point here. The silence into which words reach is, so far as it is attended to, their meaning, not their defeat:

> Only by the form, the pattern,
> Can words or music reach
> The stillness, as a Chinese jar still
> Moves perpetually in its stillness.
> Not the stillness of the violin, while the note lasts,
> Not that only, but the co-existence,
> Or say that the end precedes the beginning,
> And the end and the beginning were always there
> Before the beginning and after the end.
> And all is always now.

In *The Living Principle*, Leavis gives an account of this passage so sullen that it drives him beyond the necessity of his argument into a commentary, finally negative, on Eliot's entire later poetry. It is clear that he reached this position for many complicated reasons, including a shift in his scale of values, such that Eliot must be diminished by a revised comparison with Lawrence—a fate that Lawrence, too, suffered by still later comparison with the Tolstoy of *Anna Karenina*. Leavis allowed himself to be scandalized, in his commentary on "Burnt Norton," by Eliot's insistence—at least it appeared to Leavis to amount to insistence—on "the unreality, the unlivingness, of life in time."[2]

Eliot is not insisting on anything of this kind: he couldn't have believed it while in communion with a church founded on the redemption of time by the Annunciation. How Eliot judged those forms of temporal life which were content to be, in every limiting sense, merely temporal and to obey the call of punctuality and immediacy, is a different matter: on that, the evidence he has left is clear. In "Burnt Norton," the words that induced Leavis to protest are those which seem to entail a claim, on Eliot's part, to know what "the meaning" is: such words as "form" and "pattern," and, from an earlier movement, "the dance." But form, pattern, and dance are merely analogies, ways of putting not "eternal reality" but the poet's striving to apprehend it. They don't denote anything; they suggest the point at which an event may be brought to disclose its meaning; brought, by exerting upon it the pressure of a more demanding moral and spiritual perspective than any judgment entailed in the immediacy of the event itself. The value of these words consists precisely in their inability to do more than suggest.

That the meaning is dynamic is clarified by the "Chinese jar" which "still/Moves perpetually in its stillness." Where Eliot fails is in his attempt to be more specific than that, distinguishing between a visible and an audible stillness, and trying to go beyond the distinction. "Not that only, but the co-existence": the co-existence of what? He finds it impossible to say just what he means, as the passage about the incapacity of words goes on to confess almost at once.

In the interval between *Murder in the Cathedral* and *The Family Reunion*, Eliot had temptation much on his mind—the temptation of Thomas à Becket, of Harry's father, of Christ in the desert, and more generally the temptation of silence to dissolve in chatter. The last lines of this movement are melodramatic:

> *The Word in the desert*
> *Is most attacked by voices of temptation,*
> *The crying shadow in the funeral dance,*
> *The loud lament of the disconsolate chimera.*

I can't find any particular—or particularly cogent—meaning in the last two lines: what the shadow is, or who or what the disconsolate chimera is. Eliot is rattling old bones.

The poem ends more quietly in another attempt to represent the pattern as dynamic:

> *The detail of the pattern is movement,*
> *As in the figure of the ten stairs.*
> *Desire itself is movement*
> *Not in itself desirable;*
> *Love is itself unmoving,*
> *Only the cause and end of movement,*

> *Timeless, and undesiring*
> *Except in the aspect of time*
> *Caught in the form of limitation*
> *Between un-being and being.*
> *Sudden in a shaft of sunlight*
> *Even while the dust moves*
> *There rises the hidden laughter*
> *Of children in the foliage*
> *Quick now, here, now, always—*
> *Ridiculous the waste sad time*
> *Stretching before and after.*

Structurally, a return to the beginning: a discursive passage about time, love, and desire, a passage in which the English language, in this respect like Mallarmé's French, seems to be intoning itself without requiring either a speaker or a listener to be in attendance. As in the first movement, we are released from its monitions to the imagery of gardens, children, laughter. The figure of the ten stairs comes from St. John of the Cross and may be left unglossed; it sustains the Heraclitean motif of the way up and the way down. It would be more useful to quote, from the third movement of "Little Gidding," the passage about the use of memory:

> *This is the use of memory:*
> *For liberation—not less of love but expanding*
> *Of love beyond desire, and so liberation*
> *From the future as well as the past.*

This is what "Burnt Norton" and the other *Quartets* are about: starting from the unquestionably rich ground of laughing children in the foliage, how to avoid losing or, worse still, humiliating the promise implicit in the sunshine and the laughter. How to convert the low dream of desire into the high dream of love.

In the chapter on *Alice in Wonderland* in *Some Versions of Pastoral*, Empson remarks how a certain feeling about children developed in England after the eighteenth-century settlement had come to seem narrow and inescapable, a feeling "that no way of building up character, no intellectual system, can bring out all that is inherent in the human spirit, and therefore that there is more in the child than any man has been able to keep." This idea of the child, "that it is in the right relation to Nature, not dividing what should be unified, that its intuitive judgment contains what poetry and philosophy must spend their time labouring to recover, was accepted by Dodgson and a main part of his feeling."[3] "Burnt Norton" is full of this feeling, along with a doomed conviction that it can't be secured, and that the only thing possible is to recover one's memory of such unity, and start again from there under better, because more exacting, auspices.

The success of "Burnt Norton" is still in dispute. The reason is, I think, that none of the critical procedures developed and employed in the fifty years since the publication of the poem has been responsive to the kind of poetry we find in "Burnt Norton." I can put this briefly by saying that nobody took up where D. W. Harding's account of the poem left off. Most of the critical procedures that have been used in the analysis of poems have concentrated upon one or another of a limited set of terms: image, symbol, and structure. No critical method has arisen that proposes to show the poetic character and potentiality of discourse. It is still an effort to take the harm out of the word "discursive," as reviews of John Ashbery's poems sufficiently indicate.

Harding's 1936 review of "Burnt Norton" was the place to begin:

> Ordinarily our abstract ideas are over-comprehensive and include too wide a range of feeling to be of much use by themselves. If our words "regret" and "eternity" were exact bits of mosaic with which to build patterns, much of "Burnt Norton" would not have had to be written. . . . One could say, perhaps, that the poem takes the place of the ideas of "regret" and "eternity." Where in ordinary speech we should have to use those words, and hope by conversational trial-and-error to obviate the grosser misunderstandings, this poem is a newly created concept, equally abstract but vastly more exact and rich in meaning. It makes no statement. It is no more "about" anything than an abstract term like "love" is about anything: it is a linguistic creation. And the creation of a new concept, with all the assimilation and communication of experience that that involves, is perhaps the greatest of linguistic achievements.[4]

Harding goes on to indicate, too briefly perhaps, how Eliot's methods in "Burnt Norton" differ from ordinary attempts "to state the meaning by taking existing abstract ideas and piecing them together in the ordinary way." It might have been expected, especially after the publication of Stevens's *Notes Toward a Supreme Fiction*, that a critical method sensitive to poetry as a work in the creation of new concepts might have been developed. It has not happened. Readers are still encouraged to believe that a poem is an action (or a structure) of words chiefly concerned with the development of the resources of imagery and symbolism within the fiction of a dramatic monologue. The discrimination of concepts (not this precisely . . . or even that) is regarded as fit matter for an essay, but not for a poem. We have not yet devised a poetics of discourse in any way comparable to the several poetics of image, symbol, and structure. The result is that we don't quite know what to do with such passages as the first lines of "Burnt Norton." The problem differs from that of "argufying in poetry"—Empson's program—because such argufying is content to take concepts as they come, and to engage in conversation with them. Quite a different matter. What Harding tried to describe, in relation to "Burnt Norton," is unfinished business.

# ON *THE IDEA OF A CHRISTIAN SOCIETY*

ತಿ೧ೂ౨౬౨౨ಲ

On March 17, 1933, Eliot gave one of his Charles Eliot Norton Lectures at Harvard under the title "The Modern Mind"; the text of the lecture forms the seventh chapter of *The Use of Poetry and the Use of Criticism*, published in November 1933. Eliot took the occasion to look again at I. A. Richards's *Science and Poetry*—a book he had reviewed shortly after it appeared in 1926—and incidentally to dissociate himself from Richards's notion that *The Waste Land* had effected "a complete severance between poetry and all beliefs." Toward the end of the lecture, having sufficiently disagreed with Richards on that matter, Eliot quoted two sentences from Jacques Maritain. In the first, Maritain wrote that "the unconcealed and palpable influence of the devil on an important part of contemporary literature is one of the significant phenomena of the history of our time." Eliot commented that he did not expect most of his readers to take Maritain's remark seriously but that those who did would have very different criteria of criticism from those who did not. In the second sentence, Maritain said that "by showing us where moral truth and the genuine supernatural are situate, religion saves poetry from the absurdity of believing itself destined to transform ethics and life: saves it from overweening arrogance." While preparing for publication *The Use of Poetry and the Use of Criticism*, Eliot added a footnote to Mari-

[235]

tain's first quoted sentence, to the effect that "with the influence of
the devil on contemporary literature I shall be concerned in more detail in another book." The book turned out to be *After Strange Gods*,
the Page-Barbour Lectures he gave some months later at the University of Virginia.

I have referred to that episode for several reasons. It is true that
Eliot became dissatisfied with *After Strange Gods*, for reasons not yet
clear, and that he did not allow it to be reprinted. But his note on
Maritain's sentence makes it clear that the theme of *After Strange Gods*
was carefully chosen, the lectures not delivered on the spur of an ex-
asperating moment. It is clear, too, that Maritain, even more than
Christopher Dawson, V. A. Demant, and the other Christian writers
whose assistance Eliot acknowledged, convinced him that if he had an
ambition to assert the primacy of ethics, he would have to approach
the task directly and explicitly; he could not rely upon poetry, even
the poetry of "Ash-Wednesday" and the Ariel poems, to do the job
for him. Eliot's note also shows that in the work of diagnosis, as in his
several attempts to straighten things out, he had already decided to
affront his readers, if necessary, rather than let down a good cause.
I can't think of any Christian writer who would now promise or
threaten to write a book about the influence of the devil on contemporary literature. Father William Lynch's *Christ and Apollo* offers perhaps the nearest comparison, at least in its intention, to Eliot's, but it
is a far more tactful and less insistent work.

It would be erroneous to say that Eliot became a social critic in
1933. Even in his apparently literary criticism, he was always alert to
the social bearing of literature and of the literary positions he took.
When he entered the Anglican communion in 1927, he lost interest,
I think, in the velleities of formal philosophy and turned to the more
urgent issues of politics and religion. The themes, large and small, that
he deployed in *The Criterion* were the public issues on which he
thought he might be competent to pronounce: the question of humanism, the nature of education, and so forth. But to Eliot the crucial
issue, from 1933 to 1948, was the possibility of founding or sustaining
a Christian society—a possibility he regarded as so momentous that,
by comparison, even the terrible events of September 1938 and the
war that followed might be deemed diversions from a much greater
question. In the poem "A Note on War Poetry," he wrote:

*War is not a life: it is a situation,*
*One which may neither be ignored nor accepted,*
*A problem to be met with ambush and stratagem,*
*Enveloped or scattered.*[1]

Throughout those appalling years, Eliot's question remained the same: What would constitute a life, as distinct from a situation, however dreadful? By what means could the Christian vision of such a life be explained? In the years following his conversion, Eliot addressed that question in poems, plays, essays, and lectures. But the question had special urgency for him, it appears, from 1933 to 1948. I refer to *The Use of Poetry and the Use of Criticism* (1933); *After Strange Gods* (1934); various essays and broadcast talks, including "Church, Community, and State" in February 1937; and a chapter in a book called *Revelation,* edited by John Baillie and Hugh Martin in 1937. During the war, Eliot wrote several essays in the same cause, notably "Towards a Christian Britain," published in *The Listener* on April 10, 1941. This discursive phase of his work culminated in *Notes towards the Definition of Culture* (1948). After 1948, Eliot seems to have felt that he had done what he could, except for whatever he might yet do, indirectly, through his plays.

The book I have omitted from this short list is *The Idea of a Christian Society,* which started as a set of three lectures at Corpus Christi College, Cambridge, in March 1939. It is a difficult book to like. Eliot assumed that he was speaking to people who regarded themselves as Christians; he apparently hoped that he could persuade the readers of the lectures to become better Christians by requiring them to think, and to practice their thinking upon certain theological lines. The immediate context of the lectures was Eliot's sense of the intolerable position of those who try to lead a Christian life in a non–Christian world. "We have today," he said, "a culture which is mainly negative, but which, so far as it is positive, is still Christian." Eliot made persistent and serious play with those terms "negative" and "positive," short of defining them. A positive value, I assume, is one by which one is prepared to live, at whatever cost. Something is negative to Eliot if in practice it is neither one thing nor another but a mere pretense of being something definite. He maintained that liberalism, for instance, was negative because it exhibited merely a tendency to go away from some value rather than a determination to seek a particular end. Similarly, but not identically, the concept of democracy, according to Eliot, "does not contain enough positive content to stand alone against the forces that you dislike—it can easily be transformed by them." A thoroughgoing secularism would indeed be possible, but Eliot maintained that it would be found objectionable in its consequences, "even to those who attach no positive importance to the survival of Christianity for its own sake." These forces or sentiments—liberalism, democracy, secularism—are, Eliot implies, nothing in themselves: they have no intrinsic character but are merely the dilution of other values as a consequence of moral inertia. It is not surprising that they provide a setting for the sentimentalities Eliot derides in *After Strange Gods*. One of these, brought forcibly to Eliot's attention by Middleton Murry's writings, entailed recourse to the Inner Light, "the most untrustworthy and deceitful guide that ever offered itself to wandering humanity." Another of these "negative" sentiments involved capitulation to the cult of personality, regardless of the quality of that attribute in any particular case—in Hardy's, for instance.

Eliot insisted that these forces are merely negative, and he was ready to suggest what would count as positive. But he was reluctant, for reasons I shall try to clarify, to put forward many specific proposals. He committed himself to "the primacy of ethics" and thought that it had the best chance of establishing itself in a certain social setting. In *Notes towards the Definition of Culture*, he maintained that "the primary channel for the transmission of culture is the family." Ideally, a family would persist, extending itself in the same place for many generations. "It would appear to be for the best," Eliot said, "that the great majority of human beings should go on living in the same place in which they were born." Some of Eliot's disgust with the anonymous and rootless factors in modern society is expressed by the reference, in *The Waste Land*, to "those hooded hordes swarming / Over endless plains." A quotation from a rather hysterical passage in Hermann Hesse's *Blick ins Chaos* gave Eliot companionship in that disgust. Not that he believed that rural societies were necessarily happy, but he thought that, for a Christian society, the best paradigm was the parish. He refers to "the idea, or ideal of a community small enough to consist of a nexus of direct personal relationships, in which all iniquities and turpitudes will take the simple and easily appreciable form of wrong relations between one person and another." Eliot valued a settled, homogeneous community—even though he chose to live in London—sustained by a sense of continuity operative through local change; a sense of tradition, which in his Christian years he chose to call orthodoxy; a community educated upon Christian principles and unified by observance of Christian doctrine and dogma.

We are coming, necessarily, to certain awkward questions about Eliot's social philosophy. My view is that if we attend to the detail as well as to the broad outline of his social thought, even his most notorious utterances become understandable, if still regrettable. If you believe that the best social unit is the family or the parish, a homogeneous community having the same religious background; and if you prefer social unity and cohesion to divisiveness, then you are bound to see any self-differentiating element in that society as undesirable. The passage in *After Strange Gods* about "free-thinking Jews" is objectionable, but not for the reasons commonly given: it is objectionable because it is badly written, and, being badly written, it leaves in disorder the feelings from which it issued. The passage does not make clear whether Eliot's objection, given that the community he has in mind is a Christian one, is to the divisive presence of Jews as such, orthodox or not; or to their being free-thinking; or to their supposedly being both free-thinking and Jews. The passage is a mess; the clearest sign of the mess is the insertion of an innocuous sentence between two sentences that cogently if tendentiously go together. I quote the passage:

> What is still more important is unity of religious background; and reasons of race and religion combine to make any large number of free-thinking Jews undesirable.'

If Eliot had in view, as I am sure he had, a predominantly Christian society, the social attitude here does not seem to me pernicious. By "free-thinking" I assume he means people who are Jews by historical or ancestral experience—their grandparents, perhaps, escaped from a pogrom in Warsaw—but who do not practice their religion. An avoidable ambiguity is caused by the inevitable pairing of "race" with "Jews" and of "religion" with "free-thinking": some of the disapproval he feels about free-thinking is bound to spill over upon the otherwise neutral term "Jews." But in fact the social philosophy is no more questionable than if Eliot, alive and writing now, were to say that reasons of race and religion combine to make it undesirable that any large number of Palestinians should live in the predominantly Jewish state of Israel, or that a large number of Irish Catholic nationalists should live in the predominantly Protestant and loyalist Northern Ireland. The resultant heterogeneity, Eliot would say, is bad for everybody, including the dominant party.*

Eliot goes on to say that "there must be a proper balance between urban and rural, industrial and agricultural development." Again, the sentiment is harmless, except that it has nothing to do with the matter in hand, and it conceals the bearing of the preceding sentence upon this one:

And a spirit of excessive tolerance is to be deprecated.

A spirit of anything excessive is to be deprecated, I suppose; the particular excess that Eliot had in mind was a matter of special concern to a writer who complained that what Christians in Britain mainly had to put up with was the condition of being tolerated. Clearly he felt that it would not be good to have Christians put in the position of implying, to other people, that what they believe, or whether or not they believe anything, doesn't matter. That would be bad for the Christians, injurious to their souls.

But Eliot's procedure was not a matter of opposing one set of sentiments with another. It was more typical of him to deal with each situation by bringing to bear upon it a higher perspective and a more

---

*Professor Ronald Schuchard has drawn my attention to some unpublished letters—in the Harry Ransom Humanities Research Center, University of Texas at Austin—between Eliot and J. V. Healy in 1940, which clarify the problem of the "free-thinking Jews." Healy wrote to Eliot to complain about some alleged anti-Semitic tendencies in his writings. Eliot replied by asking Healy to cite any relevant passages. Healy then referred to the "free-thinking Jews." (I can't quote the correspondence, but this is the gist of it.) Eliot said, in effect: I supposed you would point to that passage, but in fact I meant exactly what I said. He then explained that by free-thinking Jews he meant Jews who no longer believed or practiced their religion and who had not attached themselves to any other religion. A large number of free-thinkers of any race would be regrettable; free-thinking Jews were only a special case. Eliot went on to say something quite interesting in view of his own religious upbringing: that Jews who gave up their religion tend to lapse into a colorless kind of Unitarianism. Europeans or Americans who give up their religion tend to retain many of the moral habits of Christianity or at least to live in communities in which those habits survive. The Jew who has given up his religion is therefore far more deracinated than the corresponding Christian. This deracination is the problem and the danger; it tends toward irresponsibility. It is quite possible, of course (Eliot acknowledged), that this distinction will in turn lose its meaning if all Christians should give up their faith.

In reply, Healy said he was not at all satisfied; the passage in question still seemed to him

demanding system of values. When he writes of the value of memory, for instance, in "Little Gidding," he doesn't locate it on its own ground but in a worthier state beyond any common understanding of its value:

> *This is the use of memory:*
> *For liberation—not less of love but expanding*
> *Of love beyond desire, and so liberation*
> *From the future as well as the past.*

It is a strange account of memory, a faculty we normally think of as enriching us in the moments in which we exercise it, or in the moments in which we recall something involuntarily, and it seems extraordinarily telling. Few of us would think of memory as a way of being liberated from desire or a way of replacing one relation to the beloved thing with another. Eliot removes the consideration of the sentiment to a higher ground than the one it normally occupies, so that he may reinterpret it according to a higher system of valuation. Similarly, in his social criticism he tended to fasten upon some public or conventional sentiment, diagnose it as neither one thing nor another, and then force the consideration of it into a category in which a deliberate choice must be made. By deeming some such sentiment to be merely negative, he could play fast and loose with it, show that it was not what it pretended to be but was rather the obfuscation of a genuine value not commonly recognized as such. He rarely looked

---

pernicious. If Eliot meant what he now says he meant, why pick on Jews as presenting a case in point? Why not pick on the free-thinking Irish, who would certainly fight back? Eliot then responded, saying that the whole tone of *After Strange Gods* was so violent as now to be deprecated but that he still abided by the sentence in dispute.

Professor Schuchard has also drawn my attention to a curious textual change in *Notes towards the Definition of Culture*. A sentence in the 1948 edition reads, "In certain historical conditions, a fierce exclusiveness may be a necessary condition for the preservation of a culture: the Old Testament bears witness to this." Eliot added a footnote at this point: "Since the diaspora, and the scattering of Jews amongst peoples holding the Christian Faith, it may have been unfortunate both for these peoples and for the Jews themselves, that the culture-contact between them has had to be within those neutral zones of culture in which religion could be ignored: and the effect may have been to strengthen the illusion that there can be culture without religion." In the 1962 edition, Eliot revised the first part of the footnote as follows: "It seems to me that there should be close culture-contact between devout and practising Christians and devout and practising Jews. Much culture-contact in the past has been within those neutral zones of culture in which religion can be ignored, and between Jews and Gentiles both more or less emancipated from their religious traditions."

back, once he had disposed of the allegedly negative sentiment. Nor did he practice much sympathy trying to understand why someone might in good faith adhere to that negative sentiment. He preferred to force the matter to a choice, according to the most exacting criteria of definition.

The clearest instance of this procedure is in his essay on Baudelaire, where he insists that "so far as we are human, what we do must be either evil or good; so far as we do evil or good, we are human; and it is better, in a paradoxical way, to do evil than to do nothing: at least, we exist." A dubious notion, I think.

Much of the argument of *The Idea of a Christian Society* is derived, perhaps too explicitly, from a metaphor. "We are living at present in a kind of doldrums," Eliot says—he is speaking in March 1939—"between opposing winds of doctrine, in a period in which one political philosophy"—he means liberalism—"has lost its cogency for behaviour, though it is still the only one in which public speech can be framed." If the wind of liberalism has failed, as Eliot maintains it has, then the only escape from the doldrums is by turning a negative into a positive condition, and the only way to do that is by presenting the real choice as one between Christianity and paganism. "The fundamental objection to fascist doctrine," Eliot says, "the one which we conceal from ourselves because it might condemn ourselves as well, is that it is pagan." So the entire rhetorical force of *The Idea of a Christian Society*, as of the books and essays surrounding it, is directed toward the conversion of political terms into religious terms, as if to say that the ostensibly real political terms are in fact obfuscations or self-delusions; the real issue, in every case of a consideration of values, is a question of religious belief and practice.

Eliot's rhetorical device is implicit in the title of *The Idea of a Christian Society*. His model, as he acknowledges, is Coleridge's *On the Constitution of the Church and State, according to the Idea of Each* (1830, but in fact published in December 1829). Coleridge's immediate provocation was the immense controversy in England and Ireland before the passage, on April 13, 1829, of the Catholic Relief Bill, colloquially known as Catholic Emancipation. Coleridge's book was one of his several attempts to define the principles that should be recognized in the consideration of church and state according to the idea of each. "By an *idea*," he said, "I mean (in this instance) that conception of a thing which is not abstracted from any particular state, form, or mode, in which the thing may happen to exist at this or at that time; nor yet generalized from any number or succession of such forms or modes; but which is given by the knowledge of *its ultimate aim.*" Coleridge's definition, in turn, involves a distinction between a concept and an idea. A conception, he says, "*consists* in a conscious act of the understanding, bringing any given object or impression into the same class with any number of other objects, or impressions, by means of some character or characters common to them all." That is, the conceptualizing act is one of classification, the recognition of a type or genre, based upon a perception of the attributes common to its members. An idea, on the other hand, is independent of whatever attributes happen to be present in a given situation; it respects only the end, the ultimate or defining purpose of a thing. To take an instance from Newman: the idea of a university is not constrained by the character of any university that exists or has ever existed. As Coleridge puts it: "That which, contemplated *objectively* (i.e. as existing *externally* to the mind), we call a LAW; the same contemplated *subjectively* (i.e. as existing in a subject or mind), is an idea."

Hence, and in a direct relation to Coleridge on this occasion, Eliot does not analyze any society that exists and thinks of itself as Christian. He asks, rather: what is the end, the ultimate aim, of a Christian society, whether or not this end is at all discernible in any existing society or any past society? What would a Christian society be if it were to come into being? And what changes in a Christian's social attitudes would be required to bring it about?

The type of intellectual activity which Eliot engages in—I am referring to *The Idea of a Christian Society* and the other writings in its vicinity—we may call, as he did, mythical; it is a procedure by which the mind adverts to contingent events but refuses to be intimidated by the particular conventions on which they operate; it calls upon a higher system of values by which the immediate event or situation may be judged. Eliot admired the working of this mythical imagination in Yeats's middle poems and—as his review of it shows—in Joyce's *Ulysses.* But his chief example of it comes from *The Republic,* book 9, where in answer to Glaucon's remark, "I understand you mean the city whose establishment we have described, the city whose home is in the ideal; for I think that it can be found nowhere on earth," Socrates says, "Well, perhaps there is a pattern of it laid up in heaven for him who wishes to contemplate it and, so beholding, to constitute

himself its citizen." Eliot thought so much, and so well, of that last example that he put it into the first version of *The Waste Land*—Pound
deleted it—and he translated it into secular terms in his essay on
Kipling, where Kipling's vision of the British Empire is "almost that of
an idea of empire laid up in heaven." The distinction, so far as I understand it, is much the same as Kant's distinction, in the *Critique of
Pure Reason*, between a concept, which has its source in understanding, and an idea, which is independent of experience and has its
source in reason. In Kant—and here I acknowledge a debt to Gilles
Deleuze's *Kant's Critical Philosophy* (1963)—reason forms transcendental
ideas that go beyond the possibility of experience: they are ideal limits
where the concepts of the understanding converge. These ideas are
not, however, fictions; they have an objective value. The purpose of
Eliot's book is to persuade his readers, Christians at least in some sense,
to contemplate a certain idea, a possible pattern, a social idea of unity,
and to move their wills in accordance with it. Indeed, the gist of what
I am saying, by way of elucidating the book, is that it tries to transform the reader, on every occasion of a dispute on the level of understanding, by appeal to the higher if more abstract terminology of
reason. This gesture, on Eliot's part, marks the fundamental character
of his imagination, in his poetry even more than in his plays and essays. The idea of a pattern laid up in heaven is always at hand, in the
later poems as in the social criticism, wherever Eliot speaks of a pattern as distinct from whatever *sensibilia* or concepts apparently hold the
ground of a dispute. He says again in *The Idea of a Christian Society*,
"Unless you can find a pattern in which all problems of life can have
their place, we are only likely to go on complicating chaos."

There is no merit in being dainty about the risks incurred by
Eliot's imagination, so far as it was—if I am right—essentially mythical. Eliot was just as capable as Joyce of recognizing an event or a feeling. Just as clearly as Joyce in *Ulysses*, Eliot saw what went on in the
streets. He saw, too, as Joyce did, the different things that went on in
a person's mind. He could well imagine, though with evident difficulty, what occurred in a mind other than his own. But there is always
a risk, if your respect for a pattern laid up in heaven compels the spirit
in which you recognize what goes on in the streets, that you will get
into the habit of thinking the events in the street unimportant. If the
pattern has priority, the immediate events are likely to appear merely

secondary. In practice, this cast of mind enabled Eliot to remain indifferent—or, if that word is too much, at least disinterested—in the presence of many events other people worried about and perhaps acted on. It also enabled him, even when he cared about the events for his own reasons, to hold himself aloof from those particular consider-ations of them that engrossed the attention of other people. The Span-ish Civil War is a case in point, to which Frank Kermode referred in a recent lecture on his early experience of reading Eliot. Many people were distressed by the apparent success of fascism. Eliot, too, was dis-tressed about it, but—as I have remarked—for his own reason: that it was a form of paganism.

*The Idea of a Christian Society* has had, on the whole, a bad press, and if it continued to be read it would probably get a worse one, but it has been condemned for the wrong reasons and left, therefore, mainly unread. Some readers—R. P. Blackmur is a case in point—simply declared themselves unbelievers, assumed that Christianity could no longer be believed, and made no serious attempt to imagine what Eliot was doing. In *The Expense of Greatness*, Blackmur wrote his review of Eliot's book on the assumption, premature and unexamined (since there are millions of orthodox Christians still extant), that "a Christian state, a Christian education, a Christian philosophy, are as outmoded as the Christian astronomy which accompanied them when they flourished." The point is a poor one, since the church had in the end no real difficulty in surviving the passage of Ptolemaic astronomy. A Christian state is, theoretically, just as conceivable as a Jewish state or an Islamic state; a Christian education is still feasible, and a Chris-tian philosophy is demonstrably available in more contemporary phi-losophers than one has time to read. But it is more to the point to note that Blackmur dealt with Eliot's book as if the idea it offered could be judged solely upon its probable results, upon the character it would acquire by being embodied in corresponding institutions. How Blackmur thought himself in a strong position to guess what form these institutions would take I can't say; because he couldn't begin to consider the possibility that the idea might be realized, it was vain for him to pronounce that the realization would be hapless. As an unbe-liever, Blackmur could not imagine that some other readers, Christians perhaps, would find the contemplation of Eliot's idea of a Christian society a chastening or otherwise edifying experience. "Mr. Eliot's idea of a Christian society—his idea of what is aimed at—cannot be realized in this world." It would be reasonable to answer: So much the worse for this world.

But I see the necessity of answering the obvious question: if Eliot's idea of a Christian society is not to be judged on Blackmur's terms, on what other terms may it be judged?

Deleuze's book on Kant is a help at this point, especially to someone like me who is not a philosopher. If we take seriously the provenance of an idea in Eliot's terms (or Coleridge's, or Kant's) and if, as Deleuze says in the context of Kant, "an end is a representation which determines the will," then the success or failure of Eliot's idea depends on the degree to which it engages and persuades the will of a reader toward that end. Further, and still from Deleuze, "in the ends of reason, it is reason which takes itself as its own end." Reason, that is, as distinct from understanding. A reader's conviction of this, in dealing with Eliot's book, would depend upon the degree to which he or she is persuaded that the idea is indeed independent of experience—that it does not derive from experience—and that it corresponds to the faculty of desire in the reader. One does not question a vision. Further still, and recurring to the notion of Eliot's higher perspective, the success or failure of the book is the degree to which the expression of its idea enables the reader to judge other things, the degree to which the reader is impelled to feel that the idea is indeed the valid perspective by which he or she will now judge various local issues in its light. The idea is the light, not the things seen in it; it enables us to see those things "under its particular auspices." Finally, and still having recourse to Deleuze:

> The categories are applicable to all objects of possible experience; in order to find a middle term which makes possible the attribution of an *a priori* concept to *all* objects, reason can no longer look to another concept (even an *a priori* one) but must form *Ideas* which go beyond the possibility of experience. This is, in a sense, how reason is induced, in its own speculative interest, to form transcendental Ideas. These represent the *totality of conditions* under which a category of relation may be attributed to objects of possible experience; they therefore represent something *unconditioned*.[3]

To this, one need only add the consideration that in Eliot's *The Idea of a Christian Society* the unconditioned character of the idea corresponds to its being "a pattern laid up in heaven." Its freedom includes freedom from the zeal with which we give an idea only the destiny of applying it in accordance with our partiality.

My remarks are the jottings of an amateur. But I take heart from a recent conversation with Robert Nozick, in which he suggested a possible line of argument. The content of an ideal, he said—I cannot quote him exactly—is not exhausted by the way or ways in which we manage to work it; it also includes its realization by better people. The idea of communism, or liberalism, or capitalism may fail for several reasons, one of which may be the fact that, in given conditions, the people who try to put it into practice are not equipped to do so. When we try to pursue a philosophical ideal, Nozick remarked, we associate our lives with how the ideal would have worked out in other and better worlds or with how it might still work in another and better world. I interpret Nozick as saying that an idea, in Eliot's or Coleridge's or Plato's terms, would if nothing else enrich the reverberation of our lives. Or, especially in Eliot's *The Idea of a Christian Society*, it might enforce upon us the scruple of attending to a daunting system of values. Aldous Huxley asked, in a famous essay, what it would be like to read Wordsworth in the tropics. Well, it would depend upon the imaginative reach of the reader. An incompetent reader of Wordsworth would merely apply intimations of the Lake District to his immediate context, hoping for an edifying fit. A better reader would imagine the forms and shapes of being, other than his own, elicited by Wordsworth's poems, and would not be deflected from this imagining even in the tropics. I don't claim that this would be as easy in the tropics as in a Windermere of the reader's choice, but the implied form of attention in each case is the same.

I feel some misgiving about this commentary. The poetry is the thing, isn't it? True indeed. But the poetry, especially that of *Four Quartets*, is implicated in the social and religious thought. Eliot is under attack mainly because he converted to Christianity. It is now not only permissible but almost obligatory, in intellectual circles, to attack Christianity and to deride any Christian's faith—and the attack is regularly made by people who claim to be appalled by anti-Semitism. To hate Christianity is not deemed to reflect badly upon the hater.

Nobody holds it against Empson that he published, with reiterated insistence, denunciations of Christianity; anti-Christianity is an entirely permissible sentiment, apparently. I was rebuked recently by Jonathan Culler for finding Empson's hatred of Christianity the most tedious part of his mind. Quoting that phrase in his book *Framing the Sign*, Culler added, "as Catholic Denis Donoghue smugly calls it." The implication, that only by being a Catholic could anyone find Empson's hatred of Christianity tedious, speaks all too clearly of a particular prejudice on Culler's part, which of course will not come in for any severe comment. I can readily appreciate the fact that, since the Holocaust, Israel is to be treated as a special case; the sensibilities of its citizens must be cherished beyond the consideration given to any other people. But the convention by which exceptional tenderness is maintained toward those sensibilities should now be questioned. The state of Israel has shown that in affairs of war and peace it conducts itself in much the same spirit as any other nation and is just as ready as its opponents to play rough and dirty. It is time to apply the same rules of discourse, and with equal decency, to everyone.

The bearing of these remarks upon Eliot and *The Idea of a Christian Society* should, I think, be clear. That he is still accused of anti-Semitism seems to me absurd: the charge is as specious as if I accused him, citing his reference to "Apeneck Sweeney," of being prejudiced against the Irish. His writings in the service of Christianity are mainly of interest to Christians. The fact that his poetry from "Ash-Wednesday" to "Little Gidding" is animated by a commitment to Christianity may be a problem for Leavis and some other readers; they must deal with that problem as best they can. It should not be impossible for a reader to imagine possessing certain convictions that he doesn't feel. The chief justification for reading literature is that it trains the reader in the exercise of that imagination.

But I continue to feel some misgiving. Eliot's writings on social, political, and religious themes—I refer to his prose, not the poetry—have been the cause of so much comment, much of it beside any reasonable point, that I sometimes wish he had never written a line on such matters. Suppose he had written only the poems and handed them over to his readers without saying a word of defense or justification. Could we not have intuited from the poems a vision, a pattern, all the better for not being explicit? I now find it regrettable not only that Eliot kept intellectual company with the scoundrel Charles

Maurras but that he allowed himself to be led—by Maritain, on several notable occasions—into explicitness far beyond need. That the social commentary has damaged his reputation, I do not doubt: it is what many readers fasten upon, as if it were the main thing. Eliot was an interesting but rarely a persuasive social critic, though the fact that English political life has moved in a direction in most respects contrary to the one he advocated is not a decisive point. I have never doubted that he was a great poet. Is it still necessary to say this, given the indisputably poetic power of the work from *Prufrock and Other Observations, The Waste Land,* "Ash-Wednesday," and the Ariel poems to *Four Quartets?*

# IS THERE A CASE AGAINST *ULYSSES*?

಼ಞ಼ಞ಼ಞ಼

I f there is, the main evidence for it must be "Eumaeus," often said to be the most boring chapter of the book, its sole contend- er the nearby "Ithaca." That "Eumaeus" is a plethora of cli- chés is the substance of common report. In mitigation, it is sometimes mentioned that Bloom is stunned by the events of the evening and by a far worse event presumed to have taken place at Eccles Street in the afternoon; and that Stephen is sunk in drink and exhaus- tion.

Notwithstanding its relation, such as it is, to a certain episode in the *Odyssey*, "Eumaeus" is first and last the story of the Good Samar- itan, as we are told, preparatory to anything else, in the first sentence. Stephen, much fallen among thieves, is rescued by Bloom, a practical as well as a kindly man, who brings him first to the cabman's shelter and buys him, at a cost of four pence, a cup of undrinkable coffee and a stale bread roll. After a long pause for rest and recuperation, Bloom brings Stephen to his (Bloom's) house at 7 Eccles Street. What more could a fellow do for son or brother?

"Eumaeus" might well have been written to illustrate an argu- ment put forward by Gilles Deleuze and Félix Guattari in *A Thousand Plateaus*: in the matter of language, the contents of one's mind are lore received from other minds. Free indirect discourse is the paradigm of

their disclosure, as in Skin-the-Goat's reported animadversions upon
the British Empire:

> But a day of reckoning, he stated *crescendo* with no uncertain
> voice, thoroughly monopolising all the conversation, was in store
> for mighty England, despite her power of pelf on account of her
> crimes.

Each of us takes the words out of another's mouth. Other voices, other
rooms: those voices have preceded us to become our voices, in notional relation to our eyes, hands, and face. In the following passage we
are to understand that the organs in question belong to Leopold
Bloom, but in respects not worth defining:

> The eyes were surprised at this observation because as he, the
> person who owned them pro tem. observed or rather his voice
> speaking did, all must work, have to, together.

Received phrases, not received ideas, set Bloom's mind astir: the ideas
bring up the rear and constitute, when seen as a farrago of lore, received wisdom. A language is a babble of hearsay from which consecutive sentences may be devised.

Hugh Kenner has remarked that "Eumaeus" is written in the
style Bloom would use if, pen in careful hand, he were in charge of
the narration. I agree that it's a written style, its main source the daily
newspaper, and that, like Mr. Deasy's letter about foot and-mouth disease, it sustains a man writing at a table rather than otherwise engaged
in thinking or talking:

> So saying he skipped around, nimbly considering, frankly at the
> same time apologetic to get on his companion's right, a habit of
> his, by the bye, his right side being, in classical idiom, his tender
> Achilles. The night air was certainly now a treat to breathe
> though Stephen was a bit weak on his pins.
>
> —It will (the air) do you good, Bloom said, meaning also
> the walk, in a moment.

The decorum of the written word sustains these sentences, commas
and interpolated phrases permitting niceties of adjudication and con-

cession beyond the resources of larynx and facial muscles. The comedy of the passage arises from the fact that the phrases buzzing around Bloom's ears before settling upon his pen may have suited some earlier occasions admirably but not this one. The decorum of conversation does not permit the swift, retrospective clarification by which "It" (presumptuously beginning a sentence) is detained long enough to have its noun supplied—"(the air)." "Tender Achilles" ends its sentence with a hum of kindred phrases in undeclared relation to vaguely recalled motifs—Achilles heel, and "the tendon referred to."

But the style, so far as it is Bloom's, is not that of narrative script or even of Anglo-Irish journalism but, specifically, of Letters to the Editor:

> A great opportunity there certainly was for push and enterprise to meet the travelling needs of the public at large, the average man, i.e. Brown, Robinson and Co.

And, two hundred lines later:

> Whoever embarked on a policy of the sort, he said, and ventilated the matter thoroughly would confer a lasting boon on everybody concerned.

The editor of a newspaper is an institution rather than a person; anonymous and therefore magisterial, a function of historical process rather than of psychological constitution. Communications addressed to the Editor are supposed to be in a correspondingly formal style; it is not an occasion for the colloquial note. It is an error, therefore, to dismiss as a dead thing the sentence just quoted; it occupies a zone between two forms of life, personal and institutional, and it protects the writer from incurring an entirely personal judgment.

It follows that the narrative voice in "Eumaeus" should be similar in kind to Bloom's, but higher in degree; that is, complete in its editorial, letter-writing style where Bloom's is merely partial. So an adequate if brief description of the narrator, or of the intimations we gather under that designation, is that he is omniscient in the mode of a Dublin gossip. Omniscient, as demonstrated by the fact that he knows what Stephen's mind's eye is engaged upon even though no evidence is forthcoming:

. . . Stephen's mind's eye being too busily engaged in repicturing his family hearth the last time he saw it with his sister Dilly sitting by the ingle, her hair hanging down, waiting for some weak Trinidad shell cocoa that was in the sootcoated kettle to be done. . . .

The narrator can even keep up with Stephen in a bout of synaesthesia:

He could hear, of course, all kinds of words changing colour like those crabs about Ringsend in the morning burrowing quickly into all colours of different sorts of the same sand where they had a home somewhere beneath or seemed to.

Not that omniscience is enough to turn its adept, a supreme Dublin gossip, into a competent reporter by the standards of *The Evening Telegraph*. Even more scrupulous than Bloom—whom he resembles in this respect—in trying to get the details right, the gossip has to take advantage of the second-chance resources of print to keep the sense of the narrative going:

He, B, enjoyed the distinction of being close to Erin's uncrowned king in the flesh when the thing occurred on the historic fracas when the fallen leader's, who notoriously stuck to his guns to the last drop even when clothed in the mantle of adultery, (leader's) trusty henchmen to the number of ten or a dozen or possibly even more than that penetrated into the . . .

Similarly, while the distinction between Parnell and Captain O'Shea is clear to Bloom, the narrator finds difficulty in keeping the clause of the relevant sentence adequately lucid:

A magnificent specimen of manhood he was truly augmented obviously by gifts of a high order, as compared with the other military supernumerary that is (who was just the usual everyday *farewell, my gallant captain* kind of an individual in the light dragoons, the 18th hussars to be accurate) and inflammable doubtless (the fallen leader, that is, not the other) in his own peculiar way. . . .

Still, the story gets told, in much the same way as Stephen gets delivered to Bloom's residence in Eccles Street; not perhaps the shortest way, but it comes out all right in the end. Meanwhile, the reader's interest is held by apparently minor disjunctions, word by word, sentence by sentence. A short list would include these: the difference in degree between Bloom as the man in charge and the narrator who is officially in charge, a difference comparable to that between the active voice and the middle voice, since Bloom, we are impelled to think, has an anterior existence and the narrator comes into temporary existence only with these words in this chapter; the discrepancy between Bloom (sober) and Stephen (sobering up, but not quickly enough); Bloom nearly as garrulous as the redbearded sailor, Stephen mostly silent; Bloom, forthcoming on issues social, political, and historical, Stephen breaking silence only in favor of metaphysics (the nature of the simple soul), linguistics ("Sounds are impostures . . . like names") and the development of Elizabethan song ("the lutenist Dowland who lived in Fetter lane . . ."). The crucial disjunction, like a toothache the tongue can't help probing, is the motif of the-returning-husband-and-the-faithless-wife. Bloom probes it on at least six occasions; when with Molly on his battered mind he asks the sailor, "Have you seen the rock of Gibraltar?"; when he muses silently on "those love vendettas of the south, have her or swing for her"; when he thinks of Molly's being Spanish "or half so . . . passionate abandon of the south, casting every shred of decency to the winds"; when he adverts to "the life connubial"; and when he recalls Thomas Moore's poem "I looked for the lamp which she told me / Should shine when the Pilgrim returned"—"Suppose she was gone when he? I looked for the lamp which she told me came into his mind but merely as a passing fancy of his." To make matters worse, Stephen mentions "Boylan, the billsticker," and the sailor claims to have a wife waiting in Queenstown, "She's waiting for me, I know."

So we have two motifs, neither of them original to their adepts. The dominant one is the Good Samaritan: it carries the story forward and associates Bloom and Stephen with one of the most popular of Christ's parables. The secondary motif, the-returning-husband-and-the-faithless-wife, is nearly as visible as the Good Samaritan, but Bloom spends the chapter obsessively internalizing it. Virtually every occasion brings his mind back to it. When he shows Stephen the photograph of Molly, the "slightly soiled photo" as he is deemed to say, the words "soiled" or "soiling" send his mind back to slightly soiled linen and Molly's soiled undergarments, her "soiled drawers" and the "striped petticoat, tossed soiled linen" which, many hours ago, Bloom transferred from the chair to the bottom of Molly's bed. The motif is an ironic reversal of the story of Hero and Leander, Hero whose lamp guided a fated lover to her bed.

We appear, then, to choose between two ways of reading the chapter. Fredric Jameson and Leo Bersani assume that "the dominant" is a speech act performed by each character, on the authority of philosophic idealism and a conservative ideology of the self, everything apparently external in the environment of the cabman's shelter finding its expressive destiny in someone's mind. According to this reading, Joyce's procedures would be open to whatever ideological objection one makes to subjectivity and inwardness: in my case, none. But it is also possible to read "Eumaeus" on the lines suggested for other purposes by Deleuze and Guattari. We start with a posited collectivity, represented in this chapter by the narrative voice we think of as gossip, lore, received wisdom, an attribute of sundry Dubliners. We then regard every apparent intervention of an individual voice —Lord John Corley's, Stephen's, Bloom's, Jack Tar's, and so forth—as an act of individuation permitted or ordained by the collectivity, the assemblage. The merit of this way of reading is that the clichés, the received phrases, mark a communal way of being alive in the world: only a snob would think such a life indistinguishable from death. "Eumaeus" is one perspective, one style, among eighteen. It makes light of the fact that our words are old and tired; it doesn't hanker after firstness. For similar reasons, it doesn't make a fuss about individuality: the fact that characters issue from leftover newspapers isn't a matter for lamentation. Indeed, a further merit of this reading is that it puts us under no obligation to hit these characters over the head with an ideology. Whether we call them characters or not, whether we find each of them manifesting the active, the passive, or the middle voice, are decisions we can take at leisure and without intimidation.

I choose a passage that includes many of the resources made available by the particular collective assemblage called the Dublin of 1904:

> All kinds of Utopian plans were flashing through his (B's) busy brain, education (the genuine article), literature, journalism, prize titbits, up to date billing, concert tours in English watering resorts

packed with hydros and seaside theatres, turning money away, duets in Italian with the accent perfectly true to nature and a quantity of other things, no necessity, of course, to tell the world and his wife from the housetops about it, and a slice of luck. An opening was all was wanted. Because he more than suspected he had his father's voice to bank his hopes on which it was quite on the cards he had so it would be just as well, by the way no harm, to trail the conversation in the direction of that particular red herring just to.

The cabby read out of the paper he had got hold of that the former viceroy, Earl Cadogan, had presided at the cabdrivers' association dinner in London somewhere. Silence with a yawn or two accompanied this thrilling announcement. Then the old specimen in the corner who appeared to have some spark of vitality left read out that sir Anthony MacDonnell had left Euston for the chief secretary's lodge or words to that effect. To which absorbing piece of intelligence echo answered why.

—Give us a squint at that literature, grandfather, the ancient mariner put in, manifesting some natural impatience.

The passage begins as if it were (or might be) detached, omniscient narration. The cadence of fastidious revision is established by way of second thoughts punctually inserted, newspaper-style, directly after the first—"his (B's) busy brain," "education (the genuine article)." But the sentence steadies itself into the mode of free indirect discourse, picking up Bloom's phrases (which he in turn has picked up from hearsay and gossip) and letting them do the work of reportage: "with the accent perfectly true to nature." The stability of print enables the reader to divine that in the sentence that begins with "Because" the first "he" refers to Bloom and the second to Stephen. The new paragraph is as close as the passage comes to detached narration, but the sentence about silence and yawns restores matters to Mr. Dublin, who treats with appropriate disdain anything read aloud from a newspaper. "To which absorbing piece of intelligence echo answered why." The collective assemblage utters itself in that sentence by gathering together several cognate notes: affected pedantry ("To which . . ."), sarcasm ("absorbing"), a phrase used in a finical sense ("piece of intelligence"), and a tag from Byron's "Bride of Abydos" ("echo answered why"). Such are the constituents of this particular assemblage; followed by the individuation called diversely Jack Tar, the ancient mariner, the seafarer, the sailor, and so forth, who takes the occasion to say, "Give us a squint at that literature, grandfather." Whereupon "And welcome" maintains the decency of the occasion and postpones, briefly, the restoration of the discourse to Mr. Dublin, who takes charge again with "answered the elderly party thus addressed."

The newspaper is just as much to the point in "Eumaeus" as it is in "Aeolus": source of the information, accurate or not, on which Dublin's social life kept itself going; the authority of the printed word, acknowledged even while mocked. Bloom moves in that world, borrows its hearsay and passes its phrases along. He does not complain about the quality of its lore. Stephen complains, but so did every member of the professionally disgruntled class, the intelligentsia, a French and Russian invention recently (in 1904) arrived in Dublin. Dublin was not yet, as London and Paris were, an unknowable city. Newspapers and magazines were still the means by which information, news, and gossip were distributed along with the official styles of their hearing—adequately, on the whole, if the criterion in that matter is the degree to which Dublin lore permitted people to talk without necessarily having much to say. In 1904, and even as late as 1922, there was no common talk of "the revolt of the masses," or indeed much of "the masses"; there was a proletariat, and there was trouble enough between workers and management to cause Jim Larkin, in 1913, to lead a strike against William Martin Murphy. But *Ulysses* testifies to a moment in the public life of Dublin when perhaps for the last time the printed word gave its readers the lore they required. There is no sign, in "Aeolus," "Eumaeus," or the book as a whole, of the exacerbations to come: mass society, facelessness, *anomie*, and so forth. That is another story, or an epilogue to this one.

Is there, then, a case against *Ulysses*? None that I can see. Charges laid by Jameson and Bersani are ideological opportunisms, the conduct of politics by other means: gestures of *ressentiment*. Talk of aesthetic ideology, bourgeois liberalism, and the recuperation of selves does not impinge on the book. I have never doubted that Joyce was a great writer and *Ulysses* a work of fiction as vital as Eliot, Pound, Beckett, and Blackmur thought it was. To be assured of that, I have only to read as far as the second chapter, where Stephen, after his class in Mr. Deasy's school, helps Cyril Sargent with his sums: "On his cheek, dull and bloodless, a soft stain of ink lay, dateshaped, recent and damp as a snail's bed." Not that that sentence indicates Joyce's style. He had no style of his own, but commanded many styles, each the hearsay of a form of life. Comedian of discrepancy, he apprehended the lives he imagined by intuiting their styles: content to come upon these as they issued from gossip, the newspaper, famous speeches, old songs, old poems, reverie, day-dreaming, the "collective assemblage" of a city.

# NOTES ON A POEM BY STEVENS

The poem is "Of Mere Being." Between its appearance in *Opus Posthumous* (1957) and *The Palm at the End of the Mind* (1967), "In the bronze distance" became "In the bronze decor," on the authority of a typescript in the Stevens collection at the Huntington Library:

> The palm at the end of the mind,
> Beyond the last thought, rises
> In the bronze decor,
>
> A gold-feathered bird
> Sings in the palm, without human meaning,
> Without human feeling, a foreign song.
>
> You know then that it is not the reason
> That makes us happy or unhappy.
> The bird sings. Its feathers shine.
>
> The palm stands on the edge of space.
> The wind moves slowly in the branches.
> The bird's fire-fangled feathers dangle down.

The textual change is regrettable, if only because "bronze distance" sufficiently indicates the scene and "bronze decor" prematurely makes a judgment upon it.

We have a poem of four stanzas—tercets—metrically so free that only the ghost of blank verse can be summoned to testify to the liberties Stevens has taken. No rule of prosodic law obtains, whether we count syllables, accents, or phrases. One line is divided from the next by virtue of the sentence which distributes its parts over the stanza. In the first stanza, a parenthetical phrase—"Beyond the last thought"— starts off a new line, and accommodates the main verb in a rhetorically stressed because grammatically isolated position at the end. The third line completes the sense but not the sentence. A comma keeps things going. In the second stanza, the first line is given to the subject of the sentence and its compound adjective. The second begins with the verb, which may be transitive or intransitive, a decision postponed by three adverbial phrases, two in the second line, the other at the beginning of the third, at which point the question is resolved—it is transitive, there is an object, "a foreign song." In the third stanza, sentences continue to dominate the meter, the division between the first and second line emphasizing the main noun, "the reason." The rhythm of this stanza differs from the norm established in the first two by having the sentence distributed over two rather than three lines, and by having the third line filled with two short and parallel sentences: "The bird sings. Its feathers shine." Finally, each line of the last stanza coincides with a complete sentence; the first two are almost syntactically identical, the third brings the stanza and the poem to an end with an elaborate flourish, the subject of the sentence being postponed to allow for alliterative splendors—"fire-fangled." The verb plays the internal rhymes and the final alliterations—"fangled . . . dangle down"—with such bravado as to recall the early Stevens of "A High-Toned Old Christian Woman" and "The Comedian as the Letter C." Meanwhile, the stanzas move along as if they were chapters in a novel, complete with titles: stanza 1: The Palm; stanza 2: The Bird; stanza 3: The Bird (continued); stanza 4: The Palm, The Wind, and The Bird.

The poem has been well read, notably by Harold Bloom in *Wallace Stevens: The Poems of Our Climate* and by James Guetti in *Word-Music*. I shall refer to these, and also to an essay that Bloom quotes and endorses, Paul de Man's "Intentional Structure of the Romantic Image," reprinted in *The Rhetoric of Romanticism*.

Stanza 1: As usual in Stevens, the palm denotes a celebration of being, "mere" because it is blessedly first and fundamental, manifestation of a first principle. It also denotes the fulfillment of desire, as in the sequence-surge of "Description without Place":

> *It is an expectation, a desire,*
> *A palm that rises up beyond the sea.*

It is surprising, I suppose, to find Stevens celebrating anything that is to be found or imagined "at the end of the mind" and "beyond the last thought." Generally, nothing is allowed to escape the mind's governance. On this occasion, Stevens means, I assume, literally one's last thought, one's mind facing death. In a certain mood, it is a consolation to know that life goes on in one's absence. But the status of the palm is a question. Guetti has argued that what he calls "noncognitive images" are crucial in Stevens's poems because of the relation between "effortful imaginative sequences and the last images that relieve us of them." Many of Stevens's poems "begin with the problematically intelligible," set out a problem, and worry it according to rational procedures; it is only "at the end of that sequence and after the intelligible motive has been tried and tried again" that we are released from the haggling. It is as if, "after exercising one faculty, we were then prepared to exercise another." After the ratiocination, we are given the palm and the bird. We run out the string of intelligible processes, and are then given the boon of a somehow satisfying noncognitive image.

This strikes me as one of the most telling observations elicited by a reading of Stevens's poems. But Guetti doesn't question the character of these images, apart from calling them noncognitive. Besides, I am not sure that the palm is such an image. It might be better to call it an emblem, in keeping with a distinction that Yeats makes in "Symbolism in Painting" between an image and an emblem. An image refers to a natural object, and if the associations of that object are sufficiently rich in the life of a culture or several cultures, it becomes a symbol. In either case, it assumes what de Man calls "the ontological priority of natural things." It gets its meaning and its force from nature, and thereafter from the human presence in a world in its first character natural. An emblem has its meaning, as Yeats says, "by a traditional and not by a natural right"; we come to the meaning by consulting literature and art, the lexicon of tradition. Nothing in nature gives the palm any special privilege; the privilege comes from Roman tournaments, the New Testament, Blake and Wordsworth and Stevens's earlier poems.

But even if we call Stevens's palm an emblem, we have not determined its status. If the palm is not as it is found in nature, by what mode of imagination has Stevens produced it? Guetti takes the palm as an unproblematic image, a happy release from intelligible but difficult issues. But it may turn out to be just as problematic, in another mode, as the ratiocination that has preceded it. I don't mean the obvious, that in "Of Mere Being" no ratiocination has preceded the disclosure of the palm. The phrase "at the end of the mind" may be taken as a summary of manifold intellections, as in Stevens's earlier and far longer poems. The point of my calling the palm an emblem rather than an image or a symbol is that it renders the status of the word questionable.

Perhaps I can clarify the point by referring to a passage in Sartre's *The Psychology of Imagination*:

> Every consciousness posits it object, but each does so in its own way. Perception, for instance, posits its object as existing. The image also includes an act of belief, or a positing action. This act can assume four forms and no more; it can posit the object as non-existent, or as absent, or as existing elsewhere; it can also "neutralize" itself, that is, not posit its object as existing. Two of these acts are negations: the fourth corresponds to a suspension or neutralization of the proposition. The third, which is positive, assumes an implicit negation of the actual and present existence of the object. This act of positing is not superimposed on the image after it has been constituted. It is constitutive of the consciousness of the image.[1]

It hardly matters whether we assign Stevens's palm to Sartre's third or fourth category; in either case, an emblem is posited rather than an object perceived, and it is posited as not being. In another idiom, we might say that it is allegorical. Or, a last shot at it, we might say that it issues from what Philip Wheelwright in *The Burning Fountain* calls "Stylistic Imagination," which "acts upon its object by distancing and stylizing it."[2] In any of these vocabularies, the palm is at a remove from existence. This is not because Stevens has failed to make his palm particular—this poem, not that one—but because the schema of his poem has removed it from perception; it cannot be posited as already existing, any more than can the bird on the golden bough in Yeats's "Sailing to Byzantium," which, as Bloom rightly says, is implicitly alluded to in Stevens's next stanza. Yeats's bird sings to lords and ladies "of what is past, or passing, or to come." Stevens's bird sings a foreign song, just as the cry of the wind in the leaves of "The Course of a Particular" is not in any sense a human cry; it is on the way to concerning no one at all. If it is song, its achievement of form and expression has to do with birds, not with us. Nightingales are not singing to us, though we write odes to them. The near-repetition of "without human meaning/Without human feeling" releases us from the question of meaning, mitigates its severity by calling it feeling, but the song is still foreign.

Stanza 3: If we were made happy or unhappy by "the reason," it would be because we insisted on finding the causes of our happiness or unhappiness intelligible. We would insist on talking about them, like one of Stevens's long poems. We don't: it is not a question of talk, of objects amenable to our most elaborate discourse, but of looking, acknowledging, as we look at a gold-feathered bird and feel that the foreignness of its song doesn't matter, what matters is life, its continuity, its changingness, our sense of it as living. Reason doesn't come into the matter, by definition it comes too late; reason can't recognize the "firstness" of any form of life; reason's categories are belated. Firstness is the first principle, call it mere being, according to which the bird sings and its feathers shine, and we are silently or at least undiscursively ready for these events. The readiness is nearly all enacted in the last stanza; three lines, each coinciding with a sentence, no enjambments, no complication of meter or syntax, three simple indicatives. The palm "stands on the edge of space"; a variant of the first line's "at the end of the mind" but more yielding since it doesn't even raise a question of the mind. If the mind has ever been present, it has let go, backed off to the point at which it merely—but this is not quite merely—records a fact, the palm and where it is. "On the edge of space" is so barely visualized that the phrase, like the palm, must be taken as emblematic rather than referential. The locale is nominal, we are not meant to see anything but to posit a relation, which need not be other than notional. One of our capacities is being exercised, our ability to abstract and to linger upon the abstraction. "The wind moves slowly in the branches": we have been through our Shelleyan years, and "moves" is just a little livelier than "stands." "The bird's fire-fangled feathers dangle down." Bloom quotes from Stevens's "Our Stars Come from Ireland," "fitful-fangled darknesses/Made suddenly luminous." It is hard to say "fangled" without seeming to say "new-fangled," a risk congenial to Stevens, who sometimes liked to think of himself as foppish and liked to entertain the thought of his foppishness only to see it perish. The word has long been close to "fashion," another venue of novelty for the sake of novelty. It has also been close, as in Stevens, to "feathers." The *OED* gives us Greene's "There was no Feather, no fangle, Gem, nor Jewell . . . left behinde." It also gives an obsolete sense of the word, derived from German *fankel*, meaning spark, and quotes Daniel in 1649: "There may we find without the fangle which Fires the dry touch of Constitution." The bird's fire-fangled feathers are Stevens's version of the phoenix, the diction flaming in a tradition that he is happy to share with Keats and Hopkins. Most of the associations of "dangle" have been playful, as in hanging loose because you feel you don't need to exert yourself. It has often been used to describe the aristocrat's way of passing the time; though of course he, too, could dangle from a gallows. Stevens lounged with it, especially in "A Lot of People Bathing in a Stream," which Bloom aptly quotes:

> *We bathed in yellow green and yellow blue*
> *And in these comic colors dangled down.*

When we assemble the line again, we have the phoenix still, but freed from its air of demented recurrence by turning into the amiable clown of life, who to be colorful and vivid doesn't need to assert himself. It is as if first things coincided with last things, the fantasia a merry-go-round.

I assume that "Of Mere Being" is a poem about coping with one's soon-coming death and making the best of it and being decent and undismal about it. If, as Stevens says in "A Mythology Reflects its Region," the "image must be of the nature of its creator," insofar as it is, the creator should make it lively rather than inflict his misery on others. Hence the gorgeousness of the last line in "Of Mere Being."

We could leave the poem at this point, except that Bloom, the poem still much in and on his mind, quotes several of Paul de Man's sentences as if they somehow, without referring to Stevens, circumscribed not only this poem but Stevens's entire work. De Man, commenting on a passage about origination in Hölderlin's "Brot und Wein," produced a vast generalization:

> It is in the essence of language to be capable of origination, but of never achieving the absolute identity with itself that exists in the natural object. Poetic language can do nothing but originate anew over and over again; it is always constitutive, able to posit regardless of presence but, by the same token, unable to give a foundation to what it posits except as an intent of consciousness. The word is always a free presence to the mind, the means by which the permanence of natural entities can be put into question and thus negated, time and again, in the endlessly widening spiral of the dialectic.[3]

Bloom receives this passage as if it were entirely convincing, but it seems to me to go into a wobble. At first, de Man appears to be saying that the trouble with language is that a word can't be identical with itself. A stone— that one over there, not the one beside it—is identical with itself, but a word can't be. Language can't give a foundation to what it posits except as an intent of consciousness. I interrupt this gloss to say that Stevens, among post-Romantic poets, was the one most content with that constraint; an intent of his consciousness was for him an entirely sufficient foundation for whatever he posited. He doesn't give the slightest sign that he thinks his "gold-feathered bird" disabled by the fact that its sole foundation is the poet's consciousness: on the contrary, he takes pride in that fact, and would not have it otherwise.

The wobble of de Man's passage is in the final sentence. It is bound to surprise many readers to find de Man saying that "the word is always a free presence to the mind." Elsewhere, he has insisted that it is not free, that one's sense of the free presence of a word in one's mind is a delusion, since the word is already inscribed there by the structure of the language one speaks. The ideological character of language is inescapable, even if we continuously engage in the deconstruction of whatever offers itself as "our" language. But in any case, if consciousness and nature are absolutely separate, as Bloom takes de Man to say, then the linguistic act of putting into question "the permanence of natural entities" is clearly futile. If that is what early

Romantic poets thought they were doing, they were spitting against the wind. Bloom quotes de Man as saying that Rousseau and Words-worth were "the first modern writers to have put into question, in the language of poetry, the ontological priority of the sensory object." I think Blake was nearer the truth of the matter when he accused Wordsworth of choosing not to do this; of taking dictation from na-ture, by giving such credence to memory; of granting too much au-dience to "the speaking face of earth and heaven." Besides, to put into question is not to negate; on the contrary, it is to establish the object yet again, on the ground of one's relation to it, however ironic or skeptical the relation may be.

The passage that Bloom quotes from de Man seems to me to be contradicted by several other passages, especially from de Man's later essays on anthropomorphism and prosopopoeia. I take prosopopoeia to be the trope that conjures or summons into presence—or into a sem-blance of presence—something that is absent. De Man regarded this trope, and not metaphor, as "the master trope of poetic discourse." Presumably, in that discourse the distinction between image and em-blem would persist, since the positing that results in an emblem makes a claim, to use de Man's phrase, "not given in the nature of things." But if the distinction persists, as I think it does, then further distinc-tions arise. De Man deals with prosopopoeia as if the only question in its vicinity were: will the ghost appear or not? Will the face of the ab-sent one emerge from the abyss or not? But the form of these ques-tions suppresses the many differences, of kind and of degree, among emanations that are summoned by such diverse acts of consciousness as perception, imagination, fancy, positing, abstraction, and so forth. As soon as we advert to this suppression, we see that one of the distin-guishing marks of Stevens's poem is what I might call its excluded first. Guetti assumes that the poem excludes Stevens's normal ratiocination or takes it for granted and offers the reader three noncognitive images as if to release him from the chore of patiently borne ratiocination. Provoked by de Man's essay, I am inclined to see the poem preceded by one of the great forms of the poetic faculty, an act of image-making or image-recognition, an assent indeed to the nature of things in that respect. If "the palm" arises from an act of positing and remains an emblem; if "the reason" is discourse too belated to make a difference to one's happiness or unhappiness; then the missing factor, the vital $X$ is the image. There are no images in "Of Mere Being": again, this is not a defect but a choice, an "intent of consciousness" on Stevens's part. But it doesn't give any warrant to the later passage that Bloom quotes from de Man's essay, where the theme is Wordsworth's imagination:

> This "imagination" has little in common with the faculty that produces natural images "as flowers originate." It marks instead a possibility for consciousness to exist entirely by and for itself, independently of all relationship with the outside world, without being moved by an intent aimed at a part of this world.

Again, this would be more convincing if it referred to Blake rather than Wordsworth. Or to Stevens, who in many of his moods aspired to such a declaration of independence. The consciousness de Man describes is what Yeats called reverie and characterized as taking the form of the gaze rather than the glance. Insofar as this consciousness would give itself any other employment than that of delighting in itself, it would have to be the one that Pater indicated by saying that all the arts constantly aspire to the condition of music. If the matter were to be argued further, and on the issue of ontology, as de Man in several contexts raised it, I would describe the motive of such a consciousness as angelic, and call it vanity.

Finally, a conjecture. Suppose Stevens were reading Mallarmé's "Don du poëme," the first five lines of which allude to—or at least could be eked out to allude to—Mallarmé's nightly work on the never-to-be-completed *Hérodiade*. In the morning, he has written something, perhaps a poem, not *Hérodiade* but a shard of it, and he brings it into the next room where his child and her mother are asleep and he offers it to the child as a gift:

> *Je t'apporte l'enfant d'une nuit d'Idumée!*
> *Noire, à l'aile saignante et pâle, déplumée,*
> *Par le verre brûlé d'aromates et d'or,*
> *Par les carreaux glacés, hélas! mornes encore,*
> *L'aurore se jeta sur la lampe angélique.*

Idumean, or Edomite, refers to the ancestry of Hérodiade. Otherwise the passage is fairly clear: "I bring you [as a gift] the child of an Idumaean night! [it is] dark, its wing is bleeding and pale, [its feathers are] plucked. Through the window [as if] burned with spices and gold; through the icy panes, still dreary alas!; the dawn hurled itself on the angelic lamp."

The next passage is more difficult:

> Palmes! et quand elle a montré cette relique
> A ce père essayant un sourire ennemi,
> La solitude bleue et stérile a frémi.

"Palms! And when it [the dawn] showed this relic to the father [who was] trying out a hostile smile, the blue and sterile solitude shuddered." The smile was hostile, presumably, because the poem was not the *Hérodiade* he wanted. Perhaps the palms can be explained as the shapes the dawn light threw upon the ceiling or even upon the lamp. In *The Poem Itself*, Stanley Burnshaw says that "perhaps *Palmes* simply occurred to Mallarmé and he retained it because he felt he had to— much as he introduced in another poem the word pytx because this pure invention struck him as being both right and necessary for his purposes." Perhaps; but note that the word, if not at the end of the mind, is outside its syntax. Every other word in the passage implies a context, a narrative setting. *Palmes* is a transgression, breaking the narrative, or at least suspending it arbitrarily. It is one word, free of syntax, either above or below the otherwise rational narrative, but in any case apart from the sequence. What, then, does it mean?

Suppose Stevens were reading "Don du poëme" and, coming upon "Palmes!" brooded not upon its meaning, or even a possible meaning, but upon its character of being beyond or apart from the official narrative. Might he not have placed the palms, for his own quite different purposes, beyond the category that meant more to him than any narrative, the category of mind? And reduced them to one, "the palm," making it in every respect singular?

# IS THERE A PERENNIAL LITERATURE?

ᔟᕮᕇᕤᕩᔢ

I

On January 23, 1956, R. P. Blackmur gave a lecture at the Library of Congress under the title "Irregular Metaphysics"; it was one of four lectures under the general title *Anni Mirabiles* in which he brooded on the conditions that beset the major works of modern literature. The political and cultural conditions in the first years of the twentieth century were mostly deplorable, he thought, but they somehow provoked the composition of *The Waste Land, Ulysses*—both of them published in 1922—and other peremptory works. Social distress is apparently good for literature, though hard on those who write and read it. In the first lecture, Blackmur named certain works only less famous than *The Waste Land* and *Ulysses* and written within a few years of them: *Charmes, Harmonium, The Magic Mountain, The Counterfeiters, Six Characters in Search of an Author, Henry IV, The Revolt of the Masses*, "Hugh Selwyn Mauberley," and *The Tower*. Presumably Eliot, Joyce, Valéry, Stevens, Mann, Gide, Pirandello, Ortega y Gasset, Pound, and Yeats represented a distinctive modern writing in a sense in which Hardy, Shaw, Wells, James, and Lawrence didn't.

Blackmur's lectures can't easily be paraphrased. They were concerned with the need felt by many modern artists to do without any large-scale working order, none being available, and to settle for local or partial orders which held good, if at all, only for the time being and

[269]

the work in hand. A version of this concern kept Blackmur going in these sentences:

> It has always been difficult to find a sure or satisfactory audience for the living artist; and this has become increasingly difficult in societies like our own where education has become both universal and largely technical—at any rate less generalizably literate—and which has at the same time enormously multiplied the number of its artists. So, too, it has always been difficult for the artist to find the means of expressing his own direct apprehension of life in conventions which were, or could be made, part of the conventions of society in general; and this, also—this problem of communication—has become excessively difficult in a society which tends to reject the kind of faithful conventions under which the artist has usually worked, and a society in which, under the urban process, and under the weight of the new knowledges, so much of thought has been given over to mechanism which had formerly operated under faith.[1]

Modern artists, according to Blackmur, have to devise various stratagems without a working convention or a principle of composition in sight. Every work achieved becomes a *tour de force*.

Blackmur evidently took it for granted that the people who attended the lectures were familiar with the literature he referred to or, even if they weren't, that they would gather from his words a sense of the cultural issues the literature entailed. He assumed that his listeners were willing to think about the conditions that called the major works of literature into embattled existence. What were the conditions from which *The Waste Land* emerged? In the third lecture, Blackmur quoted several short poems and passages from longer ones, including the fourth section of *The Waste Land*, the last stanza of Frost's "Stopping by Woods on a Snowy Evening," Pound's "Medallion," Yeats's "Leda and the Swan" and "A Deep-sworn Vow." The quotations were supposed to illustrate certain values which Blackmur announced on his own authority and left otherwise without elucidation. Here is "Medallion":

> *Luini in porcelain!*
> *The grand piano*

*Utters a profane*
*Protest with her clear soprano.*

*The sleek head emerges*
*From the gold-yellow frock*
*As Anadyomene in the opening*
*Pages of Reinach.*

*Honey-red, closing the face-oval,*
*A basket-work of braids which seem as if they were*
*Spun in King Minos' hall*
*From metal, or intractable amber;*

*The face-oval beneath the glaze,*
*Bright in its suave bounding-line, as,*
*Beneath half-watt rays,*
*The eyes turn topaz.*

Blackmur said only a little about that poem. He didn't indicate whether the words were to be assigned to Pound in his own name and voice or to his invented personage Mauberley. He was thinking of Pound along with Whitman and remembering Santayana's *Interpretations of Poetry and Religion,* in which Whitman and Browning are rebuked as barbarians, poets who regard their feelings as beyond question and self-evidently just. So he called Pound "a crackerbarrel Mencken proceeding by crotchets and *idées fixes.*" On the level of notions, arguments, and bright ideas too fixed for any good, Pound is no better than Mencken. But "he is also *Il miglior fabbro* and at that level knows everything, and knows besides all that his ears and eyes could tell." Blackmur recited "Medallion" without further comment but with an implication that Pound's mastery in placing word beside word makes up for everything he doesn't otherwise know. Blackmur didn't say whether "Medallion" solved the problem of communication or exemplified it.

When I met Blackmur in Cambridge several years later, I asked him how he could have assumed that his audience at the Library of Congress would cope, at first hearing, with those four lectures, with themes so difficult, sentences so compact and arcane, citations so opaque. "I wanted to do the best I could," he said. I took this to

mean: "I wanted the audience to get a sense of the difficulty of reading those works, and how hard I tried to rise to the particular occasions." I didn't ask him a better question: "How did you decide that
your audience could make anything of 'Medallion,' understand the
poem while merely hearing it line by line, and judge the force of its
artistry?" A better question, that, because it would have turned upon
local possibilities of interpretation, allusions that couldn't have been
clear to everyone. Who is Reinach, which pages are referred to, who
is Anadyomene, what precisely is the grand piano doing? Perhaps these
questions don't matter. Blackmur seems to have been content to let
Pound's words play, for their rhythm and *sprezzatura*, on the ears and
minds of his audience. Maybe he trusted his listeners to take every local problem of interpretation in their stride and to enjoy the acoustic
plenitude of those *s*-words and *z*-words in the last stanza, the eyes
turning topaz. But I wonder about Blackmur's insouciance, given that
his theme was the difficulty of communication. Surely he took an in-
ordinate risk that his audience, shaking baffled heads, would drift away
down Capitol Hill.

The reading of "A Deep-sworn Vow" offered, I assume, a different experience and pointed to a different moral:

> *Others because you did not keep*
> *That deep-sworn vow have been friends of mine;*
> *Yet always when I look death in the face,*
> *When I clamber to the heights of sleep,*
> *Or when I grow excited with wine,*
> *Suddenly I meet your face.*

Here, Blackmur said, "the senses have given a new order to thought
of all time and all eternity":

> It is not from wine to sleep to death, as thought without the
> senses might say; it is from death to sleep to wine, which the
> senses create the thought to say. In (this) poem we have what
> Milton wanted poetry to be: the simple, the sensuous, the pas-
> sionate. We have made the potential, within its own limits so
> endless, real; it is the thought which was *first* in the senses."[2]

Blackmur didn't confess to a prejudice, that the only thought he valued was one that started in the senses and retained, all the way through, its sensory affiliation. He had no respect for thought without the senses. Eliot's pupil in this respect, he agreed with him that a dissociation of sensibility had set in, sometime in the seventeenth century, and that thereafter feeling was practiced without relation to thought and—an even more drastic consequence—thought without relation to feeling. But Blackmur believed that occasionally a form of thought might be practiced that was first in the senses, as in Yeats's poem. Here and there a sensibility might be felt as unity, a capacity not necessarily dissociated. Language as gesture: that was Blackmur's phrase for a mode of language that begins as energy—sensuous, sensory, on the quick of feeling—and develops other powers as idea or abstraction but never loses connection with its first stirring. In Yeats's poem the intuition that goes from death to sleep to wine doesn't brook a question; it ignores the convention of discursive thinking by which one starts with the small occasion, wine, goes to the more general one, sleep, and ends where everything supposedly ends, in death. The senses on this occasion have determined otherwise, and they make the thought to say it that way.

I have alluded to Blackmur's lectures mainly to mark the common association of modern literature and criticism with a sense of crisis in communication and knowledge and yet to note that some of the poems that Blackmur quoted ignore every crisis except those we share by being human. In Yeats's poem the senses "have given a new order to thought of all time and all eternity." How could Blackmur know that there is such thought and that it comprehends time and eternity? Presumably this thought bears witness to what it means to be born human, to grow in that state, to get old, and then—though only Lazarus knows what this means—to die. The governing motif of Yeats's poem is "always." Blackmur assumes, without making a fuss of it, that there is knowledge cognate with a few such experiences, forms and paradigms. The thought he refers to presumably addresses "the human condition as such," not in its differences but in its sameness, its repetitions. I have put the phrase in quotation marks to mark its contentiousness. It has become a matter of acrimony in the years since Blackmur's lecture. Some critics would regard the phrase as offensive or at best prejudicial. They would say: anyone who refers to "the human condition as such" is a bourgeois humanist warming himself by an ideology. There is no essentially human state, there are only lives and the conditions under which they are individually lived.

I know the contention without being convinced of its necessity. For the moment, I shall assume that "the human condition as such" means "what every human being has in common despite the differences between them." Blackmur's reference to thought of all time and all eternity is more dashing than it needs to be, but I propose to retain it. A poetry of such thought, of the process of such thinking, is a perennial poetry. Or at least a poetry that changes so slowly that literary history can hardly make anything of it. Yeats's poem is perennial because it enacts a particular experience of what one can't help knowing, the quick of love, the self-sustaining force of memory. It is conversable, it assumes that most people live by rhythms and patterns of feeling to which names may be given: desire, fear, resentment, faithlessness, the face-to-face of love. The names are never accurate enough, except to be going on with. It is poetry because it gives that knowledge as experience, personal, irregular, but imaginable in that character. Pound's "Medallion" is not a perennial poem; it addresses itself not to what I can't help knowing but to what I can easily help knowing and probably don't know unless I have read the books he has read. The knowledge I need to have, if I am to receive "Medallion," is coincidental to my being alive; it is a caprice of my general experience. I could be fully alive without it; many people are. So what am I saying? That a perennial poetry refers to what the speakers of its language can't help knowing: mother knowledge, as native as one's mother tongue.

What Blackmur's audience made of "Medallion" I can't say: very little, I imagine. It is implausible that they noted, as Marianne Moore did on reading the poem, "the identical rhymes in close sequence without conspicuousness."[3] That is what a poet notes in someone else's poem, that "Medallion" is the work of a professional poet and that it presupposes adroit readers, well read not just in general but in relation to Pound's literary ambience. Moore showed no interest in what Pound was saying, a matter to which an unprofessional reader would presumably attend.

What Blackmur's audience made of "A Deep-sworn Vow" is easier to guess. They had no difficulty in making sense of it. They had only to act upon their general understanding of English and their general sense of life and deem these to make an available convention. The poem enacts Yeats's particular apprehension of an experience as common as loss or promises not kept. But it is not enough to let the poem sink into its themes; it still has to be read or listened to. It is not as direct as it appears. The poem is the imaginary speech of someone, man or woman, addressing his or her beloved, starting with rebuke, a self-justification, "others" set in a causal relation to "you." Others came into my life because you left it, you didn't keep that deep-sworn vow. "Friends": an equivocation, a euphemism for lovers, surely, since to have a lover doesn't preclude having friends. The rebuke covers the equivocation without concealing it, as if the one under rebuke had lost the right to be kept informed. "Yet" is the pivot of the poem; it sets aside the logic of cause and consequence that the first lines insisted on. "Always" turns from rebuke to tribute. The three "when" clauses refer to recurrent occasions on which the speaker is driven beyond the syntax of ordinary experience: each is a token of the sublime or the abysmal. "Suddenly" shows a different order of cause, beyond or beneath that syntax. "I meet your face." Not: "I see your face." I meet it as if it were a ghost, like and unlike the face of death earlier in the poem. It is a poem about conjunctions in life as in grammar.

I may as well acknowledge that a distinction between perennial and capricious experience goes against the modern grain. It is fashionable to ascribe every state of being to history and culture and virtually nothing to nature. Since the decline of natural law as a moral imperative, it has become nearly impossible to appeal to nature or "the same" or a mode of being that persists through every differentiation. By "difference" we are supposed to mean the difference between one thing and another found on the same level of being, or the different interpretations of the "same" thing. Death is one thing to a devout Roman Catholic, another to a pagan or an agnostic. We are admonished to note these simple facts. We are not encouraged to ponder the respects in which each of these things differs from a putative original, founding, and continuing form of itself. Edward Said's *Beginnings* and Catherine Belsey's *Critical Practice* express this prejudice well enough. According to Said, we should think of beginnings, because they are historical, but not of origins, because they are mythic. According to Belsey, if I say that there is a perennial literature, I am claiming that this quality inheres in a subject, fixed and unchangeable, an element in a system of differences which is human nature and the world of human experience. Possible action then becomes an endless repetition of "normal familiar actions."[4]

For another reason, it is a scandal to advert to a perennial literature. If I invoke such a literature, I respect that past from which it has emerged. Nor can I decry the social character of language. The qualities of speech that we find in perennial literature are social and sociable; they are held in common over a period perhaps of several centuries. In *A Thousand Plateaus*, Gilles Deleuze and Félix Guattari maintain that the authority of speech at any moment is the "collective assemblage" in which it circulates and from which it comes. They refer to it as hearsay, the audible circulation of lore among speakers of a language. An individual speech act is entirely possible, and it may be creatively daring, but it is always an act permitted by the collective assemblage. What I say, when I intend to be heard and understood, is allowed by my society, those who together keep the words current. But Deleuze and Guattari are exceptional in this emphasis. More generally, critical theorists resent the communal character of a language and the continuity of experience to which it apparently testifies. They regard it as an obstacle to one's desires; they treat it as an oppressive institution, an ideology, a force of culture that pretends to be a force of nature. One of the motives of Deconstruction, as a case in point, is to demonstrate the opacity of language and thereby to show that the impression of its translucence, in any social practice apparently achieved, is illusory.

I shall repeat myself to say that Blackmur's main theme in those lectures was the conviction, held by many modern poets and novelists, that they must do without a general or accepted habit of thought. They acted instead upon various irregular forms of metaphysics which would have to do the job at hand while being merely provisional and otherwise partial. They could not rely on any official order and had to allude to fragments of some lost order, which might be good enough for the occasion of the poem without being good for anything else. As a motto for this need, Blackmur quoted Shelley's remark, in *A Defence of Poetry*, that the poet's words "unveil the permanent analogy of things by images which participate in the life of truth."

Blackmur didn't quote Shelley beyond that point, but I take the occasion to cite another passage from the *Defence*:

A poem is the very image of life expressed in its eternal truth. There is this difference between a story and a poem, that a story is a catalogue of detached facts, which have no other bond of connexion than time, place, circumstance, cause and effect; the other is the creation of actions according to the unchangeable forms of human nature, as existing in the mind of the creator, which is itself the image of all other minds. The one is partial, and applies only to a definite period of time, and a certain combination of events which can never again recur; the other is universal, and contains within itself the germ of a relation to whatever motives or actions have place in the possible varieties of human nature. Time, which destroys the beauty and the use of the story of particular facts, stripped of the poetry which should invest them, augments that of poetry, and for ever develops new and wonderful applications of the eternal truth which it contains.[5]

Blackmur didn't quote that passage or any other in which Shelley takes the perennial quality of human nature for granted. But he settled upon Shelley's word "analogy" and made of it a perception grounded in a sense of human continuity. Analogy, he said, "is exactly the putting of things side by side." In analogy "we get the relation of attributes, not substances; we get the *form* of reality as if form were itself a kind of action." If we put two feelings together, we get a third feeling that differs from each but with attributes common to both. So Blackmur quoted the last stanza of "Stopping by Woods on a Snowy Evening":

> *The woods are lovely, dark and deep,*
> *But I have promises to keep,*
> *And miles to go before I sleep,*
> *And miles to go before I sleep.*

—and said that it made "a revelation in feelings; what you cannot otherwise touch; only *so*; and the analogies multiply and deepen into surds of feeling."

Blackmur compared analogy to the under-plot or secondary plot in Elizabethan drama, and I think he remembered Yeats's essay "Emotion of Multitude," in which a similar comparison is made. Emotion of multitude is Yeats's phrase for the qualities of a work of art which I have been calling perennial. Shakespearean drama got this emotion from "the sub-plot which copies the main plot, much as a shadow on the wall copies one's body in the firelight":

> We think of *King Lear* less as the history of one man and his sorrows than as the history of a whole evil time. Lear's shadow is in Gloucester, who also has ungrateful children, and the mind goes on imagining other shadows, shadow beyond shadow, till it has pictured the world. . . . Indeed all the great masters have understood that there cannot be great art without the little limited life of the fable, which is always the better the simpler it is, and the rich, far-wandering, many-imaged life of the half-seen world beyond it.[6]

The double plot depends upon analogy, putting like beside nearly like. Presumably, there have been societies in which these constituents of analogy came together easily and as if the association were so customary as to appear natural. Blackmur's theme is that modern writers have to put things together by will and yet make the juxtaposition seem natural. Yeats doesn't appeal, as Shelley did, to human nature, but he believes that the emotion of multitude is still available, as in the practice of symbolism by Ibsen and Chekhov—"the wild duck in the attic . . . the crown at the bottom of the fountain, vague symbols that set the mind wandering from idea to idea, emotion to emotion." A symbol is an object in the world that people over many centuries have taken to themselves as marking a fundamental experience: the rising of the moon, the recurrence of the seasons. If the object comes from history and culture rather than from nature, Yeats calls it an emblem.

But it was Wordsworth who made the most deliberate appeal to human nature as a moral criterion. In a letter to John Wilson in June 1802, he refers to "human nature as it has been (and ever) will be." He tells Wilson that a great poet should rectify men's feelings, "render their feelings more sane, pure, and permanent, in short, more consonant to nature, that is, to eternal nature, and the great moving spirit of things."[7] In the preface to the second edition of *Lyrical Ballads* (1800), Wordsworth referred to a belief, on the part of some friends, that if the views with which his poems were composed were to be realized, "a class of Poetry would be produced, well adapted to interest mankind permanently."

It is unnecessary to quote the many sentences in the preface in which Wordsworth takes human nature for granted and appeals to "the primary laws of our nature," "elemental feelings," "the essential passions of the heart," the "great and simple affections of our nature." He concedes that these laws may for a while be thwarted or occluded by social conditions, especially in modern cities. He refers to "the increasing accumulation of men in cities, where the uniformity of their occupations produces a craving for extraordinary incident, which the rapid communication of intelligence hourly gratifies." He means newspapers, first gestures of the yellow press, "gross and violent stimulants." "Humble and rustic life" had a better chance of practicing the primary laws of human nature. Wordsworth knew that this life was under threat as farm laborers moved to find work in the cities and cities encroached upon villages, but it was not yet defeated. It is still not defeated, though the danger of it is a concern of English literature from Jane Austen, George Eliot, and Hardy to Edward Thomas and Charles Tomlinson. It is not true that Wordsworth could find evidence of the primary laws of human nature only in lives already gone, or that the burden of his poems is incontinent nostalgia. *Lyrical Ballads* is a book of situations, anecdotes, arising, Wordsworth validly claimed, from his sense of a life in common—not a life already divided between lawyer, physician, mariner, astronomer, and natural philosopher but a life lived by people as if prior to those separate callings. There is a certain knowledge that men and women carry about with them, Wordsworth says, and the poet speaks to that. Wordsworth's problem was to find words for the primary feelings and affections. These words would then transform their readers, many of whom are now corrupted by journalism and false literature. Transformed, readers would appreciate the truth of the lyrical ballads, so far as the poems succeeded in translating the primary feelings and passions into decent verse. A society would be renewed on the basis of those truths, held in common. The matter is familiar. It is not necessary to rehearse it or to adjudicate between Wordsworth and Coleridge's dissenting view of the character of rustic life and speech.

After the publication of *The Origin of Species* it became harder to invoke "the primary laws of human nature." In 1867, Henry Adams asked the geologist Sir Charles Lyell to give him the simplest case of uniformity on record, and Lyell chose a shellfish named *Terebratula* that appeared to have remained unchanged from the beginning to the end of geological time. One's earliest ancestor, according to T. H. Huxley, was a kind of sturgeon called *Pteraspis*. Adams found these creatures, as Blackmur notes, "standards or symbols to set against fresh bewilderments." *Pteraspis* was "himself stopped short, man at his limits, and a warning of fresh limits to come." *Terebratula* was "the energy in man that never changed, as other energies changed from diffusion to intensity when charged with intelligence, but changed only from torpor to violence and back again." *Terebratula* was "the incalculable element of pure energy in other human beings: the natural man."[8] But man as such could not be invoked as Huxley pointed to the *Pteraspis* and Lyell to the *Terebratula*. Darwin might propose a law of natural selection, but the word "natural" was not supposed to endow with any authority the nature to which Shelley, Wordsworth, Ruskin, and many other writers appealed. The first effect of Darwinism was that the reach for value turned away from nature toward culture and history. It took a few years before this prejudice became a habit, potent without the necessity of being understood. By 1926, when I. A. Richards published *Science and Poetry*, he thought it obvious that the "neutralization of nature" was now complete and that it should never again be possible to attribute to nature any quasi-sentiment or otherwise Wordsworthian stirrings. Richards thought Yeats and D. H. Lawrence regressive for that reason: Lawrence with his solar myths, Yeats with his belief in magic, the *anima mundi*, and other occult forces. But Richards later conceded that Yeats wrote major poems while persisting in those intellectual practices. Still, *The Origin of Species* made it harder to appeal to human nature: the hypothesis of evolution is inimical to any "essentialism" but its own. Culture must proceed, it is asserted, not in relation to an idea of man but to what particular men and women have done. It is rarely asked whether what men and women have done is influenced, to any degree, by the idea of themselves they profess.

But poets will not be bidden. As late as 1915, Hardy wrote "In Time of 'The Breaking of Nations' ":

I

*Only a man harrowing clods*
*In a slow silent walk*
*With an old horse that stumbles and nods*
*Half asleep as they stalk.*

II

*Only thin smoke without flame*
*From the heaps of couch-grass;*
*Yet this will go onward the same*
*Though Dynasties pass.*

III

*Yonder a maid and her wight*
*Come whispering by:*
*War's annals will cloud into night*
*Ere their story die.*

Perennial experience, according to Hardy in that poem, is embodied in the continuity of work, the tilling of land, appearances of landscape, thin smoke from heaps of couch-grass, a girl and her lover. These are examples. But a reader resentful of such proclaimed continuities might remark: "Isn't it significant that in reporting the last of these apparently categorical experiences Hardy uses a noun no longer in common speech—'wight'—such that one has to go to the O.E.D. to find out what it means? It comes, one gathers, from the Anglo-Saxon *wiht*, meaning a creature. Hardy recalls from Jeremiah 51:20 the phrase about the breaking of nations, but not the nearer fact that *wight* has virtually been lost to modern English."

The point is well enough taken. But a trace of particular words is often retained long after they have disappeared from common speech. The editors of *The Norton Anthology of Modern Poetry* haven't thought it necessary to gloss any word or phrase in Hardy's poem except the reference to Jeremiah. "Ere," "maid," and "wight" remain without comment. Still, certain words are forgotten or displaced, and that makes for difficulty. Nouns, mostly, lose their place in speech, displaced by new ones that seem to name their referents more accurately. Some other parts of speech are more secure.

Christopher Ricks has argued that while all parts of speech change, "the language of prepositions changes strikingly less than most":

If as a poet you seek the simplest and most permanent forms of language, you are bound to give special importance to prepositions and conjunctions.[9]

Prepositions and conjunctions express not things but relations. An example from Wordsworth: "felt in the blood and felt along the heart." One would have expected, as Ricks says, "felt in the heart, and felt along the blood," since the heart is static and the blood diffused. But Wordsworth knows that the relation between the heart and its blood is more intimate, more reciprocal, than that:

> The heart has no blood that is not coming from and going to; the blood's coming and going are dependent upon the heart; and this reciprocity, like that of the "affections sweet," can be subtly and touchingly signalled by interchanging their prepositions.[10]

It is worth noting that Wordsworth's line is based upon a physical fact. Harvey's discovery of the circulation of the blood was common knowledge when Wordsworth wrote the line, so he could invoke it without making a fuss. In the preface he says that when a scientific discovery becomes common knowledge, poets will be ready to involve it in the general stock of assumptions and sentiments. This is what he means by claiming that the affecting parts of Chaucer are "almost always expressed in language pure and universally intelligible even to this day." *The Canterbury Tales* arises from common lore or from knowledge that has become sufficiently available to be referred to. Wordsworth didn't inquire further, beyond noting that modern poets, unlike Chaucer, were addicted to gaudy and inane phraseology, perverted diction, and other excesses. Nature remained Wordsworth's court of final appeal, guarantor of his poetry in the multiplicity and quality of its moral relations. But he took this as axiomatic; he didn't ask whether it depended upon the theology of natural law or upon moral relations historically ascertained.

It is time to say what the argument is. I am not claiming that there is a kind of literature that never changes. No modern Greek speaks as Euripides did. Nor am I appealing to some "essentialism." The debate has been confounded by the vocabulary of essence and existence. Anthropologists who search for some human universal, in principle or practice, may or may not be wasting their time. I have no opinion on that. But the continuity of feeling to which Wordsworth appeals is just as clear as the spinning jenny and the French Revolution. The fact of sameness and repetition doesn't entail a claim upon essence. I am merely suggesting that there are forms of literature that change far more slowly than literary historians are inclined to say, and that this fact should modify their (our) account of modern literature. Literary historians find satisfaction in revolutions, formal disjunctions, experiments in diction and syntax: they are like war correspondents who are irritable when nothing much is happening. It is not surprising that these historians take their analogies from war, political and social change, revolutions, *coups d'état*. They cannot deal with continuity, because it brings narration to an end. "A Deep-sworn Vow" and "Stopping by Woods on a Snowy Evening" could have been written at any time in the last two hundred years, so these poems are embarrassing to literary historians who have nothing to say until they can point to disruptions (which they like to call trangressions) in the structure, syntax, and diction of poetry. Nothing else makes news. In point of form or diction, Yeats's poem, like Frost's, testifies to "the same" rather than to difference or change, it doesn't fulfill evolutionary or revolutionary expectations. The poem moves through its conjunctions: "because," "but," "when," "or." These sustain, while they qualify, the bearing of "always" and carry perennial intimations into the structure of the poem. "You" can remain unspecified; so can "that deep-sworn vow"; and the beloved face can be met without anticipation or description, because of the allusive force of the conjunctions and the different recognitions of "always" and "suddenly." Frost's poem does similar work with "but" and "and" and "before," which hold their course when every noun and adjective in their vicinity changes. The uncoercive charm of "lovely," "dark," and "deep" is that Frost accepts them as gifts of a certain poetic tradition, and thinks them good for the occasion. The promises are not specified. And the feeling that goes into the repetition of the last line is an ancestral sigh that amounts to whatever a reader wants it to amount to. The poetry is not in the statements or the descriptions but in the turnings from one to the next, the torsions of "but" and the two "ands." So much depends on these. But literary historians like to report that everything changes because everything is in history and has a look of contingency. It is not true.

The question is: if literary history presents the history of literature as a story of changing forms and modes, what can we say of writers who don't take part in the revolution? Virginia Woolf rebuked Arnold Bennett, in effect, for not joining it or perhaps for not adverting to the fact that a revolution was under way. For much the same reason, Eliot dismissed most of the poets who were in the news when he settled in

London. Yeats and Pound were the only poets writing in English from whom he could learn anything worth knowing. How could he have been so sure that Pound, Yeats, Wyndham Lewis, and Joyce were the main characters in the story of modern literature and that Frost, Stevens, Edward Thomas, and A. E. Housman hardly rated mention?

But this isn't quite the point or the question. In later years and more relaxed moods, Eliot was willing to praise Walter de la Mare's poems and Marianne Moore's without asking whether they came into the story of modern literature. I'll try to frame a better question. Does the standard account of the history of literature in terms of eras, periods, and revolutions take decent note of the forces in life and therefore in literature that remain much the same over relatively long periods and survive the most abrupt changes? I mean: continuities of feeling, desire, and need, and the words that perform them. If there are such forces and such words, where do the forces come from and how do writers find words for them?

They come from our constitution as bodies. Where else? I agree with Kenneth Burke's argument in *Language as Symbolic Action* that each of us is a "body that learns language." I recall an occasion on which Burke said that we need a metabiology, not a metaphysic—or rather, that in default of an agreed metaphysic, we could manage pretty well with an agreed metabiology, posited on the basis that whatever we are in addition, we are bodies to begin with and to end with. We live and we die. We could maintain adequate forms of cooperation and sociability, Burke argued, by agreeing on that much, that little. Each of us learns to take some part in language or "symbolic action." What Habermas calls "communicative action" is possible on the basis of a metabiology, though I have indicated that there are difficulties to which Habermas hasn't adverted beyond that formula.

## II

Now I come to a more personal consideration. For the past several years I have been teaching a course in modern poetry at New York University. The course is called "Modern British and American Poetry," and I feel embarrassed in agreeing to regard Yeats and Irish poetry as covered by that designation. I deem "modern" in the title of the course to mean, roughly, from *Leaves of Grass* to *The Waste Land*.

I have also taught the second part of the course, running from *The Bridge* to, say, *Self-Portrait in a Convex Mirror*. Now, it would be convenient if I could teach this two-part course in narrative and descriptive terms, pointing to some poetic project more compelling than any other, or to one "common pursuit" that made sense of the poems. I could then show this project as the true history of modern poetry. But it is not plausible. The claim that modern poetry is "one story and one story only" can be maintained only by a rhetoric of wrenching and suppressing. Hugh Kenner proceeds in this way in *The Pound Era*. He regards International Modernism as the crucial movement in the history of modern art and literature; it was an affair of cities, he says— London, Paris, and Dublin. Its chief exponents in English were Pound, Wyndham Lewis, Joyce, and Eliot. One effect of this declaration is that Pound's Imagism is supposed to lead to the Objectivism of Williams, Marianne Moore, Zukofsky, and Bunting, and these to mark the true direction of modern poetry. In modern literature, according to this reading, Yeats, Frost, and Faulkner are anomalies. Stevens doesn't come into the reckoning; he had nothing to do with cities, except that he ordered a few paintings from the Paris he never visited. Kenner treats him as a minor comic poet.

If I take up an older book, F. R. Leavis's *New Bearings in English Poetry*, I find that modern poetry begins with Hopkins, whose chief claim to this office is that he was not Tennyson. In due time Hopkins leads to Pound and Eliot, who lead to Empson. In another part of the library I am instructed by Harold Bloom that the best of modern poetry comes from Emerson and Whitman, that the whole project is an extension of Romanticism, and that the crucial poets are those who effect the most daring subjective transformations of their material, no opacity being allowed to persist. Stevens is the major man, and he makes possible Elizabeth Bishop, Robert Penn Warren, Ashbery, Ammons, and Hollander. Not Robert Lowell or John Berryman: too much opacity remaining there. English poets don't come into the story. But then Philip Larkin edits *The Oxford Book of Twentieth Century English Verse* and the great poet there is Hardy, whose *Collected Poems*, by Larkin's judgment in *Required Writing*, is incomparably the greatest book of modern poetry. In Larkin's version, the Modernists are seen wilting in Hardy's strong light. Yeats appears in company with A. E. Housman and Kipling. Eliot gets more space than Edward Thomas, Wilfred Owen, Graves, Betjeman, Auden, or Dylan Thomas, but he doesn't dominate the book as, in Leavis's early account, he should. And while Larkin doesn't use the word "perennial," his claim for Hardy is based upon the range of those poems, such as "In Time of 'The Breaking of Nations,' " in which Hardy gratifies our sense that there is indeed "human life as such."

It seems necessary to take a different approach. It is an embarrassment to historians, but it can't be helped: the trouble with a broad historical narrative is that many different events take place at the same time. There is no *Zeitgeist*. Edward Thomas's poems are contemporaneous with Pound's and Eliot's and unlike them in nearly every respect. No single narrative makes sense of modern poetry. We should acknowledge several more or less distinct lines of relation and affiliation. Teaching the first part of the course in modern poetry, I need at least five affiliations or trajectories: Emerson-and-Whitman, considered as if they were a composite poet leading to Dickinson, Pound, Frost, and Stevens; Hopkins, for the reason Leavis gives; Hardy, for Larkin's reason; Tennyson, for the obvious reason, that his poems and especially "In Memoriam" haunted even the poets who disowned him; and Baudelaire-and-Mallarmé, another composite poet, whom Arthur Symons interpreted for Yeats's benefit (and later Eliot's) in *The Symbolist Movement in Literature*. There is no need to haggle over these "lines," provided it is agreed that more than one is necessary.

Why these lines, these poets, rather than others? Because these provoke a wide rather than a narrow range of interests, including mine. Reading these poets, I find it exhilarating to see what they have done, productively and performatively, in a language. If I thought that a work of literature should serve a religious or political cause, or be available mainly to readers who look to literature for that service, I would make a different choice. But I don't think so. Literature is life deliberately placed in the parenthesis of form: it is best understood as antinomian in its dispositions and ceremonies. If we want a motto for this prejudice, we find one in Kafka: "What is laid upon us is to accomplish the negative; the positive is already given."[11] Literature stands aside from the general culture and is ready to suspect its own purposes when they show any sign of being socially accredited. It invites aesthetic attention, and the main difficulty is to discover what that entails. But these are commonplaces. I recite them only because so many teachers of literature are more concerned with politics than with literature. They take their teaching seriously, but they think they can be serious only when they serve a political cause, effect changes in legislation, and make other people ashamed of practicing an aesthetic interest.

So where are we? Still in the course on modern poetry. It is misleading to present the history of a literature in narrative or otherwise consecutive terms, as if one were reciting the development of English legislation from, say, 1832 to 1913. In legislation, one act leads to another or to its amendment or repeal. But no bibliography of English literature corresponds, for discipline and definition, to the statute books of Westminster. The books we talk about are those we choose to talk about: there is no obligation. Appeal to a canon can easily be resisted. If I think, as I sometimes do, that Tuckerman's poems should be read in a course on modern poetry, I am free to include them. Instead of telling one long story as if it were the authorized version of a literature, I tell many short ones, draw short lines of relation, marking episodes, anecdotes, occasions. The most significant of these describe particular relations, especially those in which choice is featured rather than chance or circumstance: relations between Blake and Yeats, Conrad and Faulkner, Donne and Empson, Whitman and Pound, Faulkner and Cormac McCarthy. But perhaps the best way of teaching a literature is to start with terms of an apparent perennial character and see how these are modified within a broad system of continuity. Start with myths, archetypes, symbols, forms, and genres, because these testify to patterns of experience as fundamental as living and dying. Henri Focillon maintained that there is a vocation of forms that corresponds to a vocation of substances. Not to make the claim outlandish, we might start with motifs fundamental in a particular community and see how these are modified in being turned to a local purpose, as the story of the Good Samaritan is turned in the "Eumaeus" chapter of *Ulysses*. This suggests the merit of dealing not with literature— except on the level of metatheory—but with genres of literature, since genres have a care for patterns or paradigms of feeling. Rosalie L. Colie's *The Resources of Kind: Genre-Theory in the Renaissance* is a model of this procedure. Or W. H. Auden's *The Enchafèd Flood*, which studies the sea as symbol in literature and finds it as variable and as constant as the tide. Or we might teach the poems as episodes in the history of various styles. Josephine Miles is our authority for this, as in *Eras and Modes in English Poetry* and many other books she attempts a discrimination of styles and thinks of each as a way of being in the world.

"Crossing Brooklyn Ferry" and "I Like to See It Lap the Miles" are poems about movement, changing scenes and sentiments. They differ not because Whitman was a man and Dickinson a woman, the one a homosexual and the other by disposition heterosexual, but because each poem takes part in a different style or mode of writing, well established in its time. To "take part" doesn't mean "to take dictation."

It may appear that I have an interest in thwarting literary historians who like to look before and after and take pleasure in transgression. I would like to see them running up and down and all around the town. I would have them reading folk-tales, fairy-stories, "once upon a time" in which the particular time doesn't matter and they are free to imagine any time they like or none. Or I would have them reading poems that float free of their contexts because we know little or nothing of the contexts. Shakespeare's sonnets make a case in point. What is he doing in them? He is writing sonnets, working out further possibilities of that genre, as we might say that Beethoven is working out further possibilities of the sonata as a genre. But what about the implied poet, the fair young man, the rival poet, and the dark lady? We know nothing about them, even after A. L. Rowse has done his best: they can't be recovered by the methods of historical scholarship or even by those of the New Historicism. They can be used as devices for talking about something else; "homosexual male intertextuality," for instance, as in Eve Kosofsky Sedgwick's *Between Men*. But that is another story.

III

A parable to end with, on the issue of continuity and change. It comes from Kafka. "Leopards break into the temple," he writes, "and drink the sacrificial chalices dry; this occurs repeatedly, again and again: finally it can be reckoned upon beforehand and becomes a part of the ceremony."[12]

# NOTES

ഗ©∂∂ഗ©

## THE MAN OF THE CROWD

1. W. B. Yeats, *Essays and Introductions* (New York: Macmillan, 1961), p. 405.
2. William Wordsworth, *The Prelude*, ed. J. C. Maxwell (New Haven and London: Yale University Press, 1981) pp. 259, 261, 287, 289, 292, 293, 295.
3. Edgar Allan Poe, *The Complete Poems and Stories*, ed. Arthur Hobson Quinn and Edward H. O'Neill (New York: Knopf, 1967), 1:314.
4. Edgar Allan Poe, *Selected Prose and Poetry*, ed. W. H. Auden (New York: Rinehart, 1950), p. vi.
5. Walt Whitman, *Complete Poetry and Collected Prose* (New York: Library of America, 1982), p. 195.
6. Baudelaire, "The Painter of Modern Life," in *Baudelaire: Selected Writings on Art and Artists*, trans. P. E. Charvet (Harmondsworth: Penguin Books, 1972), pp. 399–400.
7. Francis Scarfe's prose translation reads:

To a Woman Passing By

The darkening street was howling round me when a woman passed on her way, so tall and slender, all in black mourning, majestical in her grief, with her stately hand lifting and sawing the scallop and hem, light-footed and noble with a statuesque leg. And I, tense as a man out of his wits, drank from her eye—a pal-

[289]

lid sky in which a tempest brews—that gentleness which be-
witches men, that pleasure which destroys. A flash of light—then
darkness. O vanishing beauty, whose glance brought me suddenly
to life again, shall I never see you once more except in eternity?
Elsewhere, far from here, too late or perhaps never? For whither
you flew I know not, nor do you know whither I am bound—O
you whom I could have loved, O you who knew it!

From *Baudelaire: The Complete Verse*, ed. Francis Scarfe (London: Anvil
Press, 1986), p. 186.

8. Walter Benjamin, *Charles Baudelaire: A Lyric Poet in the Era of High Capitalism*, trans. Harry Zohn (London: Verso Editions, 1983), p. 125.

9. W. H. Auden, *Collected Poems*, ed. Edward Mendelson (New York: Random House, 1976), pp. 145–6.

10. Gerard Manley Hopkins, *Poems and Prose*, ed. W. H. Gardner
(Harmondsworth: Penguin Books, 1953), p. 64.

11. John Bayley, "Embarrassments of the National Past," *Times Literary Supplement*, February 23–March 1, 1990, p. 187.

12. Hermann Hesse, *My Belief: Essays on Life and Art*, trans. Denver Lindley
(New York: Farrar, Straus and Giroux, 1974), p. 85.

13. Susan Sontag, *On Photography* (New York: Farrar, Straus and Giroux,
1977), p. 9.

14. *Simone Weil: An Anthology*, ed. Siân Miles (London: Virago Press, 1986),
p. 183.

## BEYOND CULTURE

1. Matthew Arnold, *Culture and Anarchy*, ed. R. H. Super (Ann Arbor: University of Michigan Press, 1965), p. 95.

2. Lionel Trilling, *The Liberal Imagination* (New York: Harcourt Brace
Jovanovich, 1978), p. 252.

3. Matthew Arnold, *On the Classical Tradition*, ed. R. H. Super (Ann Arbor:
University of Michigan Press, 1960), p. 1.

4. Georg Simmel, *The Philosophy of Money*, trans. Tom Bottomore and David
Frisby (London: Routledge & Kegan Paul, 1978), pp. 296–7.

5. Henry James, *Novels 1881–1886* (New York: Library of America, 1985),
p. 388.

6. Henry James, *The Portrait of a Lady* (New York: Random House, Modern
Library, 1966), pp. 190–1.

7. Walter Pater, *The Renaissance: Studies in Art and Poetry*, ed. Donald L. Hill (Berkeley: University of California Press, 1980), pp. 108–9.

8. W. B. Yeats, *Essays and Introductions* (New York: Macmillan, 1961), p. 163.

9. James Joyce, *A Portrait of the Artist as a Young Man* (reprint, London: Cape, 1954), pp. 199–200.

10. T. S. Eliot, *The Complete Poems and Plays* (New York: Harcourt, Brace & World, 1962), p. 5.

11. Elizabeth Sewell, *Paul Valéry: The Mind in the Mirror* (New Haven: Yale University Press, 1952), p. 33.

12. Allen Tate, *Essays of Four Decades* (Chicago: Swallow Press, 1959), p. 403.

13. Fredric Jameson, *Fables of Aggression* (Berkeley: University of California Press, 1979), p. 2.

14. Lionel Trilling, *The Last Decade: Essays and Reviews, 1965–1975* (New York: Harcourt Brace Jovanovich, 1979), p. 141.

15. Lionel Trilling, *Beyond Culture* (New York and London: Harcourt Brace Jovanovich, 1978), p. 165.

## Ariel and His Poems

1. "What Is Enlightenment?" in *The Foucault Reader*, ed. Paul Rabinow (Harmondsworth: Penguin Books), p. 42.

2. "The Painter of Modern Life," in *Baudelaire: Selected Writings on Art and Artists*, trans. P. E. Charvet (Harmondsworth: Penguin Books, 1972), p. 403.

3. G. W. F. Hegel, *The Phenomenology of Mind*, trans. J. B. Baillie (New York: Humanities Press, 1971), p. 570.

4. Jean François Lyotard, *Tombeau de l'intellectuel et autres papiers* (Paris: Éditions Galilée, 1984), p. 81.

5. *The Collected Poems of Theodore Roethke* (New York: Doubleday, 1966), p. 92.

6. John Crowe Ransom, *The World's Body* (New York: Charles Scribner's Sons, 1938), p. 116.

7. Wallace Stevens, *The Collected Poems* (New York: Vintage Books, 1982), p. 503.

8. Laurence S. Lockridge, *The Ethics of Romanticism* (Cambridge: Cambridge University Press, 1989), p. 455.

9. Wallace Stevens, *The Necessary Angel* (New York: Knopf, 1951), p. 32.

10. Stéphane Mallarmé, *Oeuvres complètes*, ed. Henri Mondon and G. Jean-Aubry (Paris: Librairie Gallimard, 1945), p. 368.

"I say: a flower! and out of the forgetfulness where my voice ban-
ishes any contour, inasmuch as it is something other than known
calyxes, there arises musically, an idea itself and fragrant, the one
absent from all bouquets.

Far from having the function of an easy and representative
currency, as it has first of all with the crowd, speech, above all
dream and song, recovers its virtuality, thanks to the Poet, and
out of the constitutive necessity of an art devoted to fictions.
[translation mine.]

11. Susanne K. Langer, *Feeling and Form* (New York: Charles Scribner's Sons,
    1953), p. 109.
12. Jürgen Habermas, *The Philosophical Discourse of Modernity*, trans. Frederick
    Lawrence (Cambridge, Mass.: MIT Press, 1987), p. 296.
13. Emmanuel Levinas, *Totality and Infinity*, trans. Alphonso Lingis (Pitts-
    burgh: Duquesne University Press, 1969), pp. 58, 55.
14. "The Other in Proust," in *The Levinas Reader*, ed. Seán Hand (Oxford:
    Basil Blackwell, 1989), p. 164.
15. Elizabeth Bishop, *The Complete Poems 1927–1979* (New York: Farrar,
    Straus and Giroux, 1983), p. 166.


# THE USE AND ABUSE OF THEORY

1. F. R. Leavis, *The Common Pursuit* (London: Chatto & Windus, 1952;
   Harmondsworth: Penguin, 1962), pp. 212–13; René Wellek, "Literature
   and Philosophy," *Scrutiny* 4 (March 1937): pp. 375–83.
2. J. Hillis Miller, *Hawthorne and History* (Oxford: Basil Blackwell, 1991), pp.
   47–8.
3. Samuel Johnson, *Lives of the Poets*, 2 vols. (1906; London: Oxford University Press, 1968), 1:123.
4. Jean Starobinski, *La Rélation critique* (Paris: Librairie Gallimard, 1970),
   p. 9.
5. Leo Bersani, "Against *Ulysses*," *Raritan* 8, no. 2 (Fall 1988): pp. 1–32
   (p. 32).
6. John Guillory, "The Ideology of Canon Formation: T. S. Eliot and
   Cleanth Brooks" in *Canons*, ed. Robert von Hallberg (Chicago: University of Chicago Press, 1984), pp. 337–62 (p. 358).
7. Immanuel Kant, *Critique of Aesthetic Judgment*, trans. James Creed
   Meredith (Oxford: Clarendon Press, 1911), pp. 175–6.

8. Quoted in John Gage, *Goethe on Art* (Berkeley: University of California Press, 1980), p. 97.

9. David Lloyd, "Arnold, Ferguson, Schiller: Aesthetic Culture and the Politics of Aesthetics," *Cultural Critique* 2 (1985–86): pp. 137–69 (p. 139).

10. Jacques Derrida, *La Vérité en peinture* (Paris: Flammarion, 1978), p. 123.

11. John Crowe Ransom, *The World's Body* (Baton Rouge: Louisiana State University Press, 1968), pp. 235–6.

12. Paul Valéry, *The Art of Poetry*, trans. Denise Folliot (London: Routledge & Kegan Paul, 1958), p. 58.

13. Geoffrey Hill, "Style and Faith," *Times Literary Supplement*, December 27, 1991, pp. 3–4.

## THE POLITICAL TURN IN CRITICISM

1. John Crowe Ransom, "More than Gesture," *Partisan Review*, January–February 1953; reprinted in his *Poems and Essays* (New York: Vintage Books, 1955), p. 104.

2. R. P. Blackmur, *Form and Value in Modern Poetry* (Garden City, New York: Doubleday, Anchor Books, 1957), p. 58.

3. Seamus Deane, *Celtic Revivals* (London: Faber and Faber, 1985), p. 33.

4. Seamus Deane, "Heroic Styles: The Tradition of an Idea" (Derry: A Field Day Pamphlet, no. 4, 1984), p. 6.

5. Northrop Frye, "In the Earth, or in the Air?" *Times Literary Supplement*, January 17, 1986, p. 52.

6. Fredric Jameson, *Fables of Aggression* (Berkeley: University of California Press, 1979), p. 2.

7. Fredric Jameson, "*Ulysses* in History," in *James Joyce and Modern Literature*, ed. W. J. McCormack and Alistair Stead (London: Routledge & Kegan Paul, 1982), p. 129.

8. Jameson, *Fables of Aggression*, p. 57.

9. Walter Benjamin, *The Origin of German Tragic Drama*, trans. John Osborne (London: NLB, 1977), p. 66.

10. Fredric Jameson, "Wyndham Lewis as Futurist," *The Hudson Review*, July 1973, p. 318.

11. Northrop Frye, *Fables of Identity* (New York: Harcourt, Brace & World, 1963), p. 238.

12. Frank Kermode, *The Sense of an Ending* (New York: Oxford University Press, 1967), p. 145.

13. Herbert Marcuse, *The Aesthetic Dimension* (London: Macmillan, 1979), pp. ix, xii, 4, 19, 72, 10, 8.

14. Paul de Man, "Hegel on the Sublime," in *Displacements: Derrida and After*, ed. Mark Krupnick (Bloomington: Indiana University Press, 1983), p. 141.
15. Paul de Man, *The Resistance to Theory* (Minneapolis: University of Minnesota Press, 1986), pp. 64, 66.
16. W. B. Yeats, *A Vision* (London: Macmillan, 1962), pp. 144–5.
17. R. P. Blackmur, *The Lion and the Honeycomb* (London: Methuen, 1956), pp. 169, 172.

## TRANSLATION IN THEORY AND IN A CERTAIN PRACTICE

1. Ezra Pound, "Cavalcanti" in *Literary Essays* (Norfolk, Conn: New Directions, 1954), p. 154.
2. Hugh Kenner, Introduction to *The Translations of Ezra Pound* (New York: New Directions, n.d.), p. 11.
3. John Hollander, *Vision and Resonance*, 2nd ed. (New Haven: Yale University Press, 1985), p. 243.
4. Hugh Kenner, "Ezra Pound and Modernism," *The World and I*, June 1988, p. 563.
5. Walter Benjamin, *Illuminations*, ed. Hannah Arendt, trans. Harry Zohn (New York: Harcourt, Brace & World, 1968), p. 80.
6. Ibid., p. 80.
7. Paul de Man, "The Translator," *Yale French Studies* 69 (1985), p. 34.
8. Ibid., p. 39.

## ON THE GOLDEN BOWL

1. *The Notebooks of Henry James*, ed. F. O. Matthiessen and Kenneth B. Murdock (New York: George Braziller, Inc., 1955), pp. 130–1.
2. Quoted in F. O. Matthiessen, *The James Family* (New York: Knopf, 1948), p. 339.
3. Ibid., pp. 339–40.
4. *The Letters of William James*, ed. Henry James (his son) (Boston: Atlantic Monthly Press, 1920), pp. 277–8.
5. F. R. Leavis, *The Common Pursuit* (London: Chatto & Windus, 1952), p. 228.
6. Henry James, *Literary Criticism: European Writers and the Prefaces* (New York: Library of America, 1984), p. 1327.

WILLIAM WETMORE STORY AND HIS FRIENDS:
THE ENCLOSING FACT OF ROME

1. Henry James, *Letters*, vol. 4, *1895–1916*, ed. Leon Edel (Cambridge: Harvard University Press, 1984), p. 302.

2. Henry James to William Dean Howells, January 25, 1902, ibid., pp. 224–5.

3. Henry James, *Letters*, vol. 1, *1843–1875*, ed. Leon Edel (Cambridge: Harvard University Press, 1974), p. 353.

4. Henry James to Henry Adams, November 19, 1903, *Letters* 4: 289.

5. Henry James, *William Wetmore Story and His Friends: From Letters, Diaries, and Recollections* (London: Thames and Hudson, n.d.), 2:87.

6. Ibid., 1:15.

7. Ibid., 1:125.

8. Ibid., 1:341.

9. Ibid., 1:224.

10. Ibid., 2:131.

11. Ibid., 2:132–3.

12. Ibid., 1:348.

13. Ibid.

14. *The Complete Notebooks of Henry James*, ed. Leon Edel and Lyall H. Powers (New York: Oxford University Press, 1987), p. 183.

15. James, *William Wetmore Story and His Friends*, 1.6–7.

16. Ibid., 1:275.

17. Ibid., 2:126.

18. Ibid., 2:3.

19. Ibid., 2:228.

20. Ibid., 1:188.

21. Ibid., 1:294.

22. Ibid., 1:333.

23. Ibid., 1:312.

24. T. S. Eliot, "In Memory," *The Little Review* 5, no. 4 (August 1918): p. 44.

25. James, *William Wetmore Story and His Friends*, 2:227.

26. Ibid., 2:55.

27. Ibid., 2:83–4.

28. Ibid., 2:216.

29. Henry James, *Literary Criticism* (New York: Library of America, 1984), p. 1173.

30. Ibid., 1174.

31. Henry James, *Novels 1871–1880* (New York: Library of America, 1983), p. 227.

32. James, *William Wetmore Story and His Friends*, 1:328.
33. Ibid., 2:208.
34. Ibid., 2:209.
35. Ibid., 2:234–5.
36. Henry James, *Italian Hours* (reprint, London: Century, 1986), pp. 217–19.
37. Ibid., 219.
38. Ibid., 217.

## ON A LATE POEM BY YEATS

1. John Crowe Ransom, *The World's Body* (Baton Rouge: Louisiana State University Press, 1968), p. 131.
2. John Hollander, *Rhyme's Reason* (New Haven: Yale University Press, 1981), p. 14.
3. *Letters on Poetry from W. B. Yeats to Dorothy Wellesley* (London: Oxford University Press, 1964), pp. 179–81.
4. Helen Vendler, "Technique in the Earlier Poems of Yeats," *Yeats Annual* no. 8, ed. Warwick Gould (London: Macmillan, 1991), pp. 3–20.
5. John Hollander, *The Figure of Echo* (Berkeley: University of California Press, 1981), p. 61n.
6. Ibid.
7. *Letters on Poetry from W. B. Yeats to Dorothy Wellesley*, p. 12.
8. William Empson, *The Structure of Complex Words* (London: Hogarth Press, 1985), p. 101.
9. Mikhail Bakhtin, *Problems of Dostoevsky's Poetics*, trans. Caryl Emerson (Minneapolis: University of Minnesota Press, 1984), p. 71.
10. Emmanuel Levinas, "The Tyace of the Other" trans. Alphonso Lingis, in *Deconstruction in Context*, ed. Mark C. Taylor (Chicago: University of Chicago Press, 1986), p. 348.
11. Walter Pater, *The Renaissance: Studies in Art and Poetry*, ed. Donald L. Hill (Berkeley: University of California Press, 1980), p. 42.

## T. S. ELIOT: THE COMMUNICATION OF THE DEAD

1. W. B. Yeats, *A Vision* (London: T. Werner Laurie, 1925), pp. 211–12.
2. W. B. Yeats, *Explorations* (London: Macmillan, 1962), p. 392.
3. T. S. Eliot, *Knowledge and Experience in the Philosophy of F. H. Bradley* (London: Faber and Faber, 1964), pp. 147–8.
4. T. S. Eliot, *Selected Essays*, 3d ed. (London: Faber and Faber, 1951), p. 21.

5. T. S. Eliot, "Literature, Science, and Dogma," *The Dial* 82 (March 1927), p. 241.
6. T. S. Eliot, "A Note on Poetry and Belief," *The Enemy* 1 (January 1927), p. 15.
7. T. S. Eliot, *After Strange Gods* (New York: Harcourt, Brace, 1934), pp. 45–6.
8. Eliot, *Selected Essays*, p. 427.
9. Ibid., p. 255.
10. Quoted in B. A. Harries, "The Rare Contact," *Theology* LXXV, no. 62 (March 1972), p. 143.
11. Helen Gardner, *The Composition of Four Quartets* (London: Faber and Faber, 1978), p. 196.
12. Eliot, *Selected Essays*, pp. 256–7.
13. Ibid., pp. 428–9.
14. Ibid., p. 275.
15. Gardner, *The Composition of Four Quartets*, p. 157.
16. *The Divine Comedy*, ed. Charles S. Singleton (Princeton: Princeton University Press, 1973), 2:270.
17. Eliot, *Selected Essays*, pp. 257–8.
18. Rainer Maria Rilke, *The Notebooks of Malte Laurids Brigge*, trans. M. D. Herter Norton (New York: Capricorn Books, 1958), pp. 26–7.
19. William Empson, *Milton's God* (London: Chatto and Windus, 1965), p. 261.

## ON "BURNT NORTON"

1. T. S. Eliot, "Note sur Mallarmé et Poe," trans. Ramon Fernandez, *La Nouvelle Revue Française* 14, no. 158 (November 1, 1926), pp. 524–6. (English text not published.)
2. F. R. Leavis, *The Living Principle: "English" as a Discipline of Thought* (London: Chatto and Windus, 1975), p. 179.
3. William Empson, *Some Versions of Pastoral* (reprint, New York: New Directions, 1974), pp. 260–1.
4. D. W. Harding, *Experience into Words* (reprint, Harmondsworth: Penguin Books, 1974), pp. 107–8.

## On *The Idea of a Christian Society*

1. T. S. Eliot, *Collected Poems 1909–1962* (New York: Harcourt, Brace, and World, 1963), pp. 215–6.
2. T. S. Eliot, *After Strange Gods: A Primer of Modern Heresy* (London: Faber and Faber, 1934), p. 20.
3. Gilles Deleuze, *Kant's Critical Philosophy*, trans. Hugh Tomlinson and Barbara Habberjam (London: The Athlone Press, 1984), p. 19.

## Notes on a Poem by Stevens

1. Jean-Paul Sartre, *The Pyschology of Imagination* (London: Methuen, 1972), pp. 11–12.
2. Philip Wheelwright, *The Burning Fountain*, 2d ed. (Bloomington: Indiana University Press, 1968), p. 33.
3. Paul de Man, *The Rhetoric of Romanticism* (New York: Columbia University Press, 1984), p. 6.

## Is There a Perennial Literature?

1. R. P. Blackmur, *Anni Mirabiles* (Washington, D.C.: Library of Congress, 1956), pp. 5–6.
2. Ibid., pp. 34, 46.
3. *The Complete Prose of Marianne Moore*, ed. Patricia C. Willis (New York: Viking, Elisabeth Sifton Books, 1986), p. 449.
4. Catherine Belsey, *Critical Practice* (London: Methuen, 1982), p. 90.
5. *Shelley's Poetry and Prose*, ed. Donald H. Reiman and Sharon B. Powers (New York: Norton, 1977), p. 485.
6. W. B. Yeats, *Essays and Introductions* (London: Macmillan, 1961), pp. 215–16.
7. William Wordsworth, *The Early Letters,* ed. Ernest de Selincourt (Oxford: Clarendon Press, 1935), pp. 295–6.
8. R. P. Blackmur, *Henry Adams* (New York: Harcourt Brace Jovanovich, 1980), p. 70.
9. Christopher Ricks, *The Force of Poetry* (Oxford: Clarendon Press, 1984), p. 121.

10. Ibid.
11. Franz Kafka, *The Great Wall of China*, trans. Willa and Edwin Muir (New York: Schocken Books, 1970), p. 167.
12. Ibid., p. 165.

PERMISSIONS
ACKNOWLEDGMENTS

ᴐᴄᴀᴄᴧᴜᴄᴝ

Grateful acknowledgment is made to the following for permission to reprint previously published material:

*Anvil Press Poetry Ltd.:* English translation of the poem "A Une Passante" from *Baudelaire: The Complete Verse,* translated by Francis Scarfe (London: 1986). Reprinted by permission.

*Georges Borchardt, Inc.* and *Carcanet Press Limited:* Excerpt from "A Wave" from *Three Poems* by John Ashbery (New York: Penguin, 1992), copyright © 1981, 1982, 1983, 1984 by John Ashbery. Rights in the UK from *Selected Poems* by John Ashbery administered by Carcanet Press Limited, London. Reprinted by permission of Georges Borchardt, Inc. on behalf of the author and Carcanet Press Limited.

*Joan Daves Agency:* Excerpt from "I Will Not Die for You" by Frank O'Connor from *Collected Stories,* copyright © 1981 by Harriet O'Donovan Sheehy, Executrix of the Estate of Frank O'Connor. Reprinted by permission.

*Farrar, Straus & Giroux, Inc.:* Excerpts from "Crusoe in England" and "One Art" from *The Complete Poems 1927–1979* by Elizabeth Bishop,

of Battle," "Ego Dominus Tuus," "Coole and Ballylee, 1931," "To Ireland in the Coming Times," "Are You Content?," "All Souls' Night," "A Dialogue of Self and Soul," "The Gyres," "Sailing to Byzantium," and "Among School Children" from *The Poems of W. B. Yeats: A New Edition,* edited by Richard J. Finneran, copyright © 1919, 1928, 1933 by Macmillan Publishing Company, copyright renewed 1947, 1956, 1961 by Bertha Georgie Yeats. Copyright © 1940 by Georgie Yeats, copyright renewed 1968 by Bertha Georgie Yeats, Michael Butler Yeats, and Anne Yeats. Reprinted by permission.

*New Directions Publishing Corporation:* "Medallion" and an excerpt from "Cino" from *Personae* by Ezra Pound, copyright © 1926 by Ezra Pound. Reprinted by permission.

*Oxford University Press:* version of "Man and the Echo" from *Letters on Poetry from W. B. Yeats to Dorothy Wellesley* (Oxford, England: 1964). Reprinted by permission.

*Random House, Inc.:* Excerpts from *Ulysses* by James Joyce, copyright © 1934 and renewed 1962 by Lucia and George Joyce. Rights outside the United States administered on behalf of The James Joyce Estate by The Bodley Head, London. Reprinted by permission.

*Random House, Inc.* and *Faber and Faber Limited:* Excerpts from "The Capital" from *W. H. Auden: Collected Poems,* edited by Edward Mendelson, copyright © 1940 and renewed 1968 by W. H. Auden. Rights outside the United States administered by Faber and Faber Limited, London. Reprinted by permission of the publishers.

*Charles Scribner's Sons* and *Alexander R. James:* Letter from Henry James to William James from *The Letters of Henry James, Vol. 2,* edited by Percy Lubbock, copyright © 1920 by Charles Scribner's Sons, copyright renewed 1948 by William James and Margaret James Porter. Reprinted by permission of Charles Scribner's Sons, an imprint of Macmillian Publishing Company, and Alexander R. James, Literary Executor of The James Estate.

*Yale University Press:* Excerpt from *Rhyme's Reason* by John Hollander (1989). Reprinted by permission.

## A Note About the Author

Denis Donoghue was born in Tullow, Ireland, in 1928. He took his B.A., M.A., and Ph.D. at University College, Dublin, and received an M.A. at Cambridge University when he joined the teaching faculty there. He was Professor of Modern English and American Literature at University College, and is now University Professor at New York University, where he also holds the Henry James Chair of English and American Letters. Among Donoghue's many books there most notably figure *The Third Voice*; *The Ordinary Universe*; *Thieves of Fire*; *The Sovereign Ghost*; *Ferocious Alphabets*; *Connoisseurs of Chaos*; *The Arts Without Mystery*; *We Irish*; *England, Their England*; *Reading America*; *Warrenpoint*; and *The Pure Good of Theory*.

## A Note on the Type

The text of this book was set in Bembo, a facsimile of a type face cut by one of the most celebrated goldsmiths of his time, Francesco Griffo, for Aldus Manutius, the Venetian printer, in 1495. The face was named for Pietro Bembo, the author of the small treatise entitled *De Ætna* in which it first appeared. Through the research of Stanley Morison, it is now acknowledged that all old-face type designs up to the time of William Caslon can be traced to the Bembo cut.

The present-day version of Bembo was introduced by The Monotype Corporation, London, in 1929. Sturdy, well balanced, and finely proportioned, Bembo is a face of rare beauty and great legibility in all of its sizes.

Composed by Creative Graphics, Allentown, Pennsylvania
Printed and bound by Arcata Graphics, Martinsburg, West Virginia
Designed by Brooke Zimmer